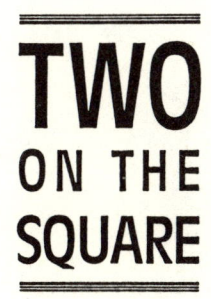

TWO ON THE SQUARE

TWO ON THE SQUARE

BILL MOORE

Illustrated by Dianne Cable

Bright Mountain Books

Published by
BRIGHT MOUNTAIN BOOKS
138 Springside Road
Asheville, North Carolina 28803

© 1986 Bill Moore

Illustrations © 1986 Dianne Cable

All rights reserved. No part of this book may be reproduced in any form or by any means without the prior written permission of the publisher, except brief quotes used in connection with reviews written specifically for inclusion in a magazine or newspaper.

Bill Moore developed the characters of Lonzo and The Pundit in his weekly columns for *The Asheville Citizen-Times*. Some episodes from those columns appear in *Two on the Square* in somewhat altered form, although many are original material written for this book. Dianne Cable's graphic interpretations of Lonzo and The Pundit were created especially for *Two on the Square*.

Manufactured in the United States of America

ISBN: 0-914875-13-2

Library of Congress Cataloging-in-Publication Data

Moore, Bill, 1923-
    Two on the Square.

    I. Title.
PN6162.M63   1986   813'.54   86-20781
ISBN 0-914875-13-2

Contents

Introduction	1
1 · Philosophy on the Square	5
2 · The Women in Their Lives	31
3 · Life on the River Bank	49
4 · Philosophy on Wheels	69
5 · Some Civics Lessons	103
6 · Philosophy Almost Anywhere	121
7 · Getaway Days	141
8 · A Little Work	157
9 · Winters in the Sun	179

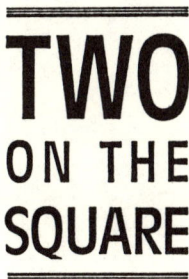

Introduction

As they say down at Tiger Murphy's Auto Body Shop, let's get a few things straight:

☐ Neither Lonzo nor The Pundit are real people. They are, instead, composed of glued-together bits and pieces of many people I have met, in everyday life and in forty years in the newspaper business.

☐ Neither Lonzo nor The Pundit are representative of the Southern Appalachians or of any other part of the country. They are, if not universal, at least transcontinental.

☐ I like them.

I have had a few problems with the identities of Lonzo and The Pundit. I have described them in some detail, but I have carefully not given either of them any singular, unmistakable characteristics. They are composites and not to be taken for real people.

Nevertheless I have, from time to time, been forced to deny that some real living person is the model for either The Pundit or Lonzo. And, in some cases, my denials have met with obvious disbelief.

I think it has something to do with the universality of the two. They are not recognizable, really, as individuals. But they are recognizable as types. Readers see the types and confuse them with the individuals.

This was demonstrated vividly to me a few years ago, not long after I started writing about Lonzo and The Pundit. Dick Kaplan, the *Citizen-Times* bridge columnist, hot horse handicapper, and bowling buff, wandered into my office and said, "Say, I just saw those two guys you've been writing about. They're sitting on a bench over in Pack Square, and they look exactly the way you described them."

I carefully explained to Dick that he couldn't have seen Lonzo and The Pundit because Lonzo and The Pundit don't exist—they are products of my imagination.

Kaplan said something like, "Oh, I see," and went away.

Ten minutes later he came back into my office and said, "I just went back to Pack Square and took another look at those two guys and I don't care what you say, Lonzo and The Pundit are sitting there on that bench."

And that's just one example. There also was the Ashevillean who went on vacation in Florida and came back swearing he had passed the Honkerbus southbound on I-95 "just a few miles north of Jacksonville and she was steaming right along, just the way you write about it."

The Honkerbus, too, is imaginary.

Because I write in Asheville, down here in the beautiful end of Appalachia, Lonzo and The Pundit sometimes talk in a way that suggests an Appalachian accent. And, naturally, many of the things they do and say are appropriate to life in the mountains.

But that is not to suggest that Lonzo and The Pundit are necessarily identified with Appalachia. I have met people very much like Lonzo and The Pundit on the broken-down concrete benches abeam of the L Street Bath House in South Boston; over in back of Signal Hill in Long Beach, California; not far from the main entrance to the race course in Brisbane, Australia; and fishing in the Ala Wai Canal in Honolulu—that was long ago, but if the Ala Wai Canal still exists, I'll bet people like Lonzo and The Pundit still are fishing for breakfast in it. And if I worked for the *Honolulu Star-Bulletin*, I'd probably be writing about that, too. You can find Lonzo and The Pundit, or reasonable facsimilies, almost anywhere.

Not everyone likes Lonzo and The Pundit. Occasionally I get a letter or a phone call from a reader wondering why I waste my time and theirs writing about "two smelly old bums . . . really!"

And once in a while when I meet someone new, I get a remark like, "I do like those things you write about your cat and your wife and your basset hound and some of your friends, but I can't stand it when you write about those two derelicts you seem to be so fond of."

Well, I write about those "two derelicts" because I like them. Oh, I know, sometimes they are just not what you might call fastidious about their persons, and maybe they are a little irresponsible. They won't work, except under duress, and they are not scrupulous about other people's property. Sometimes they step over the line into outright dishonesty.

They probably wouldn't pay their bills if they got any bills, but that's not a problem because no one in Asheville would dream of extending them any credit. And sometimes they tend to overindulge in the use of alcohol. No, to be accurate about it, they just flat get drunk.

On the other hand, they are not violent. They never steal anything that's really needed by the owner. Maybe they don't wash often, but there's no running water in a Dempsey Dumpster.

Perhaps their appeal is in the fact that they are free agents. They have no ties to jobs or homes or families or the other constraints most of us acquire in life. They come when they please, stay as long as they want, and go when they please. And perhaps that quietly appeals to some people, people who maybe have been fighting deadlines, or tax payments, or those little coupon books from the bank all their lives.

It is mind-boggling to imagine Lonzo and The Pundit in nightshirts flying over the Botanical Gardens in Asheville, but those two are as close to the carefree vision of Peter Pan as any of us is likely to get in this century.

There are a few things about Asheville, North Carolina, that should be understood before reading this book.

Oh, of course, you can go ahead and read the book without reading these footnotes, and you'd probably understand most of what you read, but I don't want you to understand most of it, confound it, I want you to understand all of it.

So, go on, read the footnotes.

PACK SQUARE: This is a large, open expanse in the approximate geographical center of town. It was named to honor George Pack, a lumber baron from Cleveland, Ohio, who moved here about the turn of the century to allow the climate to restore his health.

The climate did, and a grateful Pack bought a lot of downtown property and donated most of it to the city as sites for libraries, fire stations, public markets, and other good things. After living here healthy and happy for a decade or so, he unaccountably decided to return to Cleveland. The climate there killed him in a year, but that's another story.

A few years ago some civic busybodies "improved" Pack Square. I liked it a lot better when it was unimproved, but it remains a good place to sit and whittle.

BELE CHERE: This is an annual civic convulsion that runs for three days during the summer, traditionally marked by thunderstorms. It is a combination of mammoth street fair, sidewalk talent show, balloon race, circus, and bunion derby.

The name "Bele Chere" sort of came about by accident. The promoters of the first edition of this shivaree were looking around for a Gaelic expression that would connote a good time. Gaelic, of course, because the first white settlers—and a lot who came later—were of Scotch-Irish derivation.

Somebody came up with the title "Bele Chere." Later it was discovered that the phrase is not Gaelic, it is a bastardized French expression that had been kicking around Scotland a lot during the eighteenth century when all of the quality folks larded their speech with French phrases whether or not the phrases fit the occasion. But it was too late to change the name of the festival and there we are.

TOM WOLFE: This is the original Tom Wolfe, the Tom Wolfe of *Look Homeward, Angel,* and not the other Tom Wolfe who came later and wrote about candy-striped orange machines or something. The original Tom Wolfe was born in Asheville and went from here to the University of North Carolina at Chapel Hill and from thence to fame and notoriety.

Tom Wolfe has not been forgotten in Asheville. His name has been given to everything from music halls to parks to streets. Many Ashevilleans speak his name in tones of reverence, despite the fact that his first book did a savage hatchet job on Asheville and many of its residents. That's why a later book by Tom Wolfe is entitled *You Can't Go Home Again.*

But he did.

THE FRENCH BROAD RIVER: There are many things that are lovable in a perverse way about Asheville, and the name of its river is one of them. It does not refer to a mademoiselle of questionable virtue.

When the early English explorers were working their way up into the mountains from the Atlantic Coast, they encountered many rivers. One was broad and it was called the "Broad River." Soon there were too many "Broad Rivers" and the explorers began to discriminate. They produced titles like the "Rocky Broad River" and the "Muddy Broad River," and, for all I know, the "Broad, Broad River."

When they came to the place that later became Asheville, they ran into another broad river. This was located in territory then thought to be the property of the king of France. So they called it the "French Broad River."

Understand? Good!

1
Philosophy on the Square

It was all Oddly's fault.

Years ago I bought an almost-new Volkswagen bug for a second car. It was white and had a black vinyl top. I never had seen a black vinyl top on a Volksagen before and I thought it was an oddly attractive combination. I said so to my kids, who thereafter referred to the automobile as "Oddly Attractive," which was quickly shortened to "Oddly."

My children, bless them, have a way of handling colorful speech.

Anyway, when we moved to Asheville many years ago, Oddly, although showing distinct signs of wear, still was part of the family and came with us.

About a year later Oddly contracted a failing of the front end, a malady peculiar to aging Volkswagen bugs. A friend of mine named Dr. Randy Foreigncar examined the patient, declared that major surgery was required, and put it in the Foreigncar Clinic for a spell.

So that my wife could retain custody of our other car, I started riding the little blue Asheville Transit buses back and forth to work.

It was fun. Not as convenient as driving my own car, of course, but interesting, nevertheless.

One balmy spring afternoon I was slouched on a bench on Pack Square, the Times Square of Asheville, waiting patiently for a blue bus to take me down Biltmore Avenue and up to Kenilworth, the neighborhood in which we live.

I was half asleep when a whiskey baritone voice croaked in my left ear, "Hey there! You got a light for this here cigar?"

It was The Pundit. I sighed, pulled some matches from my pocket and handed them to him. He struck a match and set fire to a two-inch cigar butt that produced a cloud of nauseating smoke.

Then I heard a thin, high-pitched voice in my right ear. "Hey there! You got a cigarette for this here light?"

That was Lonzo.

And that was how I met Lonzo and The Pundit.

If a car named Oddly had not started to fall apart, I might never have met that particular version of "The Odd Couple."

At least that's the way I remember it now.

Maybe it was different, though. Maybe I met them in the parking lot of a restaurant on the Outer Banks. Or maybe they showed up one day at my house looking for work mowing lawns and trimming hedges.

The whole thing is complicated because, as I said at the outset, Lonzo and The Pundit are not real people, except that they're very real.

They're really nobody, except that they could be anybody or everybody.

It doesn't make sense?

It wasn't intended to.

"Of course I remember how Lonzo and I first met each other," said The Pundit. "It wasn't back in the dark ages, you know."

"Yes, it was," said Lonzo sleepily. "It was in Minnesota." He shivered gently, although it was warm under the bridge that afternoon where we sat watching the French Broad flow through Asheville.

"What in the world were the two of you doing in Minnesota?" I asked. "That's about the last place I'd expect to find you."

"It was the last place I expected to find myself," said Lonzo, " and I ain't never going back there.

"I got there when I took a job as driver and mechanic for the Swiftsure Magazine Subscription Company, J. Huddleston, Prop. Huddleston went all over the country with a bunch of young people he used to sell magazine subscriptions. Huddleston had to be swift for sure because he had to get into a town, sell a lot of subscriptions, and get out of town quickly before anyone discovered that Huddleston didn't believe in sharing the subscription money with any old magazine publisher.

Philosophy on the Square

"We moved around in an old school bus Huddleston had bought and fixed up. We started down around Atlanta in the early spring and by that October we had worked our way north to Minnesota.

"Then, halfway between Mankato and Fandango, in the heart of Torgerson County, one of the connecting rods in the bus engine came out through the oil pan. I had been telling that danged fool Huddleston that the motor was just plain wore out and he ought to do something about it. But he didn't pay me no never mind.

"Well, after the engine come apart, Huddleston told us to sit tight, that he'd hitch a ride into the next town down the road and arrange for a wrecker to come out and tow us in. It wouldn't take me more'n a couple days to install a new motor in the bus, he said, and then we'd be on our way again.

"Three days later we come to the conclusion that we wasn't ever going to see Huddleston or a wrecker or any of the money he owed us.

"The kids in the sales crew just took off, hitchhiking down the road. I started walking. After I walked a longer ways than I really wanted to, I turned into a nice-looking farmhouse alongside the road and asked for work.

"As luck would have it, the lady who owned the farm was looking for a handyman and hired hand and she figured I would qualify on both counts.

"Her name, she said, was Gertrude Lavransdatter, or something like that, and she offered to feed me, let me sleep in the barn, and pay me a little walking around money for my work. I didn't have nothing else on my social calendar at the time, so I said it was a deal.

"Gertrude was a good cook, too, except she cooked more fish than I really care for. Lutherfish, she called it. Said all of her six previous husbands loved it. I figured out right quick that Gertrude was looking for another husband and that as far as she was concerned, I could be Old Lucky Seven.

"I refused to apply for that job, however, so I continued to sleep in the barn. But winter came, and when winter comes in Minnesota, you really know it's there. My Lord, I never been so cold in my life! I thought the sun had retired and the heat had leaked out of the world.

"I was just plain miserable. On one side I had Old Gertrude, just yearning and slavering for matrimony. On the other hand, sleeping in that barn was becoming impossible. On the third hand, I was flat broke, all alone, and had no way to get out of the fix I was in.

"One night at supper in early December, we was watching the weather on the TV, and the weather lady said the temperature was going down to twenty below that night. I told Gertrude I had come to see things her way and I was willing to get hitched. So I moved into the house.

"In mid-January we got what they laughingly call the 'January Thaw' in Minnesota. The weather moderated from unbearable to only impossible. 'Get the car started and warmed up,' said Gertrude. 'Why?' I asked. 'We're going to town to let Reverend Johannsen marry us,' said Gertrude. 'I changed my mind,' said I.

"Well, she really pitched a fit. I tell you, that lady was mad. She threw everything in the kitchen at me. Then she threw everything in the living room at me. She called me everything under the sun. She used some words I even didn't know.

"Then she says I had lionated her affection and comprised her in front of her friends and neighbors, and she then called the sheriff."

"You didn't comprise her," I said, a little awed. "What she meant was that you had compromised her."

"I didn't do that, neither," said Lonzo. "Sometimes I just wish I wasn't so attractive to those darn women. I get in trouble all the time that way.

"Anyway, that was the first time I seen The Pundit. He come out from the sheriff's office in town to arrest me."

I stared at The Pundit. Finally I said, "I find it extraordinarily difficult to picture you as a deputy sheriff."

"Why? Who do you know that has had more experience in the field of law enforcement?"

"Well, there's that, of course," I said, "but I always pictured you as the object and not the verb."

"Ridiculous!" said The Pundit. "I got a lot of experience in law enforcement when I was serving in the Philippine Constabulary. Believe me, we chased them insurrectos from the Sulu Sea to the Straits of Johore and we always got our man."

"But how did you get to Minnesota, too?" I asked.

"It involved a violation of a Federal Aviation Agency regulation," The Pundit confessed.

"See, I had just concluded a land transaction up in Johnson City. I sold a man up there an option to buy 3,000 acres of wooded land down near Erwin. When I got the option money I decided to leave the area for a while because I didn't own the land in question. Now, mind you, I did nothing dishonest, really. I didn't tell the man I owned the land; I just told him I'd sell him an option to buy if he wanted one. I couldn't tell him I owned the land. The federal government owns the land; it's part of the Cherokee National Forest.

"Nevertheless, it was a good idea to go away before the option buyer discovered that the option was worthless except maybe as a souvenir. So I went to Seattle where the World's Fair was going on and rode that monorail until I was seasick. I tried to buy the bar in the Space Needle, too, a drink at a time. Finally I got tired of Seattle and Seattle got very tired of me, so I used nearly all of what was left of my money to buy an airline ticket back to Asheville by way of Chicago.

"Well, when the plane took off from Seattle, the stewardess sold me two drinks. I drank them and took a nap. When I woke up, I tried to buy two more. No soap, said the stewardess. Two drinks per flight was the limit, she said. If the plane landed somewhere like say, Minneapolis, and then took off again, she could sell me two more drinks, she said, but the plane was scheduled to fly directly from Seattle to Chicago.

"I said that was a stupid rule. No, she said, the rule was all right but every now and then she ran into stupid people. Land the plane in Minneapolis, I said, and take right off again, and we could all have another drink.

"No soap, she said. I said I didn't want to wash my hands, I wanted a drink and they should land at Minneapolis. We debated that idea for a while and then she invited the pilot to join the debate and he came back and we discussed it with him for a while, and by grannies, they did land the plane in Minneapolis.

"And they threw me off it.

"Well, there I was, in the middle of the airport at Minneapolis one cold night in October and I didn't know a soul. So I cashed in what was left of my ticket and used the money to rent a car and drive to Fandango, where my uncle, Thorwald Bjornesen, was the sheriff of Torgerson County.

"I hadn't seen Uncle Thor for years and he hadn't seen me neither, and it was hard for him to recognize me. In fact, he didn't want to recognize me.

"But my Aunt Elfreda, the one that's my mother's sister and Uncle Thor's wife, worked on him, and it wasn't long before I was sleeping in his house with my feet under his table. Course I didn't have no money and I had to borrow from him. That lasted for a week, then he put me to work. The county wouldn't pay deputies enough, he told me, so he was always shorthanded. And, seeing as how he was supporting me, the least I could do was help him out. It was that or hit the road, Aunt Elfreda or no Aunt Elfreda, he said.

"Well, it was already pretty cold up there, so I allowed as how I'd do a little work for him, long as it wasn't too onerous. He swore at me, swore me in, gave me a pistol and a badge and a uniform, and told me to get out and patrol the roads.

"He said the uniform belonged to a deputy who had retired, but I found out later it had belonged to a deputy who let his cruiser run out of gas the winter before and, as a result, had frozen to death.

"Well, there's not much going on in rural Minnesota in the dead of winter—well, at least nothing the sheriff had to worry about—and I almost started to enjoy the work. But the cold was fierce and I was scared of making a mistake with my cruiser. I filled the gas tank three times a day.

"Then one afternoon the dispatcher radioed me to go to Gertrude Lavransdatter's farm and referee a domestic dispute. When I got there, I found this poor, skinny geek dodging around on the front porch, trying to get back into the warm house, while Gertrude was hurling assorted crockery at him to keep him out.

"I put the handcuffs on him and threw him in the cruiser. Then I tried to talk to Gertrude, but she didn't want to talk, she wanted to throw. I let her roar along for a while, but when she whanged a steam iron off the top of the cruiser, I blew my whistle and made her stop.

"Then she told me the charges she was preferring against Lonzo and to take him away to jail. Then she come out on the porch herself and took a long look at me.

"'How do you feel about Lutherfish?' she asked. I told her I couldn't stand the stuff, and her charges against Lonzo wouldn't hold up in court and I was going to let him go. Gertrude, she started throwing stuff again, this time at me. So I retreated to the warm cruiser, intending to throw out Lonzo and go back to the sheriff's office for a cup of coffee.

"But Lonzo was now sitting in the driver's seat behind the steering wheel. I started to pull him out but he just pointed to his left wrist. It was handcuffed to the steering wheel. I asked him how in the Sam Hill he managed that, and he said he had took the handcuff key out of my pocket while I was throwing him into the cruiser.

"So I told him to just produce that key again and I would unlock him and he could go back and negotiate with Gertrude. He turned white and said he didn't want to negotiate nothing with Gertrude and that he couldn't produce the handcuff key right then because he had swallowed it.

"Well, I ranted and roared around for a while but by that time it was getting colder and the daylight was beginning to go, so the only thing to do was to go back to the sheriff's office. Lonzo drove, of course.

"It was sort of humiliating and I didn't want anyone, least of all Old Uncle Thor, to find out about me being outwitted by a prisoner. So when we got there, I sneaked into the garage, got a hacksaw, and cut out a piece of the cruiser steering wheel to get Lonzo loose. Then I escorted him into the sheriff's office.

"There was a holding cell not far from the front door. The cell door was open and Lonzo made a bee-line into the cell, wrapped three blankets around him, laid down on the bunk and seemed to go to sleep.

"'Who's that?' demanded Uncle Thor. 'It's Gertrude Lavransdatter's hired hand,' I said. 'She called in and wanted him arrested. Said he was guilty of alienations of affections and I don't know what all.'

"Uncle Thor's face got red. He ground his teeth. He threw his big sheriff's hat on the office floor. 'Confound it,' he said. 'That's about the umpteenth time Gertrude has had us arrest her hired hand. It's always the same story. She tries to get them to marry her and no one wants to do it. They can't take that lutefisk diet she feeds 'em. She just can't find no more good Norwegian farmers. I told her a dozen times that I'm a sheriff and not a marriage broker and this here is a jail and not a matrimonial bureau. Now I'm through playing. I don't care what charges she filed. You take that drifter out of that cell and throw him out. I don't want nothing to do with him. For all I know we violated his constitutional rights about nineteen times already.'

"I heard a click from Lonzo's cell. When I tried to get him up on his feet, I couldn't. He had handcuffed himself to the bunk. 'How did you do that?' I said. 'You told me you swallowed that key!'

"'I lied a little,' said Lonzo.

"'Well, give me the key now, and I'll turn you loose,' I said. But Lonzo said he couldn't; that this time he really did swallow the key. So I went and got the hacksaw and started to saw the cuffs off Lonzo. But Uncle Thor made me stop. He said those cuffs cost the taxpayers of Torgerson County $44.95 and he'd be danged if he'd let me destroy them. Lonzo would just have to wait around until he could produce the key natural like.

"So Lonzo stayed in the warm jail and so did I. I was on the night shift, but the weather was too cold to just go out and roam around looking for trouble. So I stayed there waiting for the phone to ring and hoping it wouldn't. Lonzo and I talked. We discovered that we was both from North Carolina and that we both was from up in the mountains and that we both enjoyed what you might call an unconventional lifestyle and that we both mightily disliked Minnesota in the winter.

"And we talked about how fine the mountains look when they heave up into view as you drive toward them from someplace else, and how sweet the air is, and how clean the rivers are, and we decided that we both wanted to get back to North Carolina any way we could. But right then there wasn't any way.

"Lonzo hung around the office. He gave me back the handcuff keys in a day or so and we freed him up and Uncle Thor said he could stay a while and make himself useful. He did. The next day the sheriff's radio system went out of commission. Lonzo fixed it. Course, for a day and a half the only thing you could get on the receivers in the cruisers was a hard rock radio station in St. Paul.

"But he got that straightened out. Then he improved the locking system on the cell block in the jail, and we had to carry food and water to the prisoners for a week because we couldn't get the cell doors unlocked, and we heard about that from the Civil Liberties Union, let me tell you.

"Lonzo continued on in that manner, just generally making life interesting for Uncle Thor there in the dead of the Minnesota winter. And he and I kept talking about how great it would be to be back in North Carolina. We were careful to have these conversations where Uncle Thor could hear them. But we really were dying to get out

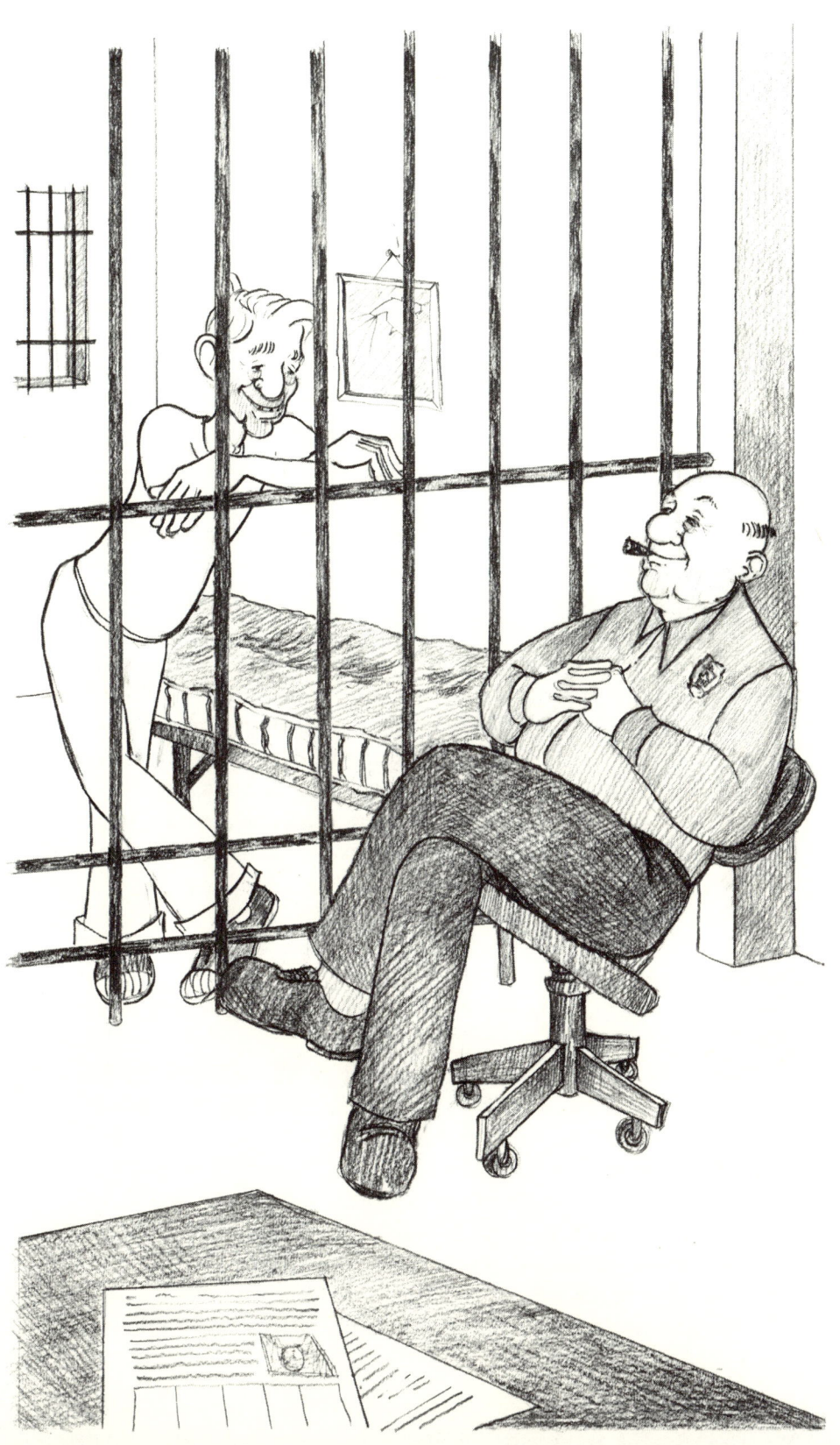

of Fandango and the great state of Minnesota.

"Not long after the episode of the lockup that wouldn't unlock, the lighting system in the sheriff's office went on the blink—literally. Every light in the building started to blink rapidly. In ten minutes we were all going nuts. Uncle Thor told Lonzo to fix it, pronto.

"Lonzo blinked, too, then attacked the main circuit breaker panel in the basement with a big screwdriver and a pair of pliers. In no time at all the lights in the sheriff's office had stopped blinking. But every traffic light in town went out. Lonzo got that fixed, too, after crashes at intersections all over town.

"While this was going on, I thought I saw Uncle Thor looking at Lonzo and me with a strange expression on his face. It was thoughtful. Usually when he looked at us, his expression was one of pain.

"The next day he called us into his private office. 'Listen boys,' he said. 'There is a law problem we need your help with. The sheriff over in St. Paul called me this morning. He has picked up a stolen car that needs to be taken back to its owner. The car was abandoned near that theater where they put on that "Prairie Home Companion" radio show. The car belongs to a woman named Carolina Bellew and she lives in Chapel Hill or some such outlandishly named place down in North Carolina. She can't come up here to get it and the sheriff in St. Paul can't spare anyone to drive it down there. He just happened to mention it to me this morning. Now this Carolina Bellew will pay $100 in expenses for the person who drives it down there for her. Are either of you interested?'"

The Pundit said there was then a great, profound silence. "Then," he said, "Lonzo did something that convinced me that we ought to be friends for life. He looked Uncle Thor right square in the eye and said, 'You sure this Carolina Bellew won't go for a hundred and a half?'

"Mind you, there it was—deliverance from Minnesota and a free ride to North Carolina, and it was all laid out before us like a dream. And there was Lonzo, working the situation for an extra fifty bucks. My heart went out to him. This, I thought, is a great man!

"Well, Uncle Thor gulped and said he was sure that she would and, if she wouldn't, he'd throw in the extra fifty himself. So about two hours later he drove us over to St. Paul and ten minutes after that we were headed down to Chapel Hill and Carolina Bellew.

"On the way down to Chapel Hill we stayed two nights in motels and Lonzo showed me a couple of things about motels and motel bills that he had learned from the magazine subscription magnate, and I showed him a couple of things about checks in restaurants, and we realized that we had a perfect partnership.

"And we've been together ever since. Ain't that right, Lonzo?"

But Lonzo didn't answer. Lonzo just snored gently, happily, free of horrifying memories about Minnesota winters, Gertrude Lavransdatter, and Lutherfish.

I was quietly reclining in one of the beaten-up benches in front of the old Pack Library when suddenly the air was affrighted with eldritch screams and wheezes, and the Honkerbus clanked around the corner and groaned to a stop in front of me, smack in a zone reserved for buses.

The Honkerbus is the latest and perhaps the most picturesque vehicle to be acquired by Lonzo and The Pundit.

It started its career as a 1952 DeSoto sedan, but later was converted into a truck of sorts. The conversion obviously was performed by some rough-and-ready craftsmen who were rougher than they were ready. Later it was given a coat of flat black stove paint by someone wielding a whitewash brush. It is now a truly astonishing conglomeration of bent metal, loose bolts, and slow leaks.

Lonzo does the driving. Lonzo is an atrocious driver, but The Pundit is worse. The Pundit is the only man I know whose driving is so bad he gets a season ticket from the highway patrol. Both of them piled out of the machine and sank into places on the bench beside me.

Lonzo was attired rather casually in paint-spattered slacks, a straw sombrero, and a T-shirt that once had been the property of a member of the Outrigger Canoe Club of Waikiki Beach. The Pundit was wearing his business suit, a rusty black serge job suitable for banking or burial.

"We figured we'd find you here," said Lonzo, exhibiting all four teeth in a smile.

"And a good thing, too," said The Pundit.

"We are on way over to Bargainjohn's new flea market in Candler, but we wanted to give you an opportunity to look over our stock first.

Philosophy on the Square

"You may purchase anything that catches your fancy," he continued, "but we must insist on a minimum sale of two dollars."

"Why two dollars?" I asked.

"Because Candler's over there a piece and one dollar's worth of gas doesn't go very far these days," said The Pundit.

Whereupon Lonzo began to show me the treasures they planned to scatter to the winds of commerce.

First I was offered a "slightly used" tractor tire, as bald as a watermelon and with what Lonzo called "just a little hole" in the sidewall.

I declined, with thanks.

I also declined a dozen used flashlight batteries, a coffee pot without a handle, and a souvenir whiskey decanter.

I showed a similar lack of interest in a single-barrelled shotgun with a broken trigger spring, a 1948 edition of the *Information Please Almanac,* and the gearbox from a 1909 Sears, Roebuck "Little Giant" cream separator.

Finally, reluctantly, The Pundit rummaged around in the front of the truck and came back bearing an object wrapped in a stained cloth.

"We had hoped we wouldn't have to sell this," he said. "It's an heirloom, an object of great sentimental value to Lonzo. But if we don't get some gas, we don't get to Candler, so we'll let it go to you.

"But you'll have to promise to treasure it the way Lonzo's mother did. She loved it. Was handed down to her and she kept it in the place of honor in her home, that grand old lady did. We are really doing you great honor in even offering this treasure to you."

I was about to decline the great honor, too, when I heard Lonzo sniff. And, to my horror, I noticed big tears forming in the corners of his eyes.

So I produced the two dollars, The Pundit handed me the treasure, and the two of them leaped into the front of the truck and started the complicated routine of getting the engine going again.

Wrapped in the dirty rag was a blue-and-white ceramic bird with a broken beak. On the bottom was lettering which said "Taiwan—1969."

I ran to the truck and banged on the door.

"What," I screamed, "is all this nonsense about heirlooms and Lonzo's dear old mother?"

The Pundit grinned.

TWO ON THE SQUARE

"In this case, son," he said, "it would seem that Lonzo's mother is the invention of necessity."

Lonzo let in the clutch and the Honkerbus disappeared down the street in a cloud of blue oil smoke.

We rounded the corner from Biltmore Avenue into Pack Square and stopped dead.

The bench was gone.

So was everything else. The placed looked as though a bomb had gone off. Huge, dish-shaped pieces of pavement three feet in diameter were piled up all over the place. In one corner a front-loader was picking up the debris and dropping it into dump trucks. Over against the wall of the old library, a small bulldozer snorted and gouged its way toward us.

The entire scene was one of dust, heat, change, and desolation. Lonzo looked toward the place where once our favorite bench had stood. His eyes bulged with surprise and his lower jaw dropped.

The Pundit stared, ducked as the front-loader snorted past, and whistled.

"The bench has gone!" cried Lonzo.

"The sidewalk under the bench has gone, too," said The Pundit.

"And four feet of the dirt that once held up the sidewalk has gone," I said.

Big, shiny tears welled from Lonzo's brown eyes.

"We have been eliminated," he said.

"We've been evacuated," said The Pundit.

"We've been excavated," I said.

"What's happening here?" Lonzo roared.

"It's pretty plain what's happened," said The Pundit. "We've been civic improved, that's what's happened!"

And so saying, he took the greasy brown fedora he was wearing off his head and threw it in the general direction of City Hall.

Just then Ken, the city manager, wearing his customary expression of faint astonishment, rounded the corner. He, too, stopped to view the excavations.

Ken was neatly attired, as usual, in pink summer suit, a crisp white

Philosophy on the Square

shirt with a collar, and a tie.

He looked as though the temperature was nowhere near 90 degrees in the shade. He looked clean and unruffled. He looked like the very model of a modern city manager.

Lonzo plucked at his elbow.

"Look there," said Lonzo. "Those people have went and demolished our bench and dug up the sidewalk and everything."

Ken looked there, nodded, and said, "Yes, it certainly does appear that this particular corner is undergoing some changes."

Lonzo snorted.

"But Ken, I've been sitting around on Pack Square for fifty years or so, give or take a few. Now these folks have come along and done away with the last and most comfortable bench on the square. Ken, what's going to become of us, The Pundit and me, that's what I want to know?"

Ken smiled reassuringly. He nodded, too. He did everything but pat Lonzo on the head.

"All we're doing," he said, "is fixing up the square some. We're making it look better. But don't you worry, Lonzo. When we get this place put back together there certainly will be a place for you and The Pundit to sit."

Lonzo brightened. "You mean," he said, "we'll get our good old rickety, rattly bench back again?"

"Well, no, I don't mean that," Ken said, sort of staring off across the square. "Maybe it will just be a nice grassy bank.

"Or," Ken said, looking even more remote, "it may not be quite that way, either.

"But don't worry. We'll have something there," he said, strolling off in the direction of City Hall.

Lonzo looked at The Pundit, The Pundit looked at Lonzo, we all three looked at each other. Then we strolled off, in search of an antidote for civic improvement.

The day they turned the water on in the new pool in Pack Square, I noticed them, over near the fountain, leaning against each other for mutual support.

They were as disreputably dressed as ever. Somehow the neatly ordered atmosphere of the newly rebuilt square made their dilapidation seem worse. Lonzo was watching the clear water cascading out

TWO ON THE SQUARE

of the fountain with open-mouthed, pop-eyed, slack-jawed awe. The Pundit seemed to be less impressed, but even he wore a smug smile.

As I came up to them, Lonzo noticed me out of the corner of his eye. He grinned. "Shucks," he said, "they didn't have to go to all of this trouble just for us."

I was about to tell him that I suspected they hadn't gone to all that trouble just for them, when The Pundit turned and said, "Yeah, that's right. We don't want to seem chinchy about this, and it's a great honor, of course, but really, we were getting along all right with the old Pack Square. However, we'll do our best to adapt to the change. It's the price of fame, I suppose."

"What in the blue-eyed world makes you two think the city went and did this specially for you?" I asked.

"Well," said Lonzo, "just a couple of minutes ago some guys came down here from City Hall and turned the water on. And I heard one of them say to the other, 'I hope this satisfies those two old characters Bill Moore keeps writing about.'"

"'Characters' wasn't exactly the word they used," said The Pundit, "but we got the message."

"Well," I said, "now that you have a pool, what you do think of it?"

"I don't know," said The Pundit. "It's nice, of course, but there are a few flaws in it. For instance, the water is too rough for the backstroke and too shallow for the Australian crawl."

"I wouldn't crawl around in there," said Lonzo with a shudder, "even if I was from Australia."

"Never mind, Lonzo," said The Pundit.

"There's a couple of things missing," he continued. "For instance, when do they put up the lifeguard's seat? And they forgot to put in a deep end so that people could dive in off the deep end."

"I don't know about that," said Lonzo. "There's still plenty of people around here who will go off the deep end, even if they have to make their own deep end."

"I haven't quite caught up with that bit of philosophy," said The Pundit, "but you're probably right."

"Anyway," said Lonzo, "that geezer's real pretty."

I looked around.

"Which geezer?" I asked. "I don't see any geezer."

"Why, that geezer right there," said Lonzo scornfully. "That place where the water is all gooshin' up. That's a geezer. Don't you know

20

no good words? Ain't you had no education?"

"I just want to warn both of you," I said, "if you ever get any notions about swimming in that pool, the boys in blue will come up here from the station, straighten you right up, and cart you off to the hoosegow. City Hall doesn't want any swimming in that pool."

The Pundit looked offended.

"Listen," he said, "the last time either of us was in water was when Lonzo accidentally rolled off the river bank back in '69. You won't find us in that pool ever. We just don't have any truck with water.

"But," he said, brightening up, "we don't have any foolish prejudices against other liquids. Did I hear you was buying?"

The Pundit shifted comfortably on the bench in the warm sunlight, chewed the soggy end of a cigar, looked out complacently over a nearly deserted Pack Square, and said, "Sure would be nice to watch people swimming in that pool after the governor took the trouble to dedicate it and all."

I looked at the reflecting pool and fountain in front of the Akzona building and sighed.

"We've been over this before," I said. "If I told you once, I told you a thousand times, that's not a community swimming pool. In fact, if the boys in blue catch either or both of you swimming in there, they'll put you so far back in the jail it will take ten dollars' worth of postage to get a nickel postcard in to you.

"And it won't do any good to tell them you're practicing for the Olympics, either."

"Forget it," said The Pundit. "That pool ain't deep enough for me to do my backstroke, so I ain't getting into it."

"Me neither," said Lonzo. "I had a bath in April."

"You couldn't prove it by me," I said.

Lonzo scowled.

"But I don't think we'll see the governor up here again for quite a while," The Pundit said.

"Why?" asked Lonzo.

"Well, the legislature just finished up, you know. They were down there in Raleigh for seven months. But they've all gone home. Now the people who work in Raleigh all the time have to figure out what the legislature did during those seven months."

There was dead silence. The Pundit stared moodily at the splashing

TWO ON THE SQUARE

water. Lonzo's eyes widened and he almost appeared to be thinking.

"That could take seven years," said The Pundit, finally.

"Sober," said Lonzo.

Lonzo shuddered.

"I rarely take the name of the Deity in vain," said The Pundit, "but I feel like it in the face of such a prospect. Think of it! For seven months they were all down there, meeting in broom closets and men's rooms and passing laws like it was going out of style.

"Man, they passed laws on laws, laws about laws, laws on top of laws. They passed a few laws nobody's ever read yet. And they passed a few nobody probably ever will read.

"It's a shame," he said, "but they seem to have forgotten the most important law of all.

"Which one is that?" I said.

"The Law of Diminishing Returns," The Pundit said.

"You're an economist," I said.

"That's a terrible thing to call a man," The Pundit said.

Lonzo and The Pundit looked downright prosperous.

Lonzo had put aside his usual battered tennis shoes in favor of a pair of yellow high-topped brogans. Over those he wore clean slacks, a clean white shirt (no tie, naturally), and a straw sombrero with the words **Viva Francisco Madero** painted around the brim.

The Pundit was wearing his customary black business suit, but it recently had been cleaned and pressed. He was wearing a tie, a green confection about the same shade as the shark repellent issued navy fliers in World War II.

Both men looked relaxed, well-nourished. Both, too, smelled of hair tonic, good cigars, and store whiskey.

"You two are dressed up like Mrs. Astor's horse," I said.

"Benny's back," said Lonzo.

Philosophy on the Square

"Benny's back?"

"My friend," said The Pundit, " is referring to the fact that Big Time Benny Biscayne once again has seen fit to grace us with his presence. It is always a joyous occasion. We love Benny dearly and do certainly welcome his yearly sojourns among us.

"Big Time Benny is well connected in some influential legal circles down in Florida," said The Pundit. "By that I mean he caddies at a country club where a good many attorneys play golf. He does real well, what with tips and other things. And every year about this time he comes up here with a pocket full of what he's done real well with. He likes to visit us mountaineers and teach us how things are done in the big city."

"That Benny, he's special, all right," said Lonzo. "Why, he even wears those little shoe coats on his feet."

"Spats," said The Pundit.

"And a big diamond ring on his little finger."

"Glass," said The Pundit.

"And a pearly gray hamburg hat."

"Homburg to you," said The Pundit.

"So how does the presence of this sharpster from down south explain your sudden affluence?" I asked.

"Benny plays cards with us," said Lonzo.

"You gamble with him?"

"Son," said The Pundit, "when we play cards with Benny there's no gambling about it. He loses."

"You bet," said Lonzo. "We got him by the tail on a downhill drag."

"Or something like that," said The Pundit.

"You always win?" I asked.

"No," said The Pundit, "only when we want to. Sometimes we just let Benny teach us a lesson. But that's not often."

"You two must have a big edge on poor Benny," I said.

"The biggest edge we have over Benny is the fact that he thinks we're stupid," said The Pundit.

"We don't dress sharp like he does and we don't talk like he does, so he thinks we aren't in his league. So far he hasn't been able to figure out how two rubes like us have been able to win from him so consistently. But Lonzo learned to play cards in the back room at Turkey's place, and I've dealt poker under a lot of bridges, so Benny is just a short word for benefactor to us."

"I think I'd like to meet this Benny," I said.

Lonzo looked startled; The Pundit looked amused.

"Benny's last name is pigeon," said The Pundit. "But he's our pigeon and we aim to keep it that way. See you around."

And they stalked off, striding across Pack Square with the measured tread of men marching toward a manifest destiny. Named Benny.

They sat in the shade on Pack Square, almost under the wings of Tom Wolfe's homeward-looking angel. The warm early afternoon sun toasted the brick sidewalk, and across the street the fountain in their favorite swimming pool made wet, happy noises.

The sky was blue, the mountains around the town were beautiful, and in the tree over their heads a songbird of some sort ignored the diesel fumes from passing buses and sang its heart out.

It was an idyllic scene. Lonzo and The Pundit seemed to be enjoying it.

Lonzo, a vacant smile on his face, was sprawled across the bench. His paint-speckled cap was pulled down low over his eyes. A paint-speckled T-shirt bearing a mystic statement about how crop-dusters do it, was stretched across his scrawny chest, and his black tennis shoes were thrust far out.

In place of his customary greasy fedora, The Pundit wore a sporty black Greek seaman's cap which he moved restlessly around on his head as if seeking the place where it felt most comfortable.

The heat rising from the warm pavement carried with it the familiar effluvium of cheap wine, ancient cigars, and lack of sanitation that has characterized them for as long as I've known them.

When I was in elementary school I was made to sit, along with the rest of the youngsters in my class, through a course called "personal hygiene." It was taught by a fastidious maiden lady who preached about the necessity for bathing with a fervor that impressed even a room full of nine-year-olds.

Since I have come to know Lonzo and The Pundit I often have wondered how she would react if she ever were confronted by that pair. But, no matter. She has long since gone to that great shower

Philosophy on the Square

room in the sky, and she isn't likely to run into either Lonzo or The Pundit there.

I slid onto the bench beside them.

"How do you like it?" I asked, pointing to the angel.

The Pundit grinned. "It's downright angelic," he said.

Lonzo stared at the angel for a moment. "Makes me feel like I was in church," he said, finally.

The Pundit snickered. "Lonzo," he said, "it's been so long since you was in church, I just don't see how you can remember."

Lonzo smiled dreamily and closed his eyes. In a minute or two he began to emit a sound like a failure in a hydraulic system. He was snoring.

"The poor man is overcome," said The Pundit. "It's the post-statue syndrome, a dreadful malady I have been hearing about."

The Pundit pulled a broken black cigar stub from his pocket and lighted it. The songbird gasped and flew away.

"Let me tell you," said The Pundit, "it was no easy task getting that statue up. It took a world of supervising, and me and Lonzo was plumb wore out by the time they finally got around to dedicating it.

"However, it wasn't a total loss. After the dedication, one of them out-of-town professors who came here for the doings took one look at my old hat, grabbed it, threw it in the sewer, and gave me this cap right off his own head. He said he couldn't bear the thought of my old hat anywhere near a monument to Tom Wolfe."

The Pundit grinned and shook his head. "After he left, of course, I got Lonzo to crawl down into the sewer and retrieve my old hat. It's been in worse places and winter's coming."

It was a warm, windy spring day on Pack Square.

It was not long after the first of the month and both Lonzo and The Pundit had money. It was evident from the bulges on their hips, the ripe aroma of grape they carried around with them, The Pundit's nose, and in the dreamy, almost stunned expression on Lonzo's face.

Lonzo was attired in his customary paint-spattered coveralls, brogans, and painter's cap. The Pundit was wearing his everyday black business suit, a string tie, and a huge, floppy planter's straw hat.

The hat looked like something worn by Ezio Pinza in the film *South Pacific*. I said something like that to The Pundit. He harrumphed and started to give me a long, involved story about how he got the hat while he was managing a sugar mill in Cuba.

I asked if this was before or after Teddy Roosevelt went to Cuba.

Eventually he fished around in one of his coat pockets and produced a mangled cigar stub and an ancient Zippo cigarette lighter. He jammed the stub in his mouth and flicked the lighter's spark wheel.

A six-inch long stream of fire erupted from the lighter. Startled, The Pundit moved the lighter away from his face. The fire streamed out in the wind.

"That," Lonzo said, addressing The Pundit, "is what you get for putting that Madison County moonshine in that contraption of yours."

The Pundit repositioned the cigar in one corner of his mouth, cranked his head over hard, and somehow lit the cigar without roasting his nose.

I felt like applauding. Instead I said, "I don't want to appear to be criticizing your technique, but I believe you just set your hat on fire."

The Pundit's eyeballs snapped to the full-up position. He looked. He said a very bad word. He pulled the hat off his head. He threw it into the street.

The blazing hat blew catty-cornered down the street for a way, then came to a stop up against the left front wheel of an auto waiting for the light to change. Four elderly, well-dressed women were sitting in the car.

There must have been grease or oil coated on the underside of the car engine. It caught fire and a cloud of greasy black smoke began to roll out from under the vehicle.

A storm of screams issued from the interior of the car. The driver jammed on the accelerator and the car disappeared over the brow of the hill on Patton Avenue heading in the general direction of the fire station.

Lonzo scratched his head. "They took that fire to the firehouse, didn't they? I believe that's the first special delivery fire I ever saw."

For a moment The Pundit looked concerned. "I certainly hope none of those ladies get singed," he said.

Then he said, "That reminds me of a thing that happened when I was drill boss on an oil rig in the Persian Gulf. We had this Ayrab

Philosophy on the Square

roustabout who was the most careless man with a cigarette I ever did see.

"Well, one day we punched down into a little gas formation there and somehow the gas started to come up between the casing and the side of the hole. We all was tippy-toeing away from that well, trying not to make no sparks with our shoes, when up comes that Ayrab roustabout with a match in his hand—"

"Save it," I said, interrupting. "I don't think those people coming up over the hill want to hear about that Arab."

And coming they were, four bedraggled, smoke begrimed women and two big, surly looking firefighters. From the way they were walking and the expressions on their faces it was obvious that we had interrupted the firemen's lunch.

By the time they turned the corner onto Biltmore Avenue, Lonzo and The Pundit were going at nearly terminal velocity in the other direction.

"Did you have anything to do with setting that car on fire?" one of the firemen asked me.

"No," I said, "but the whole episode reminds me of the time I was executive office on an oil tanker in the Straits of Magellan. You see, it was about four bells . . . "

But they didn't seem to want to hear the rest of the story. That was a shame, too. It's one of The Pundit's best.

The Pundit obviously was angry.

His arms waved frantically. His normally pink, bulb-shaped nose glowed crimson. At one point, he took off his grimy gray fedora, threw it on the sidewalk, stomped on it, then plunked it back on his head.

Lonzo stood in front of him, a picture of dejection. His chin drooped onto his chest. He was clutching what appeared to be a map, holding it up to his chest, defensively.

The Pundit's voice rose and fell in the cold winter air. He was taking inventory of Lonzo's character. Words like *idiotic*, *stupid*, and *imbecile* were the kindest he was using.

TWO ON THE SQUARE

"You seem to be disturbed," I said to The Pundit.

The Pundit's nose grew even redder.

"You doubtless have heard," he said through gritted teeth, "of the Lost Dutchman gold mine in Arizona." I allowed that I had.

"And possibly you also have heard about the Lost Spaniard gold mine in New Mexico?" I admitted that I had heard of that mine, too.

"Well," yelled The Pundit, throwing his hat on the sidewalk again, "meet the simpleton who just bought a secret map showing the location of the Lost Lithuanian Gold Mine of Western North Carolina."

Lonzo's chin sank even lower. A tear appeared in the corner of his eye.

"No doubt you have noticed that the weather is getting colder," said The Pundit, continuing the catechism. I said that, yes, I had noticed that the weather was cold.

"Well, this moron and I have an invitation to go down to Florida for a couple of months and help his Uncle Cloyd wash yachts at Marathon Key.

"So we scrubbed a million floors, cleaned a billion windows, and raked a zillion piles of dead leaves to get up the bus fare.

"Well," said The Pundit, "on the way to meet me at the bus station, Lonzo was a little early, so he stopped in the Deadfall Literary Club for a little refreshment. When he finally came out, the bus money was gone but he had this map—this confounded secret treasure map to a lost gold mine. It's not worth a Continental whoop nor holler."

"I just ran into a feller who showed me the map," said Lonzo. "He said he didn't want to sell it, but he needed money to get back to Lithuania to look after his dear old mother. She has complications of lumbago and is suffering something terrible. So I used the bus money to buy the map. Look at the price of gold these days."

The Pundit groaned.

I looked at the map. It was a chart-sized piece of paper obviously folded and refolded many times. It had coffee stains and grease spots and something that looked like catsup on the margin. It was hand-printed. There was lettering on the map in a language I didn't recognize. Written along the bottom of the map in pencil in English were the words "Josef Kervils—Riga—1963."

"It might be a very valuable map," I said, "if you happen to be driving a taxicab in the capital city of Esthonia."

The Pundit groaned again.

Philosophy on the Square

Lonzo walked over to a trash can on the curb and was preparing to ditch the map when The Pundit shot up from the bench.

"Hold it," he said, "just hold it. We don't want to throw that thing away. Lonzo, a little while ago I said you were the dumbest man in the state. I probably was wrong. You and I are going back to the Deadfall Literary Club. When we get there we'll find the guy who really is the dumbest man in the state."

"Then what?" Lonzo asked.

"When we find him, Lonzo," The Pundit said, "we are going to sell this priceless treasure map to him. That's what! Come on, Lonzo, the warm sun and the blue water of Florida await. And do you think you could possible fake a Lithuanian accent for a while?"

"It's Esthonian, really," I said. But I don't think they heard me.

2
The Women in Their Lives

I suspected it was not a happy morning when I saw Lonzo spring up from the bench, scrabble across the sidewalk, and kick the tire on their old truck.

"Green is green, gol dang it," Lonzo snorted, giving the tire another kick. "And gray is gray, dad blame it!"

"What ails your buddy?" I asked, sliding onto the bench.

The Pundit, wearing an unhappy look, replied, "We have suffered a grave set-back, you might say, and Lonzo is merely giving vent to his feelings."

"I presume you'll tell me all about it," I said.

"You couldn't stop me," said The Pundit.

"It all started back in 1776," said The Pundit, settling more comfortably on the rattly bench. "That was the year when on the Fourth of July, the American colonies declared their independence from England. Ever since then, we Americans have been celebrating on the Fourth of July. This year was no different. We celebrated.

"Lonzo and me, we probably celebrated harder than most people did. In any case, along about the middle of July we discovered that we had dipped too deeply into our monthly remittances. We were, to be exact, broke."

"Distressing," I murmured.

"Indeed," said The Pundit. "Things were almost desperate. We were in danger of having to start sleeping again in the stairwell at the city parking garage. And, let me tell you, that's not very nice. The concrete is terribly hard."

"I can imagine," I said.

"No, you can't," said The Pundit. "Anyhow, we decided to go into the interior decorating business, Lonzo and me. Lonzo knows

TWO ON THE SQUARE

a widow woman up in Whiskey Cove who's been sort of house proud since she got electric lights and running water a couple of years ago. She also has some money and she's always been a little sweet on Lonzo."

Lonzo smirked modestly.

"So we sold her on the idea of Lonzo and me painting the inside of her house. Let me tell you, it took a lot of time and patience. She spent days just looking at paint chips and trying to make up her mind. And, shucks, there's only three rooms in her house. Finally she settled on Mediterranean sea mist azure for the bedroom, dove wing taupe for the living room, and Samarkand sunset for the dining room. She gave us the money to buy the paint and we went down to see Midnight Mowrice, the second-hand king.

"Mowrice, unfortunately, didn't have any Mediterranean sea mist or Samarkand whatever. What Mowrice did have, was some green paint, some gray paint, and some pink paint. He got it from some fellow who just happened to have seen it fall off the back of a truck on a dark night. And the price was right," The Pundit said. "So we bought it, took it back to the widow's house, and started painting. We had been hard at it for a couple of hours when the Widder Lady came back from the wine and cheese tasting party she had been attending.

"She took one look at the wall I was working on and started making noises like a leaky boiler. Then she skittered into the other room and looked at the wall Lonzo had painted. The she started to speak English—old English. The upshot of it was that she wanted her money back. But we already had spent some with Mowrice for paint and had spent the rest for refreshments. So we got out of there in a hurry, just before she threw the piano at us.

"And I just don't think she's going to pay us for all the labor we done," The Pundit said gloomily.

"Back to the stairwell at the parking garage, I guess," I said.

"No," said The Pundit. "I think the high sheriff is going to take care of our lodging for a while. I hear the Widder filed a charge."

"I see," I said. "You might say the widow has raised a great hue and cry."

"Don't get smart with me," said The Pundit. "We raised a great hue: the Widder raised the great cry."

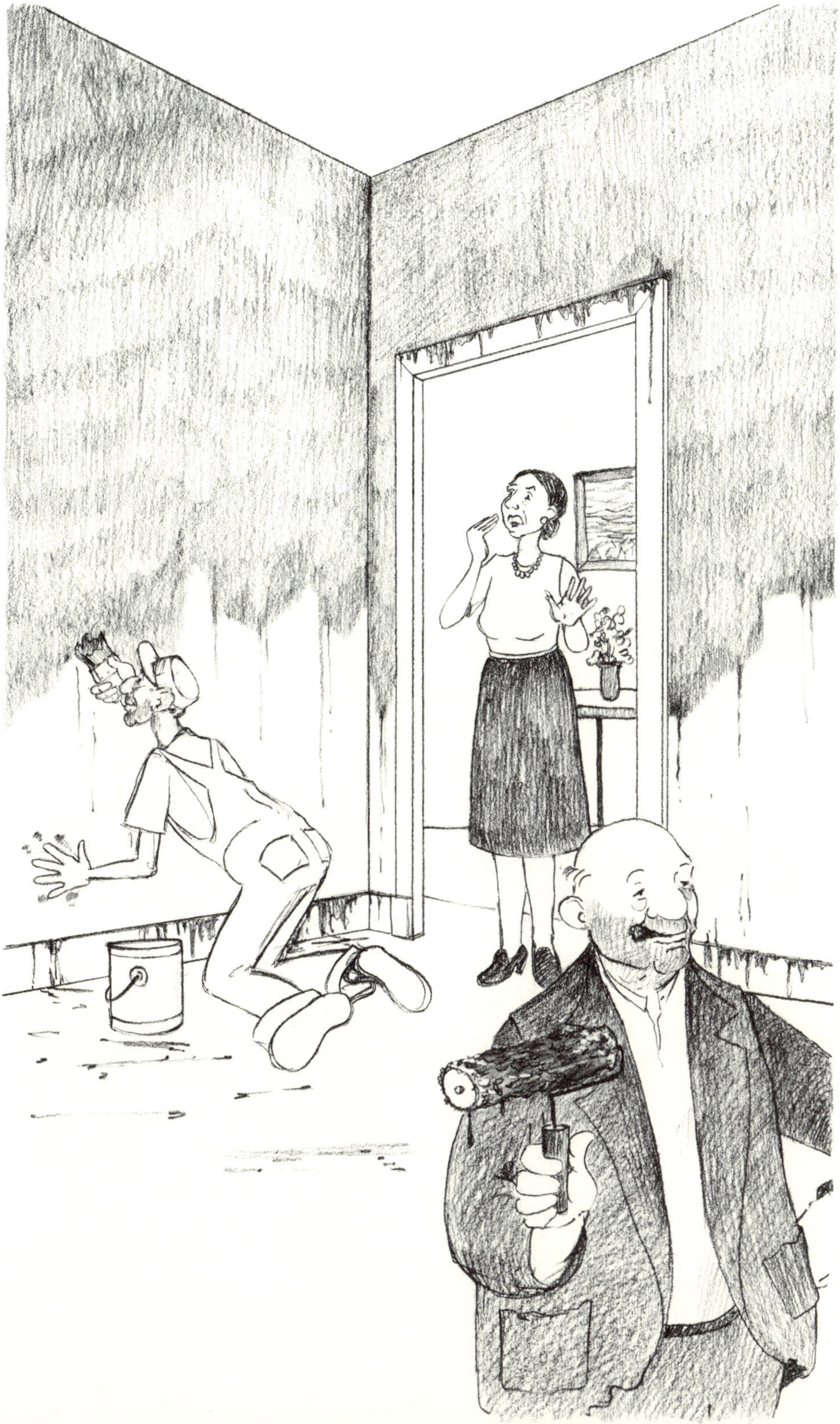

Lonzo, seated comfortably on the rickety old bench, was helping one of the Pack Square pigeons pass the time.

Lonzo would say something to the pigeon in a soft, low voice. The pigeon would gargle something in reply. Lonzo would feed it some crumbs and say something else.

The Pundit, on the other hand, was slumped bonelessly on the bench, wearing a smug smile.

"You seem pleased with things," I said as I sat down. "What's happening?"

"Not much," said The Pundit. "Except that Lonzo and me have once again escaped the clutches of matrimony."

"Somehow I hadn't thought of either one of you as prime matrimonial timber," I said. "What happened?"

"Well," said The Pundit, "it's the Widder Lady from up in Whiskey Cove. Every year about this time, when the leaves start to turn and the geese fly south and the temperature drops, she gets a notion to marry Lonzo. She gets to thinking about those long, cold winter nights, I guess. And she's always been sort of sweet on Lonzo.

"Anyhow, we happened to run into her over in West Asheville the other day, and she made a big fuss over Lonzo. Finally she ended up by inviting both of us to supper at her house. Well, we haven't been invited out to supper since the Salvation Army fed us last Christmas, so we went. We even took baths before we went."

"I see," I said. "It was a formal affair."

"Sometimes you got a big mouth," he continued. "That Widder Lady may never have been a candidate for Miss America, but when she tackles a cookstove, she's an All-American.

"We started in on her biscuits. They were so fluffy and light I thought I'd have to glue them to the plate to put butter on them. I complimented her on them."

"'Oh, it's really nothing,' she says. 'I may have put a little too much baking powder in them. I was in such a hurry.'

"Lonzo, who had demolished a half-dozen of them, chomped on another and said, yes, he saw what she meant about the baking powder. In fact, he said, she could have put a little more salt in the biscuits, too. Well," said The Pundit, "there was what they call in the novels a 'pregnant pause.' The Widder Lady got red in the face and her hands clenched.

"Then she laughed and changed the subject. We got to the fried ham and it was heaven. The Widder Lady cures her own hams, old-time mountain style. I complimented her on the ham. She laughed and said it was nothing special. She said she had trouble getting decent hams to cure last year. Lonzo chewed about a half pound of ham, swallowed it, and said he could see what she meant about getting second-rate hams, all right, and she could have used more salt in the curing, too.

"There was another pause. The Widder Lady got real red in the face and started making whistling noises through her teeth. Then she sort of shook herself, like a dog coming out of water, smiled again, and started talking about how cold the weather has been getting. Then we went on to the dessert. It was key lime pie and it was marvelous. I told her it was.

"She smiled and asked did I really think so? She was a little flustered about cooking for company, she said, and had been afraid she'd used too much sugar. Before I could say anything, Lonzo chewed up half a piece of pie in one bite, and then said, yes, he did believe that she'd used too much sugar, and were the limes real fresh when she squeezed them?

"Then the Widder got very, very red in the face. Under her breath she said something like, 'It ain't worth it. It's just not worth it. I'll get an electric blanket instead.' Then she threw us out of the house."

"I'm surprised she didn't throw the cookstove at you on the way," I said.

"If she'd left the pie on the stove when she threw it I wouldn't have minded," said The Pundit.

It was a Saturday evening in the high summer. The Chief of Staff had gone to Ohio to visit the kids, and I was sitting on the front porch letting the bees buzz me to sleep.

I had just about dozed off when I heard the unmistakable rattling, wheezing, clanking noise that signals the proximity of the Honker-bus. Thirty seconds later it pulled up in front of the house. Lonzo was at the wheel and, as the car stopped, he reached over his head, grabbed a cord, and pulled it down.

The roar that followed almost knocked me off the porch. Several shingles were torn loose from the roof. Inside I could hear Spats, our cat, going crazy, trying to get out to attack whatever it was that had made the monstrous noise.

All up and down Buckingham Court people came out of their houses to see what the racket was. When they saw the Honkerbus, a couple of the more savvy ones immediately started to lock up their cars.

The Pundit appeared from the back of the Honkerbus, dismounted, and came up to the porch steps, grinning.

"What in the blue-eyed world was that noise? And whatever it was, don't do it again," I said.

"It's our new air horn," said The Pundit. "We found it laying around loose near a boatyard in Morehead City when we went down there for the deep-sea fishing. We think it came off a shrimp boat. We also found an air tank with it and it wasn't no trouble at all for Lonzo to rig up a compressor and the tank and the horn in the Honkerbus.

"Lonzo kind of figured a way to improve the equipment, too. It's a lot louder than it ever was on that boat.

"It does have a penetrating sound, don't it? We have to be careful with it, though. It violates the city's noise ordinance. Course, ain't nobody enforced that ordinance since Sherman burned Atlanta, but the cops probably would make an exception in our case."

As if to underscore that statement, Lonzo, wearing a big grin, yanked the horn lanyard again. A shower of leaves fell off the oak tree in Marie From Philadelphia's front yard. The cat squalled again. Weaubleau, our basset hound, set up a deep, mournful howl. So did some of the neighbors.

"What we came about was to borrow a couple of lawn chairs to take to the Shindig with us."

"Let's take three and we'll all go," I said, eyeing two neighbors coming up the hill. One was carrying a two-by-four; the other was toting two sidewalk bricks.

Lonzo wheeled the Honkerbus down the court, around the corner, and out onto Biltmore Avenue. Then we stopped for a light. "I can blow that horn with my feet, too," he said. He flung his right foot into the air. He was wearing high-topped black leather shoes without laces. Adroitly he hooked the shoe heel over the horn cord and pulled down.

The blast peeled the paint off the back of a city transit bus in front of us. A dozen starlings, stunned by the noise, crashed onto the hospital lawn across the sidewalk. On the other side of the street, an elderly gentleman ran away screaming something about how the end had come and we should all repent mighty fast.

The Pundit retrieved his greasy black felt hat from the back of the car where the sonic wave had thrown it and sternly ordered Lonzo to lay off the horn. I seconded the motion as soon as my ears stopped ringing.

When we got to the Shindig at the City-County Plaza, most of the good places down near the stage had been taken.

"Looks like we'll have to go back up the hill," I said.

The Pundit examined the situation carefully. "Maybe not," he said.

He moved unobtrusively in the gathering dark to a point upwind of the third row back from the stage, squatted down, pulled one of his ropy black cigars from a breast pocket, lighted it, and puffed hard.

In thirty seconds people in that row started to cough. In sixty seconds it sounded as though a pneumonia epidemic had broken out. In ninety seconds a lot of angry people, with streaming eyes, coughing and choking, were carrying their lawn chairs far, far away from that cigar. And we unfolded our chairs and sat down in spacious comfort.

It was "long about sundown" by that time and the stage lights came on and Joe Bee started his routine. Joe Bee is local talent. He is an emcee, and orator, an inspirational leader, whatever.

Joe could, if he wanted to, discuss the relative merits of the fifteenth century Italian poets in an accent suggestive of the Harvard Yard. But the Shindig is a country event featuring folk and country music, and when Joe Bee works the Shindig, he makes "Hee-Haw" look like a seminar on urban design.

Joe Bee used to work at keeping the postal service hereabouts out of trouble. Then he retired. Now he goes all over the country making after-dinner speeches and orating and inspiring, usually for a fee. But the Shindig is his first love and he throws himself into it.

He had the microphone in a death grip and was just about to deliver the evening's first load of corn, when Jack Walker, one of the police officers on foot patrol in the downtown area, appeared and tapped The Pundit none too lightly on the shoulder with his nightstick.

"Some folks back there complained to me that you just about gassed them with that cigar of yours," Jack said to The Pundit. "You pull that trick one more time and I'm going to make you eat the cigar, lit end first, understand?"

The Pundit said mildly that every man has a constitutional right to smoke.

"You give me any trouble and I'll give you a constitutional right," said Jack, "closely followed by a looping overhand left, closely followed by my stick on your shinbone. Keep those cigars in your pocket or I'll run you in for aggravated air pollution."

Lonzo grumbled something and Jack walked away, swinging his stick with the cool competence of a Wyatt Earp wading out of the OK Corral.

Joe Bee introduced the first artist and the Shindig got going with a swing. The performers are all volunteers, but the music is far from amateurish. In this part of the country, kids start twanging a banjo or picking a guitar a little earlier than they start playing basketball in Indiana.

We had two country music combos and a clog team. Then there was a pause between acts. In the silence that prevailed I heard a girlish voice say loudly, "Mama, look at that man in front of me. Look at him!"

I looked over my shoulder. The voice belonged to a female child of about nine years sitting right behind Lonzo. Sitting next to her was a matronly looking woman who obviously was the child's mother.

"Mama, that man looks just like Uncle Harry! And Daddy says Uncle Harry's a bum. Is that man a bum, Mama? Is he? A bum?"

She was pointing at Lonzo, who slid down in his seat and tried to pretend he wasn't there.

"Hush up, Gretchen," said her mother. "You got no call to talk about your Uncle Harry like that."

"Well, I think he's a bum and that man sitting next to him looks like one, too," said Gretchen in a childish treble that carried across the audience like the public-address system at a horse track.

The Pundit cranked his head around at Gretchen and smiled weakly.

"Gretchen, you be quiet," said her mother in a tone that carried no conviction at all.

"Yeah, Gretchen, be quiet," said The Pundit with another smirk.

"Shut up, you bum," said her mother.

Joe Bee got the next act on, a virtuoso who performed with spoons

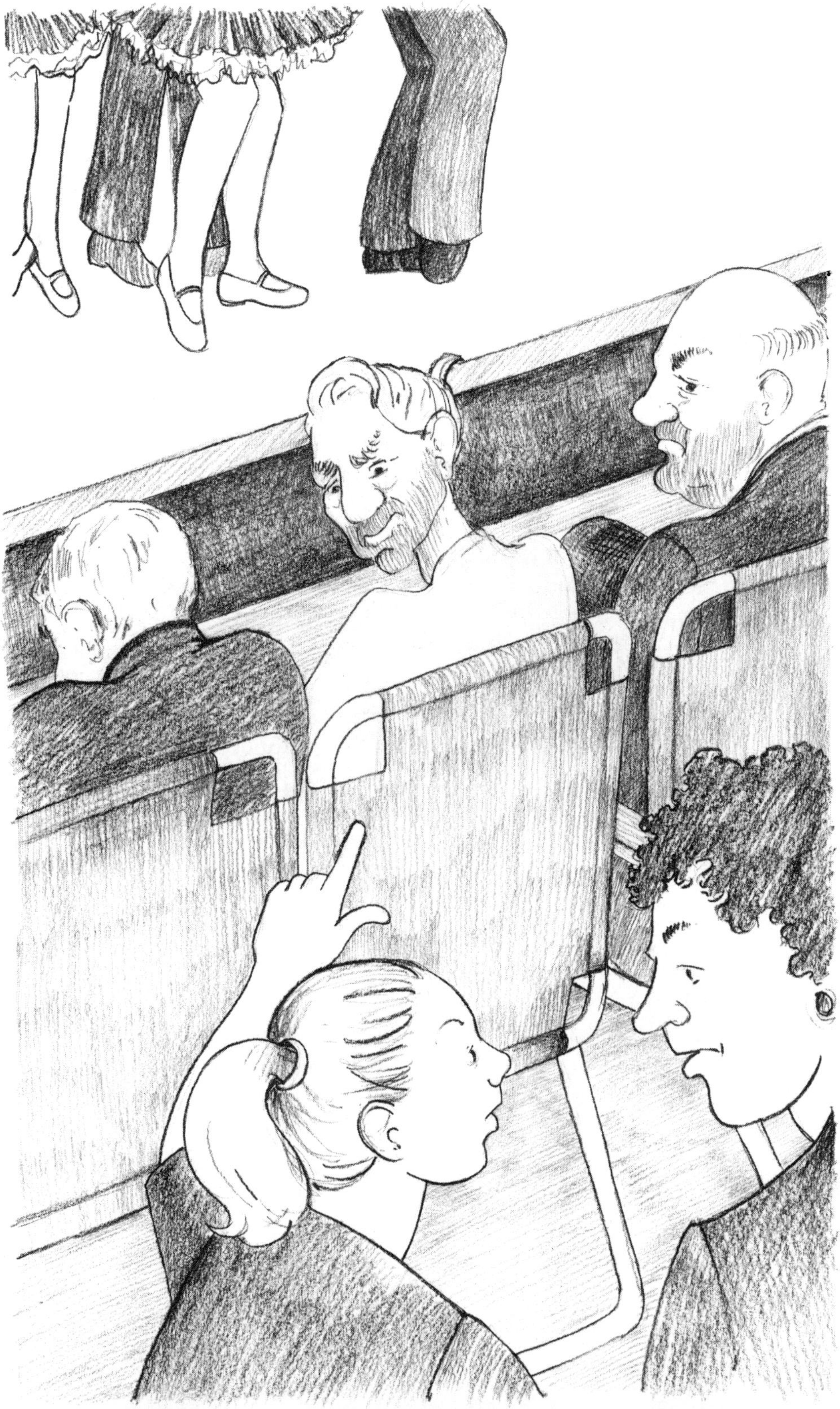

TWO ON THE SQUARE

and a Jew's harp. The act was not the most successful of the evening.

Instead of applause, the audience was treated to Gretchen saying, "Mama, that man sitting in front of me smells like a bum, too."

Lonzo crouched down lower in his seat. The Pundit ground his teeth in helpless rage. Instinctively he reached for a cigar. From out in the darkness beyond the seats came a low, warning growl. The Pundit sadly put the cigar away. Officer Walker was on the job.

Two more acts went by. Then Joe Bee introduced the next act, a well-endowed woman singer in a low-cut gown. Lonzo straightened up in his chair, naturally, and the chair moved.

Before the woman could start singing, Gretchen let out a wild scream. "You got your chair on my foot and it hurts!" she said. "Get your chair off my foot! Get it off, off, off!"

Lonzo instantly stood straight up. "All right," said Gretchen, sweetly. "It's all right now. You can sit down."

Lonzo sat down but the chair wasn't there. At the psychological moment, Gretchen hooked her toe around a chair leg and pulled it out from under him. Lonzo landed with a crash on the blacktopped street. There was the sound of breaking glass. There was the smell of cheap wine. A pint of Thunderbird drained out of the back pocket of Lonzo's overalls.

The female singer wordlessly handed the microphone back to Joe Bee and walked off the stage.

The Pundit covered his face with his hands. Lonzo painfully crawled back onto his chair.

"Gretchen, that wasn't a nice thing to do at all," said her mother.

"I know," said Gretchen. "Mama, get me something to drink. I'm thirsty and I want something cold to drink. I want it, want it, want it, Mama!"

"All right, Gretchen," said her mother. "You wait here. I'll go get us some nice cold drinks."

A tall, graying man behind her who had been watching the whole thing said gently, "Ma'am if I were you, I wouldn't leave that little girl alone. No telling what one of us is likely to do to her."

So both Gretchen and her mother went for cold drinks which effectively spoiled the next two acts for the rest of us, because they had to barge out and barge back in again.

When Gretchen finally got back with her cold drink, she decided, of course, that she didn't want it, so she poured it into the back pocket of Lonzo's overalls.

The Women in Their Lives

The evening wore on.

Finally Joe Bee announced the final act of the evening. They came on stage. They played. They danced. They sang. They were good. They finished up with a huge flourish. They looked out expectantly for applause. But before that could happen, Lonzo rose straight up about six feet in the air, came down whopperjawed across two chairs, tore the shoe off his left foot, and began hopping up and down on his right foot and moaning loudly.

"My God!" said Joe Bee, who normally does not invoke the Diety for secular matters, "I never seen an audience reaction like that before."

As the howls of laughter and catcalls and hoots and cheers died down, I heard Gretchen's mother say in a really awed voice, "Gretchen, give me back those matches. You really have done it this time. We better get out of here right now."

But just about that time Joe Bee said, "That's all and good night, folks," and we all started out, Lonzo limping, The Pundit steaming.

We walked through the warm summer night up the hill and across Patton Avenue to the parking lot. Lonzo sat in the driver's seat and said he'd drive, sore foot and all. We were in no mind to argue with him. He got the Honkerbus started and pulled out into traffic. We went a half a block and had to stop for a red light at a passenger crosswalk. We were the first vehicle in line.

Across the street, just stepping off the curb in the pool of illumination made by a street light, were Gretchen and her mother. They were going to pass right in front of the Honkerbus. Lonzo saw them about the same time I did.

His skinny, grimy hand rose and took firm hold of the air horn lanyard.

"Don't do it, Lonzo," I said. "We'll get arrested for sure."

Lonzo's normally undershot jaw was stuck out a mile and the hot, white light of madness gleamed in his watery eyes. "I'm gonna!"

"Forgive and forget, Lonzo," I said.

"Forget, hell," said Lonzo. "I was the guy who got the hotfoot, remember?"

Gretchen and her mother were moving ever nearer to the front of the Honkerbus, sweetly oblivious to their peril.

"Don't do it, Lonzo!" I said. "Pundit, tell him not to do it."

"Don't do it, Lonzo!" said The Pundit, "unless you're sure we got enough air pressure in the tank to make it worthwhile."

"I'm gonna!" said Lonzo.

I leaped down from the front seat and raced around in front of the Honkerbus. My hand was extended in a stop signal and my mouth was framing a warning just as Gretchen and her mother came directly in front of the vehicle.

My memory of what happened next is like one of those stop-action frames in a sports movie. I recall vividly how Gretchen's mother's hair sparkled in the street light as they were blown toward West Asheville. I remember how little Gretchen's eyes bulged and her cheeks puffed out and her ears bent back around her head.

I remember hearing faintly the sound of cars crashing in the parking lot and the screams of panic from people still in the dark in the City-County Plaza.

I don't remember much else.

Lonzo got back on the street after only two weeks. Violating the city noise ordinance is, after all, only a misdemeanor and not a felony. The city attorney said he would gladly have prosecuted Lonzo for something more serious, but he couldn't figure out what.

They confiscated the horn, of course. They classified it as a concealed weapon and buried it under twelve feet of used coffee grounds in the Solid Waste Disposal Facility that used to be the City Dump.

There almost was some trouble with Gretchen and her mother. Jack Walker told me a month later that Gretchen had been speechless since the night of the incident. "Hasn't said an everloving word," he said, "and she hasn't been mean to anyone since, either. Looks like losing her speech sort of took the heart out of her," he said.

He said Gretchen's mother wanted to file a civil suit against Lonzo and The Pundit, but that Gretchen's father wouldn't hear of it. The father, Jack said, was sort of on the lookout for an air horn off a shrimp boat for his ownself. Planned to try it out on his wife's brother, Harry, Jack said.

As for me, well, my left ear hasn't won any prizes since that day many years ago when, in a fit of youthful folly, I tried to set a world's altitude record for the B-17G on a day when I also was suffering from a bad head cold.

The night of the air horn didn't improve that, but I still can hear thunder, and I guess I'm lucky.

The Women in Their Lives

They were huddled together on their favorite bench, swathed in raggedy white blankets bearing the words **U.S. Navy**, knitted caps pulled down over their ears, shoes covered with old-time, four-buckle galoshes.

They looked for all the world like football fans at an Ohio State-Michigan game. They looked cold and miserable.

It was the fifth straight day of cold weather and Pack Square was almost deserted at 9 a.m. The wind whistled around the old library building and the few pedestrians in sight hurried along their way, anxious to get into a heated office or store. I was in a hurry to get to a heated office myself, but I stopped long enough to talk.

"You two look like Napoleon's retreat from Moscow," I said. "Why aren't you in Florida? Why aren't you in front of the fire in the living room at the Widder's farm in Whiskey Cove? Did Lonzo say something about the Widder's cooking again? How come you're sitting here in this wind tunnel?"

Lonzo sniffed. The Pundit sniffed. They both sniffed.

"We was out at the Widder's farm," said The Pundit. "We been there for four straight days. We couldn't get away because the Honker-bus ain't running right. And we was in the Widder's living room. It's too blame cold to sit in the barn all day.

"But we ain't going to do that no more, no sir. No more long days in the Widder's living room for us, not if we have to retreat to a Dempsey Dumpster again. We are a-plumb TV'd out, me and Lonzo, and we can't take no more."

Lonzo sniffed again and nodded in agreement. "No more of that Frances Farmer," he said.

"How did Frances Farmer get into this?" I asked. "She hasn't made a movie since 1937."

"And we seen all the movies she did make," said The Pundit. "Her and that Joel McCrae. And a few others. They was all black-and-white, though, which was a blessing. I don't know if we could have stood them all in glorious Technicolor."

Lonzo made a retching sound.

"The Widder Lady is a TV maniac," said The Pundit. "She gets up at 5 a.m. and gets all her day's chores done before 8 a.m. At 8:01 the TV set goes on and it runs from then until midnight. While she fixes breakfast she also fixes a sandwich for lunch and throws it in the refrigerator. At lunchtime she eats the sandwich without missing any TV. That's a busy time for watching, she says.

"From 5 to 6:30 p.m. there's nothing on she wants to watch, so she fixes and eats supper during the break. Then it's back to the TV until midnight or until she falls asleep in her chair.

"But the best time for her, she says, is in the afternoon while the soaps is on. Once in a while she'll miss the TV in the morning if she has to go shopping or something. And once in a while she'll miss it in the evening to go to a church meeting. But most of the time she's a non-stop, iron-bottom, bullet-proof TV addict."

"You know what's on the TV at 8 in the morning?" Lonzo asked. "Old movies, that's what's on. And that's what the Widder watches."

"That's how Frances Farmer and Joel McCrae got into this," I said.

Lonzo nodded. "Also Percy Kilbride, Guy Kibbee, Beulah Bondi, Helen Twelvetrees, Dame May Whitty, Ward Bond, Sidney Toler, Jackie Coogan, Eduardo Cianelli, Edward Everett Horton, Richard Arlen, Marie Dressler, Eddie Foy, Nigel Bruce, Judy Canova, Carmen Miranda, Lash LaRue, Gene Autrey, Trigger, and The Sons of the Pioneers . . . to name a few."

He groaned.

The Pundit said, "Them old movies is bad enough after a couple of days, but them soap operas is unbearable.

"The Widder Lady just dotes on them, though. She says those people are just like family to her. Shucks, if I had a family like that I'd change my name and emigrate to Australia. But the Widder just eats that stuff up.

"Them people in the soaps, they do awful things, you know. Why half of them belong in a penitentiary or a mental hospital or a clinic of some sort. From murder right down to casual adultery, it's all there, all afternoon long.

"They've been talking a lot about cleaning up magazines and such because they're pornorific or something. Maybe those cleaner-uppers ought to look at a TV set around 3 p.m.

"But they sure are real, those soap opera people, to the Widder. Yesterday afternoon I was taking a nice nap in the middle of one of them soaps when the Widder woke me up with her elbow. 'Look there,' she said, all excited. 'That hussy is pregnant, I just knowed it. Why, my land, she's been showing for a month! And her sweet-talking that nice young doctor about how she needs to go on a diet! Oh, she's a slick one! And her with a husband who's been away for

The Women in Their Lives

a year building a dam in Borneo. How's she going to explain away a baby when he gets back? Oh, there's going to be a day of reckoning, all right!'

"Well!" said The Pundit, "four days of that really makes a body feel young and restless. So this afternoon we're going to be watching how the world turns right here on Pack Square, not in some TV set, even if the cold sends us later to a general hospital."

"What you really ought to do is get away to Florida again before that TV rots your minds for all the days of our lives," I said.

"That's it," said The Pundit. "You said it all, right there. That idea about getting off to Florida is going to be our guiding light."

Lonzo choked again.

"Long about 4:30 this afternoon it's going to get dark in that lot down in back of City Hall, and we are going to get a carburetor that will fit the Honkerbus. Tonight we'll install it. Tomorrow morning the post office will be open at 8 a.m., and 8:01 Lonzo and me will be there, picking up our checks. By 8:05 we'll have them cashed at Dirty Eddie's Cafe, and by 8:06 we'll be headed down I-26, bound for another world.

"After all, we only have one life to live and we don't propose to live it dangling somewhere between frostbite and brainwash."

"You two have taken a noble position about this," I said, "and it's one I'll tell all my children about. So, bon voyage, and give my regards to the alligators."

They may have answered me, but Lonzo's few teeth were chattering so loudly I couldn't be sure.

The Pundit and Lonzo were, for a change, eminently presentable. They were washed and shaven and combed and otherwise groomed.

Lonzo had just gotten a haircut and was redolent of rum—bay rum, I think. The Pundit doesn't need haircuts anymore.

Both wore clean shirts. Lonzo had a sprig of holly stuck in his battered felt hat. I looked at them; they grinned back.

"Where's the wedding?" I asked.

The Pundit said, "We're not going to any wedding, and you know it. We are, however, on our way to spend Christmas with the Widder

Lady of Whiskey Cove. We have been invited out for the holiday.

"There will be a grand gathering of people there at the Widder's. Her daughter, Mary, who lives up in Detroit, is coming with her husband, Joe, and their little boy. He's just a baby. The Widder hasn't even seen him yet.

"Sounds like a lot of people to crowd into the Widder's house," I said. "You sure there'll be room for you?"

"Not to worry," said The Pundit. "We'll be staying in the Widder's barn. It's heated and she has a couple of cots in there. We'll be quite comfortable."

"It's a lot better than some places we slept lately," said Lonzo.

"I don't think I ever asked you before," I said, "but where exactly is Whiskey Cove?"

"It's not hard to find," said The Pundit. "You just go out beyond Oteen, turn north a little until you come to Starr Road, then just follow Starr Road east. You'll come to the place soon enough."

"Well," I said, "I'm delighted that you two have a nice place to go for the holiday."

"Oh, it's nice enough," said The Pundit in the offhand manner of a man accustomed to dashing off to Acapulco on a whim, "but Lonzo and me, we're old soldiers. We just don't make much of a fuss about Christmas anymore."

"I'm sort of surprised that the Widder Lady invited you two out to her place again after the way Lonzo bad-mouthed her cooking on Thanksgiving," I said.

The Pundit grinned again. "Well," he said, "she's still a little sweet on Lonzo, and the nights have been getting longer and colder. But for this holiday, she's promised not to go fishing for compliments about her cooking."

"And I promised not to give her none," said Lonzo.

"How are you going to get out to Whiskey Cove?" I asked. "You need a ride?"

"Kind of you to offer," said The Pundit, puffing mightily on a cigar butt, "but our transportation has already been laid on, as they say in England.

"The Widder's brother, Melchior, is going to pick us up in his automobile in a couple of hours."

"Melchior—now there's an odd name," I said.

"Odd names seem to run in the Widder's family," The Pundit said.

"There's Melchior, of course, and her two other brothers are named Gaspar and Balthasar. They'll probably be out at the Widder's farm on Christmas, too. They usually are."

Something about the names clicked.

"Now let me get this straight," I said. "You two are going to follow Starr Road to the east until you come to the Widder's farm where you will stay, for all I know, in a manger. You will be seeing Mary and her husband, Joseph, and their new-born son. And you will be joined there on Christmas Day by Melchior, Gaspar, and Balthasar. Is that it?"

Lonzo nodded gravely.

"You got it," said The Pundit.

"And you two have the nerve to tell me you don't make much of a fuss about Christmas anymore," I said, a little wistfully.

I couldn't resist asking, "So what brought you here to my office?"

"Well," said The Pundit, looking at me coolly over the ropy remains of the cigar, "we were sure you wouldn't want us to go out there empty-handed."

"That's right," said Lonzo. "Stuff like that frankincense and myrrh costs money."

Sighing, I paid.

I decided that I might just run out to the Widder's farm myself on Christmas.

3
Life on the River Bank

The air down under the I-240 bridge was pleasantly damp and cool. A little breeze ruffled the surface of the water and big, white cumulus clouds chased shadows over the French Broad River.

The Pundit, perched precariously in a folding aluminum porch chair, stared dreamily out over the water, half asleep. His rusty black fedora was pulled down over this forehead, his black high-topped shoes were unlaced, and he had even unbuttoned his dingy black suitcoat. He looked like a deacon at a church picnic.

Lonzo was bent over a metal tackle box, rummaging. He dragged out a hook that looked big enough to catch a whale. Near his left heel was a coil of new clothesline. Near his right heel was a cylindrical shape hidden by a brown paper bag. Occasionally he would put the cylindrical shape to his mouth.

He was attired in his customary paint-spotted pants, a green baseball cap advertising a popular brand of chewing tobacco, and a T-shirt that was a souvenir of something called the Port Saint Lucie Yacht Marina and Used Car Company.

He fastened the hook to the end of the clothesline. Then he pulled a piece of rancid salt pork from the tackle box and speared it with the hook. Then he tied the loose end of the clothesline to the tackle box.

I hunkered down beside him. "We're a mite far north to catch alligators," I said.

Lonzo glared at me with owl-eyed concentration.

"Gonna catch the biggest fish in this river," he said. "Gonna win first prize in that there fishing contest."

"The only fishing contest I know about is the one the Land-of-Sky Council is sponsoring for French Broad River Week."

"That's the one," said Lonzo, excitedly. "The landasky big fish contest. And I aim to win it. I'm practicing. I'm going to catch a whopper just like my great-uncle Forbish did in 1909. He caught one that weighed a hundred and sixty pounds and was five feet long." So saying, he threw the hook and the bait out into the river.

"That fish your great-uncle Forbish caught really must have been a big one," I said. "Was it a bass or a muskie?"

"It was a surgeon," said Lonzo.

There was a metallic clatter as The Pundit fell out of his aluminum chair. "A surgeon?" he roared.

"Sure," said Lonzo. "It was a female surgeon, too. It was stuffed full of eggs. I hear they make caveat out of fish eggs like that in Russia."

"Are you sure it wasn't a cuttlefish instead of surgeon?" I asked.

"No! No!" howled The Pundit, stretched out on the concrete apron under the bridge. "It wasn't neither of them. It was really a nurse shark! But beware nurse sharks and caveat!" He roared with laughter.

Lonzo's lower lip protruded.

"Gol dang it!" he said. "I said it was a surgeon and that's what it was." He stomped over and kicked The Pundit's chair about fifty-three yards.

His reedy voice quavered with indignation as he discussed his generally low opinion of The Pundit and me. He had reached the part about matrimonial prospects of our parents when the tackle box clattered across the concrete a couple of feet, moving toward the river.

All three of us silently watched the box. It moved six inches more toward the river. Then it whipped out across the surface of the water, moving almost too fast to watch, and disappeared under the surface.

There was not even a bubble to mark its passing.

There was a long silence. The Pundit wordlessly picked up Lonzo's cylindrical object and drank deeply.

"Maybe there is a surgeon out there," he said. "Something certainly severed us from that tackle box. But whatever it is, I'm sure I don't want to catch it.

"In fact, I believe I'm going back to the farm."

And he walked up the river bank and disappeared down the road.

Life on the River Bank

The Pundit's gravelly voice on the telephone was terse. "Lunch. You're invited. Tomorrow—1 p.m. Under the bridge. Bring the wine. Goodbye."

It was an offer I couldn't refuse. The next afternoon, clutching a bottle of an unassuming burgundy, I climbed out of Hirohito's Revenge and dropped down under the bridge. I was guided by a beguiling aroma, a pungent fragrance, the irresistible smell of good things cooking.

The three of them were seated in the shade under the bridge. In front of them, propped up on an arrangement of sidewalk bricks, was a large lard can. Under the can was a small, almost smokeless fire. In the can a white, mucilaginous substance simmered.

My arrival was greeted with cries of welcome and expressions of thirst—about half and half.

"What's cooking?" I asked.

"Bullybase," said Lonzo, plucking the wine bottle out of my hand.

"Indeed, it's a sort of perloo, fashioned around a cat Lonzo caught in the river this morning," said The Pundit. "And a few potatoes, a touch of onion, a tad of this, and a pinch of that, and we will have a meal fit for the most demanding gourmet. It will be ready in a little while, but first, let's enjoy the wine."

Lonzo poured the wine into jelly glasses he extracted from a fishing tackle box. I declined. As they sipped, I inspected them. Clearly it was an occasion of some sort.

The Pundit was dressed formally. He wore a tie. Lonzo had on clean white sailing pants, black high-topped sneakers, a painter's cap, and a white cook's apron that bore evidence of the fact that he had been cooking.

The Little Old Lady wore blue jeans, T-shirt, and white, high-topped sneakers. On her head was a battered straw skimmer with a garland of daisies woven around the crown.

It was pleasant in the cool shade beside the slowly flowing water. The Little Old Lady took an appreciative sip of the wine and smacked her lips. "My land, but this is festive, just festive. Wine and all for lunch by the riverside. It reminds me of my undergraduate days at Sweet Briar."

She turned her snapping black eyes on The Pundit and said, "And I do believe that we really have you to thank for all of this. How did

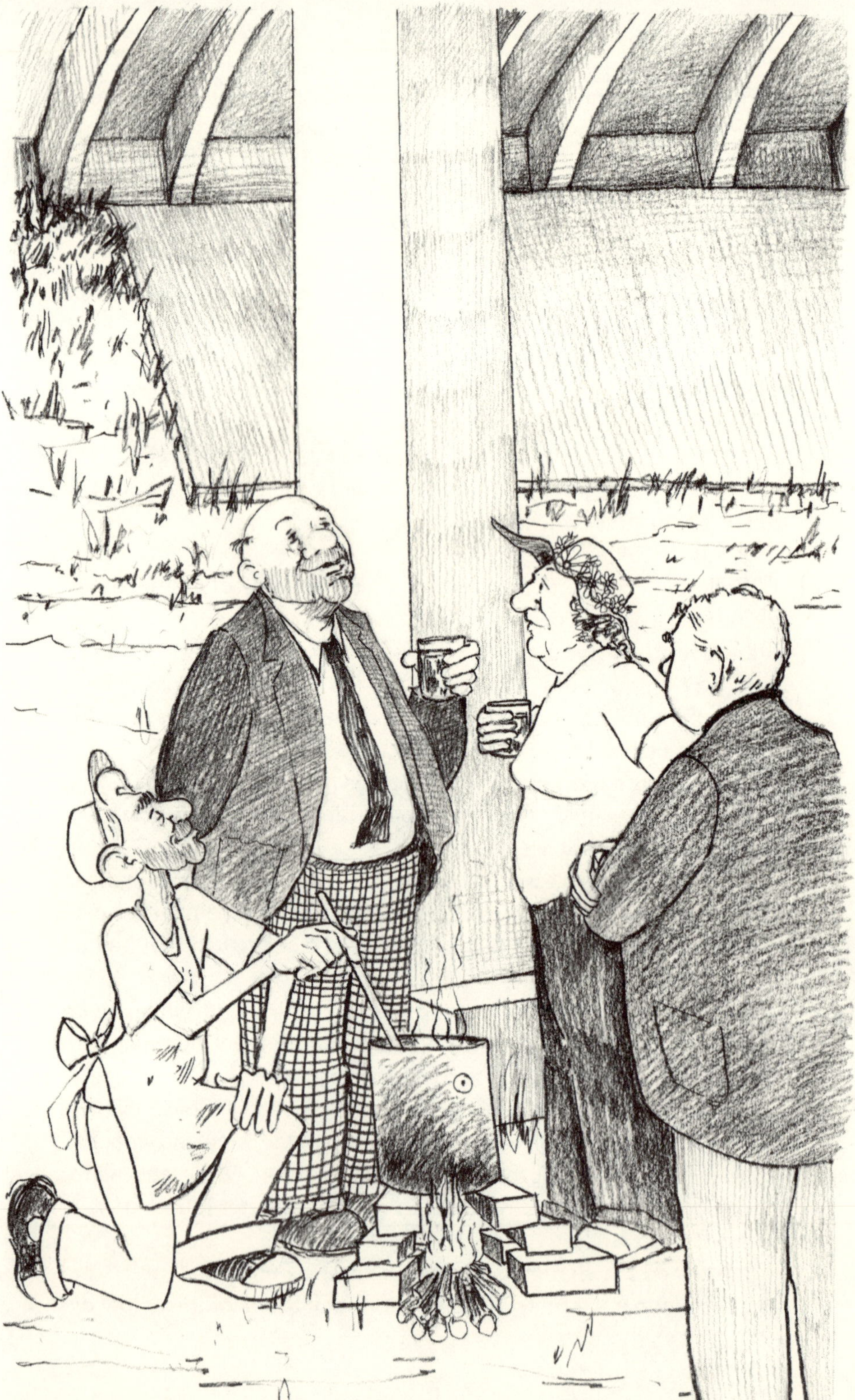

Life on the River Bank

you ever remember to bring everything? I'm sure I would have forgotten a dozen things. You're so efficient!"

Lonzo snorted derisively. The Pundit grinned. "Think nothing of it, my dear," he said. "It was nothing. In my time I have organized much bigger and more complicated events. Not more important, of course. Nothing could be more important than luncheon with you and my friends here, but they were more complex, you know.

"It's not generally known around here, but I was in charge of the foodstuffs and supplies on the Third Byrd Expedition to the Antarctic, and that was a big, big job."

Lonzo choked on his wine and I couldn't stay quiet.

"Wait a minute, here," I said. "Now just hold the phone a minute. Pundit, I've let you get away with some whoppers. The time you told us you were in charge of military intelligence for Black Jack Pershing in Mexico, I never said a word. And when you told us how you helped Alexander Fleming invent penicillin, I never argued a bit. But this is too much. I just don't believe you were in charge of anything on the Third Byrd Expedition to the Antarctic."

The Pundit stared at me. "Do you happen to know," he asked, "the name of the man who really was in charge of the foodstuffs and supplies for the Third Byrd Expedition?"

"Well, no," I said.

Behind me I heard Lonzo chuckle and say softly, "Gotcha!"

"As I was saying, my dear," The Pundit said, turning back to the Little Old Lady, "when I was in charge of the foodstuffs and supplies for the Third Byrd Expedition, I had to think of all the things one hundred fifty men would need during a whole year on the ice at Little America. Now that was a big job!"

The Little Old Lady took a hefty swallow of the wine and said, "I used to know a Byrd. Maybe it was the same one that went on that expedition. All the girls at Sweet Briar were swoony about him, but he was *my* beau. He was my escort the night I came out at the cotillion in Richmond. My, he was something splendid—tall and handsome and rich and just so sweet! 'Dicky Byrd' I used to call him."

Her smile faded. "Sometimes I wonder what happened to Dicky Byrd. Sometimes I wonder what happened to me."

There was silence. The Pundit cleared his throat and said, "I don't think the Byrd of the Third Antarctic Expedition was the same Byrd who was your beau, really."

The Little Old Lady fastened her black eyes on him and snapped, "Did you ever meet my Dicky Byrd?"

"Well, no," said The Pundit.

"Gotcha," said Lonzo.

"I'm sure my Dicky Byrd was a very fine man to work for when you and he went to the South Pole, Mr. Pundit," she said, "and please pass the wine."

In about ten minutes Lonzo assured us that the bullybase was ready to cut. The Pundit produced four plastic bowls and four spoons from the tackle box. The silverware was embossed **U.S.N.** I was afraid to ask if they were left over from the Byrd expedition.

The Little Old Lady dug into her big canvas handbag and extracted a loaf of bread. Lonzo dished out salt and the stew and, with some trepidation, I tasted it.

It was sheer ambrosia. It had several flavors, all cunningly mixed, but all separate, too. I couldn't exactly tell what the flavors were, but the combination was magnificent. The bread was fresh and crusty and for a few minutes there was silence on the river bank, broken only by a few contented burps.

As I got to the bottom of my bowl, I noticed that I had been given a bone. It was about three inches long and a quarter of an inch in diameter. I could not imagine where it fitted into the body of a fish. Then I had another idea and my stomach churned.

"Pundit," I said carefully, "when you said Lonzo caught this cat in the river this morning, you did mean cat*fish*, didn't you?"

"Well, of course," said The Pundit. "What else would I me—" And he began to roar with laughter.

"Good Lord!" he said, "you really don't think we'd feed you stewed cat, do you?"

The Little Old Lady made a choking noise.

"Why not?" asked Lonzo.

"If that was a fish in the stew," I said, "where did this bone come from?" I held it up to them. "That didn't come from any catfish."

"Of course not," said The Pundit. "That particular bone came from the Liberty Chicken."

"The what chicken?"

"The Liberty Chicken. Listen, while we were driving down here from the farm this morning, we spotted a chicken alongside the road.

Life on the River Bank

It seemed to be at liberty. So Lonzo took liberties with its neck and we cleaned it and threw it in the pot with the catfish.

"A Liberty Chicken seemed to be very appropriate for the day."

"I don't get it," I said.

"Sometimes," said The Pundit, "you betray the fact that that college you went to was for plumbers and not scholars. Today is the fourteen of July. It's Bastille Day and we struck a blow for liberty this morning. That's what this festive occasion is all about. We are observing a great French holiday, and we invited you because you brought a little of that great nation with you."

"Formidable!" I said.

"Vive la France," said the Little Old Lady, finishing the wine in her glass.

"And here's to the Third Byrd," said Lonzo, finishing the wine in the bottle.

They were sitting almost out from under the bridge, in the warm autumn sunlight. Their backs were propped against a concrete retaining wall; their legs were splayed out. Their heads were together and they seemed to be studying something in The Pundit's lap. Every once in a while The Pundit would say something and Lonzo would cackle his nervous high-pitched laugh.

The Pundit was arrayed in his usual funeral garb of rusty black suit, battered black fedora, and white shirt buttoned at the neck but absent a necktie.

Lonzo wore a baseball cap bearing the emblem of the Chicago Cubs, a blue T-shirt with the message **UNCA Blue Streaks**, and tattered canvas pants. One grimy, sockless big toe peeped coyly out from the end of one of his well-worn tennis shoes.

They each had cylindrical objects wrapped in brown paper bags close to hand, and as I got closer it became obvious that they had been enjoying the wine of the country. Maybe the wine of several other countries, too.

Then I noticed that The Pundit was holding a pocket calculator. Lonzo, astonishingly, was clutching a tooth-marked pencil and occasionally making marks on a piece of paper.

The Pundit punched at the calculator and said something to Lonzo. Lonzo scratched with the pencil. They both examined the results and howled with laughter.

"What's happening?" I asked.

"It's budget time," said The Pundit. Lonzo giggled.

"I didn't know you had that problem," I said.

"We are not entirely indigent," said The Pundit with a touch of indignation. He spoke slowly and clearly, but his eyes were focused on a point ten feet behind my head. "It ain't easy when 70 percent of your expenses goes for refreshments. And we have a real bad cash flow problem just now."

"Yeah," said Lonzo. "The outflow is bigger than the inflow, so there's no cash flow." The humor of his remarks appeared to overcome him. He rolled over on his side, cackling insanely and clapping his hands.

The Pundit manfully tried to muffle a belch. He said, "I get my pension from my service with the Philippine Scouts, of course, and Lonzo gets money regular from the veterans, so we have some money coming in.

"But it ain't enough," he said mournfully. "It just ain't enough." A big tear cut a track down his cheek.

"How do you manage to live?" I asked, although I knew the answer.

"We resort to mendicancy," said The Pundit, recovering his good humor quickly.

"He means we begs it," said Lonzo.

"That's no way to say it, Lonzo," said The Pundit.

"We steals it?" said Lonzo.

"No, not that, either," said The Pundit. "We simply rely on the kindness, understanding, and generosity of our friends and benefactors to enable us to make our modest ends meet."

"Is that what we do?" Lonzo inquired.

"Certainly," said The Pundit, taking a swallow from his bag. "By the way, this one's almost dry," he said, looking at me. "How's your cash flow?"

"It's the same old story," I said. "I'll stake you to hamburgers or doughnuts and the coffee's on me, but I won't buy you any Old Popskull."

"Did you say 'benefactor?'" Lonzo asked The Pundit bitterly.

Life on the River Bank

I found them down under the bridge, huddled under Lonzo's drop cloth, morosely staring at the gray, rain-swept river. They had a fire going in an old paint can. Lonzo had a big stack of what appeared to be left-over political campaign fliers. The words *Vote For* were prominent, but I couldn't make out the rest of the message.

Lonzo was steadily feeding the fliers, a sheet at a time, into the fire. As I hunkered down beside him, he grinned. "Ain't much heat in these things," he said.

"Nor light, neither," growled The Pundit in his gravelly voice.

"Next time, I hope they use better paper," Lonzo said.

"Maybe we'll get some better candidates," I said.

"You're still a tourist," said The Pundit.

A heavy truck rumbled overhead. The bridge structure vibrated. The Pundit looked out at the driving rain.

"I know we've been behind on our rainfall for a while, but do they have to make it all up in one week?"

Lonzo threw another flier on the fire.

"Perhaps you should have stayed in Florida longer," I said.

"No," said The Pundit. "Things there ain't much better. We got a letter from Big Time Benny Biscayne the other day. Benny and some of his colleagues on the beach invested in a jai-alai fronton over near St. Citrusburg. They sank a lot of money into the building, but the day they held the grand opening the building sank, too.

"The north end of the fronton fell into one of those sinkholes that have been opening up down there in Florida. Instead of playing jai-alai there, they're playing high-low."

"But it still takes jacks to open," said Lonzo.

"You're thinking of a different game," said The Pundit.

"No, they're really all the same," said Lonzo. "No matter what they call them, Lonzo loses."

"Anyhow," said The Pundit, "Benny said he and his associates are out looking for the guy who sold them the land. But he appears to have sunk out of sight, too. Benny's kind of worried. Some of his colleagues are not the type to lose money without making a fuss over it. And you can lose more than a jai-alai court in one of those holes. We may see Benny. He might come up here too for a while, until things cool off down there in Florida."

Lonzo shivered and threw a whole handful of fliers on the fire. "If he wants to cool off, this is the right place," he said.

TWO ON THE SQUARE

The Pundit pulled the drop cloth higher on his shoulders, pulled his battered felt hat down over his ears, and looked at me.

"What brought you out of a nice warm office to come down here and associate with us poor unfortunates?" he asked.

"Oh," I said, "I just thought I'd slip over here to see how you two are getting along and maybe interview you about the state of affairs in the area, get your views on local politics and the weather and so forth."

The Pundit laughed. It was a dreadful sound, a compound of the sounds made by breaking glass and clogged hydraulic lines.

"I'd rather talk about the weather. It's bad, but not as bad as local politics. And when I think about what they're up to down there in Raleigh . . . well, it just makes me wish I really was Dooley and Lonzo was Hennessey."

Lonzo smiled his dreamy smile. "Who's Hennessey?" he asked.

"Back around the turn of the century, when I was living in Chicago," said The Pundit, "there was a newspaper editor there named Peter Finley Dunne, and he wrote a column about an old Irishman named Mr. Dooley.

"Dooley was supposed to be the owner of a saloon in Chicago's South Side which, in those days, was more than somewhat Irish. Dooley was forever having conversations with a customer named Hennessey who, judging from the number of times he appeared in the column, must have been a lush.

"Anyhow, they'd get started on politics or who won the Spanish-American War, and Dooley would lecture to Hennessey about it for a column and a half of six-point type.

"If your eyes didn't crack up on that small type and if you could untangle the Irish brogue in which the columns were written, the columns were funny—and smart. Perceptive, you know.

"I almost used the word *insightful*, for which I'd never have forgiven myself."

The Pundit huddled more closely under the drop cloth.

Lonzo cleared his throat. "The only Hennessey I ever heard of made brandy," he said.

"That's the best idea you've had all day," said The Pundit, scrambling out from under the drop cloth and heading up the river bank toward the street.

"I never heard of that Dooley, neither," said Lonzo, "but I'll go

Life on the River Bank

along with this guy Hennessey." He trailed off after The Pundit.

"I wonder what Peter Finley Dunne would have done with those two?" I thought, as I trudged after them.

The Pundit rose majestically, strode purposefully down the concrete slab to the water's edge, stopped, and filled his black hat with river water.

Then, slowly and with evident relish, he poured the water over his head, clapped the dripping hat back on his few remaining gray locks, and resumed his seat under the bridge.

"Refreshing," he said, sighing a little.

"Another triumph for the inventor of drip-dry fabric," I said.

The Pundit smiled serenely, then looked thoughtful. Carefully he put his hand in his hip pocket and withdrew a still-squirming minnow.

He gazed at it for a minute, apparently perplexed. They he got up again, walked to the water's edge, and carefully restored the minnow to the river. "Wasn't big enough to be a keeper," he explained gravely.

It was hot. Eddies of pure heat, mixed with tendrils of water vapor, rose from the river. The leaves on the trees on the river bank were motionless. Even the shady underside of the bridge was hot to the touch. The mountains that surround Asheville were invisible behind a screen of haze, smog, and water vapor. It was a day to make automobile air conditioning almost worth the money.

Lonzo was flat on his back with his bare white feet in the river. His straw cowboy hat was pulled down over his eyes. A tall bottle of murky brown fluid stood at his elbow. "Pundit, it's right hot here today. I wish we was at the beach."

"It is a mite warmish here today," said The Pundit judicially. "But I wouldn't come right out and call it hot. My no, this is nothing compared to what I've seen in other places.

"Why, I recall one time whilst I was still serving with the Philippine Scouts. We camped in a coconut grove near Zamboanga. That afternoon the weather got so hot the milk in the coconuts turned to steam and the nuts started exploding all over the place.

"Lonzo, I tell you, it was like an artillery barrage. Jagged pieces of exploding coconuts was flying every which-away, just like shrapnel. Now they was thousands of monkeys turned tail and run. This naturally made their tails the most vulnerable parts of their anatomies, and thousands of monkeys had their tails shot off. It was just plain dreadful, Lonzo, absolutely pitiful."

There was a catch in The Pundit's hoarse voice. He used the grimy cuff of his shirt to wipe away a furtive tear.

I thought I heard Lonzo groan faintly.

The Pundit sniffed hard a couple of times and then, his composure regained, continued. "Now to be truthful, I only saw the coconuts explode that one time, but after the barrage was over, one of the natives told me it happened sort of regular in that area.

"And that, Lonzo, is why the monkeys have no tails in Zamboanga!"

There was a long, long pause.

Lonzo arose, hoisting himself to his feet in awkward, lanky hitches.

He pulled his prized cowboy hat down firmly on his head, made sure that the cap on his bottle was tight, clamped it under his elbow, and, without a word, started wading down the river bank.

"Where in the Sam Hill are you going?" asked The Pundit.

"The shrapnel from the nuts around here is getting too thick for me," said Lonzo.

"I read that piece you did last week about earthquakes," said The Pundit, keeping one bleary eye firmly fastened on his fishing line, "and I didn't believe a word of it. Not a word."

Lonzo, flat on his back on the river bank with his straw cowboy hat down over his eyes, giggled.

"What I don't understand," said The Pundit, "is why you keep writing these things that call for expert knowledge without ever consulting me first."

"Yeah," said Lonzo.

"Wait a minute," I said. "Everything I wrote in that earthquake column was supported by science. Surely you believe in science, don't you?"

"Hah!" said The Pundit, lighting an El Ropo cigar. "Science got me where I am today."

Life on the River Bank

"And just look at him!" said Lonzo.

"Let's not get personal," said The Pundit. "We was talking about earthquakes."

"I was in a earthquake once," said Lonzo, sitting up. "Leastways, I thought it was a earthquake. It was back in '28 or maybe it was '29. I can't exactly remember which, but I went to live at my Uncle Cloyd's place on Whippersnapper Creek over in Sevier County.

"As I recall, it was just after my third wife had thrown me out of the house for the fifth time, or maybe it was that my fifth wife had thrown me out for the third time. I can't exactly remember . . .

"Well, anyway, I went over there to stay with Uncle Cloyd. And that first night, I woke up with a sort of feeling that something was wrong. I didn't know what, exactly, but I knew something was wrong. Well, in a minute or two, the whole cabin started to shake. Then the north end of the cabin heaved up and down. The windows rattled. The crockery clattered. If Uncle Cloyd had had any pictures on the wall, they'd have fallen down, I bet.

"Quick as a wink, I suspicioned that we was having a earthquake and I commenced to yell. Uncle Cloyd, he woke up then and he started yellowing, too. He yelled, 'Thunderbolt, dern you, git out from under the cabin!'

"And pretty soon, the biggest boar hog I ever saw crawled out from under the cabin and went and lied down in a mud puddle over by the fence. Uncle Cloyd said Thunderbolt liked to sleep under the cabin, but sometimes he got restless and when he rooted around he sort of lifted up the whole building. So it wasn't no earthquake, after all. Sure felt like one, though."

The Pundit threw his fishing pole into the river and glared.

"Lonzo, I've always suspected that you wouldn't know a pig from an earthquake and you just proved it. Why don't you let someone who knows something about earthquakes talk for a while?"

So saying, he relit his cigar. I moved out of the smoke cloud, coughing. Lonzo flopped back on the bank, tilting his hat back over his face.

"All right," I said to The Pundit, "tell us all about earthquakes."

"That's a downright dumb thing to say," said The Pundit. "How can a man with my vast knowledge tell everything he knows about earthquakes? We ain't got all year here, you know. That's like asking Albert Einstein to explain the theory of relativity in twenty-five words or less.

"However, I will tell you about one particular earthquake. It happened at Iloilo on the island of Mindanao while me and General Eisenhower was serving in the Philippine Scouts.

"We was camped in a coconut plantation when the earthquake hit and, boys, I tell you she was a corker!

"The ground shook and so did those coconut trees. In fact, they shook so hard that the milk in the coconuts turned to butter."

Lonzo jerked upright, climbed to his feet, threw his fishing pole into the river, and stalked away.

In the shade under the bridge, The Pundit was holding court, his broken baritone rising and falling across the barely moving brown water. Slouching around him in attitudes reminiscent of students at the feet of a master, were some other members of the Under-the-Bridge Philosophical and Recreational Society.

"Yes, it's sad but true that envy does terrible things to a man," said The Pundit, shaking his head sagely.

"Why, just last week I was relating an experience I had whilst I was on the far-off Philippine Islands, when my old friend Lonzo was so overcome by envy that he took to the river.

"Didn't manage to get himself out until he was passing Hot Springs, neither," said The Pundit.

"Didn't want to come out. It was nice and cool in the river and too danged hot ashore," said Lonzo, sitting a little apart as befits an aggrieved person.

"My friend Lonzo lost his straw cowboy hat in the bargain, didn't you, Lonzo?" said The Pundit, smiling.

"Didn't neither lose it," snarled Lonzo. "A danged shark et it."

"Well, anyhow, today, since it's still a mite warm, I thought I'd start the discussion among us world travelers with a little talk about the time I used Baffin Bay lamp fish to survive a winter in the Arctic."

Lonzo groaned, stood up, and moved closer to the water's edge.

"It was about the summer of '33 or '34, sometime around there," said The Pundit, "when I went north on the schooner Gertrude Bluenose under the command of Captain Bob Bartlett. Our mission

Life on the River Bank

was to bring Bibles, blankets, and biscuits to a little-known tribe of Eskimos who lived on the north shore of Baffin Island."

"What was you doing on a expedition like that?" asked Lonzo.

"I went along as spiritual adviser, of course," said The Pundit.

Lonzo started to wade into the river.

"Well," said The Pundit, "we pushed far to the north of the Arctic Circle. After bouncing off a few icebergs and repelling a few polar bears, we finally found the tribe we was looking for. So we unloaded the Bibles and stuff. But one evening while I was giving spiritual guidance to the elders of the tribe, Captain Bob sailed away.

"He later said winter was coming on early and he didn't want to get trapped up there. Besides, he said, at the rate I was giving spiritual guidance, it looked to him I could go on all winter. And there I was—without food, without fuel, without hope, almost.

"But them Eskimos filled my igloo with Baffin Island lamp fish and I never had a day's distress. As soon as the water in Baffin Bay froze over, they chopped holes in the ice and started catching these long, skinny lamp fish. The fish froze solid as soon as they hit the air.

"These fish were just about the oiliest critters on the face of this earth. What you did was, you sawed off the tail of the fish, then you stuck the long, spiky head of the fish into the snow wall of your igloo. Then you just touched a match to the place where you sawed off the tail. There was so much oil in them fish that each one of them burned like a big torch. All winter long I had more light and heat than I could use.

"I came out of the igloo that spring with a tan like I had been at Miami Beach the whole winter."

"It's Belcher," said The Pundit.

"It's not neither," said Lonzo. "It's Belly Cheer, that's what."

"Well, whatever it is," said The Pundit, taking a sip from a bottle wrapped in a brown paper bag, "I don't think I'll be able to include it on my social schedule this season."

I shifted my seat, trying vainly to find a soft spot on the concrete apron that runs down to the French Broad under the bridge.

"I went to one of them things a couple of years ago," said Lonzo,

TWO ON THE SQUARE

musingly. "First thing that happened, there came a sharp-looking lady who had me carrying folding chairs all over downtown. I swear, I toted so confounded many folding chairs I was ready to fold myself. Then I went and got something international to eat and got the worst case of indigestion I ever had in my life."

"What did you eat?" I asked.

"I dunno exactly," said Lonzo. "It was called Whisker Bob or something like that. It was like pieces of meat on a stick. The meat was all right, but the stick didn't have no flavor at all."

There was another silence.

Then The Pundit, a little awed, said, "Lonzo, that stuff was called shish-ka-bob and you wasn't supposed to eat the stick."

There was another silence.

Lonzo took a sip from the brown paper bottle. "No wonder I didn't feel so good afterward," he said.

"The last time I went over there for the Belcher thing," said The Pundit, "some guy with a loudspeaker kept trying to get me to pay three bucks to go up in a balloon. The thing wasn't going very high. They kept it tied to the ground pretty good. It just sort of whooshed up about twenty feet and then slid back down again. But, shoot, I don't need a balloon to get twenty feet high . . . nor three bucks, either."

"I still don't know what makes them things go up in the air," said Lonzo.

So I explained to them about how the warmer air in the balloon displaces the cooler air in the outside atmosphere and how the result is a positive increment of lift in the balloon and how, with the judicious jettisoning of ballast and the careful application of heat from the gas burner, a free balloon can be maneuvered.

I gave them a brief review of the history of ballooning, starting with the brothers Montgolfier in Paris and running through Professor Picard and his high-altitude flights.

When I got through, Lonzo was goggle-eyed with amazement. The Pundit was making low, gutteral noises that I thought were expressions of admiration until I realized that he was aleep and snoring.

"Speaking of gas bags . . .," said Lonzo, softly.

The Pundit made a gargling noise, awoke, and sat up.

I snapped the cap back on my bottle of Perrier water, reeled in my fishing line, put my hat on my head, and got ready to leave.

Life on the River Bank

"Where you going?" asked The Pundit.

"To the Bele Chere thing," I said. "I promised to work in the beer booth for the Hospice people, and it's about time I showed up over there."

"Beer!" they said in unison, their eyes gleaming.

"Forget it," I said. "Hospice is a good outfit and I wouldn't slip Leopold, King of the Belgians, a free one. Not at the Hospice booth."

"It was just a thought," said The Pundit.

The balloon pilot pulled the trigger on the propane tank, a long spear of flame shot into the neck of the balloon, and the whole thing rose majestically.

As the balloon reached the end of its tether, I smelled something that was not hot air or burned gas. It was an unmistakable mixture of grime, grease, and muscatel.

Sure enough, there across the circle of balloon watchers were Lonzo and The Pundit.

The Pundit was attired in a rumpled, scuffy seersucker suit topped with a battered straw hat. Lonzo was wearing a T-shirt emblazoned with the words **Wyoming Blew It In 1896**.

Keeping carefully upwind, I sidled around the circle.

"Hey," I said to Lonzo, "I thought you two had taken off in the Honkerbus to attend the Democratic convention in New York."

"Oh, we was going to go," said Lonzo, his eyes riveted on the balloon, "but someone put a new lock on the gas pump down at the bus gar—garrouch!"

The cry of pain was caused by The Pundit who stopped firmly between me and Lonzo, stomping hard on Lonzo's instep.

"There's no need to bother you with mundane details about our travel arrangements," The Pundit said with a smirk. "The truth is that Lonzo and I had planned to drive up to Fun City, but we discovered at the last moment that our social secretary had made a serious error. We would not dream of leaving Asheville while all this (He took off his Panama hat and waved it in the general direction of the downtown.) was going on. Why, it would be positively disloyal for us to neglect this annual extravaganza, this municipal spectacular, this Belcher celebration."

Lonzo, hopping on one foot, snorted indignantly.

"You old phony," he said to The Pundit. "You don't even know

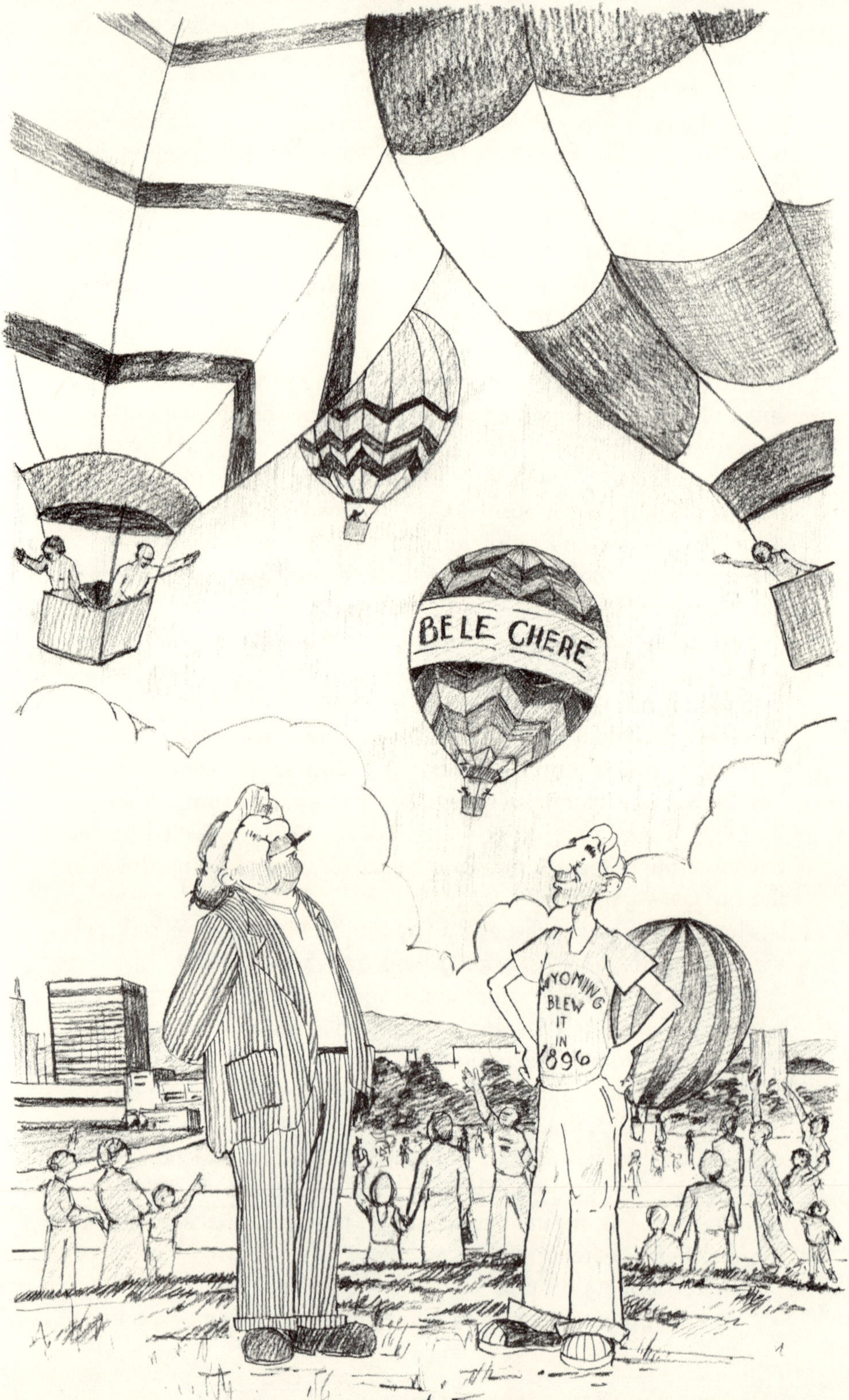
BE LE CHERE
WYOMING BLEW IT IN 1896

how to say it. It's not a Belcher celebration, dang it! The thing is called the Belly Cheer!"

"Well," said The Pundit to me, "it's been pleasant talking to you here at the balloon accessions, but Lonzo and I have to go over to Haywood Street now to hear the singing dog."

"Wait a minute," I said, clutching at The Pundit's coat sleeve. "What's this about a singing dog?"

"It's true," said The Pundit. "There's a man in town who has a singing dog. The dog's repertoire is pretty limited, though. It will only sing opera, and then it only sings music by one composer."

"I'll bet the name of that composer is Poochini," I said.

"You must have heard the dog already yourself," said The Pundit as he walked away, followed by Lonzo, hopping along on one foot.

4
Philosophy on Wheels

I was waiting for the bus to pull out when Lonzo and The Pundit got aboard. When the bus driver demanded money, The Pundit gave him a cock-and-bull story about how he and Lonzo had just been held up and robbed of their transfers.

"And in broad daylight, too," said The Pundit, rolling his eyes in mock distress.

Lonzo smiled and nodded. But it didn't work. The driver insisted on the fare. So The Pundit dragged out a battered snap-top change purse and reluctantly counted out sixty cents.

Then he made a remark about "blood-sucking public utilities." The driver offered to draw some of The Pundit's blood, perhaps for comparison purposes. These social amenities concluded, the two of them then made their way toward the back of the bus.

Both of them were heavily tanned. Lonzo wore his usual dreamy smile and a fisherman's cap with the words **Welcome to Pompano Beach** embroidered on it.

Spotting an empty seat next to me, The Pundit flopped into it with a gusty sigh. Lonzo, moving with his boneless glide, slid into a seat across the aisle.

"You two have been in Florida," I said.

"True," said The Pundit, "and it was perspicacious of you to notice. We have been down there, Lonzo and I, enjoying the climate and reviewing some business opportunities we felt were worth our personal attention. We had expected to return after a sojourn of only a week, but circumstances forced us to stay much longer. Transportation problems, you know."

"The airlines canceled your flight?" I asked.

"No," said The Pundit. "The truck drivers went out on strike. Most annoying. Lonzo and I were obliged to accept employment in agriculture."

"You got work picking oranges?"

"No, lettuce. And never again. However," The Pundit continued, "there is always an advantage in adversity. While we were engaged in that bucolic pastime, I got the idea for the biggest, most sensational deal Lonzo and I have promoted yet. It's the **OTAPLC**, and just as soon as we clear up a few details with the Securities and Exchange Commission, we'll start selling stock."

"What in the world is the **OTAPLC**?" I asked.

"It's the Orlando to Asheville Pipeline Company," said The Pundit.

"Pipeline?" I asked.

"Pipeline!" The Pundit said.

"Pipeline for what?" I asked.

"For orange juice, naturally," said The Pundit. "Do you have any idea how many oranges there are in Orlando? Do you have any idea how much orange juice is drunk every day in Asheville? Why not a pipeline?"

I thought it over for a while. Then I asked, "Does this pipeline pipe dream have any connection at all with that other nutty scheme you had of putting Lonzo to work making gasahol out of moonshine whiskey?"

The Pundit's booming voice lowered to a conspiratorial growl. "Sort of," he said. "That's one of the details the Securities and Exchange Commission won't hear about, though. It's just that if we pipe all that orange juice up here from Florida, we ought to have something to send back. And Lonzo, bless his 100-proof head, can take care of that. Now how many shares of stock shall I put you down for?"

But we had come to my stop and I had to get off the bus then.

The Honkerbus heaved into view, made a two-wheel turn onto the square, and came to a dead stop in the bus lane.

"Hold on, there," shouted The Pundit.

"Yeah!" yelled Lonzo.

"I'm glad we caught you," said The Pundit, alighting from the truck.

"Yeah," said Lonzo.

Philosophy on Wheels

"We wanted to tell you goodbye," said The Pundit.
"Yeah," said Lonzo.
"Yes, indeed," said The Pundit. "We have had a little windfall and we are going on a trip."
"What windfall? What trip?" I asked.
"Well," said The Pundit, "the other day we ran into some humanitarians who call themselves the Society for the Improvement of Pack Square. These fine, public-spirited people gave Lonzo and me four retread tires for the truck, $50 for gas, and half a ham. Then they suggested we might want to go to Florida for the season."
"Yeah," said Lonzo.
"Wait a minute," I said. "Seems to me that the last time you two went to Florida you went broke in a hurry and wound up working on your knees in a bean field to get carfare home."
A grimace of remembered pain flickered across The Pundit's face.
Then he smiled. "That won't happen this time," he said. "This time we have a rock-solid business opportunity waiting for us down there."
"That's hard to believe," I said. "As I remember it, you had a big deal waiting down there for you the last time, but it didn't work out."
"This time is different," said The Pundit. "This time we got the truck and we are going to set up our own hauling business."
"Yeah," said Lonzo.
"This time," the Pundit said, "we have an agreement with Lonzo's nephew, Luke. Luke is a stonecutter. He supplies most of south Florida with gravestones. He calls his business the Last Word Company of Dade County, and this time of year he's a very busy man. Ain't that right, Lonzo?
"This time of year is when Luke's business really comes alive," said The Pundit. "All those people from New York and New Jersey go down there and spend two or three weeks in a Miami Beach hotel. Then they get ready to check out and they ask for the hotel bill. That's when we get their business."
"Yeah," said Lonzo.
"Old Luke said he can give us a lot of work delivering gravestones from his factory in Homestead to places all over south Florida," The Pundit said. "It's piecework."
"Yeah," said Lonzo.
"As soon as we get down there, Lonzo and me are going to incorporate. We're going to call our business the Monumental Drayage

and Cartage Company, Unlimited," said The Pundit.

"I just hope Luke's business doesn't die after you get there," I said.

"It won't," said The Pundit. "Luke's famous down there in south Florida. He specializes in marble angels carved on the gravestones. They're called Luke's Homestead Angels, and people are dying to have them."

"Well," I said, "if business is that good down there, you may find you can't come home again."

"Stop it," said The Pundit.

"Yeah," said Lonzo.

Lonzo and The Pundit, both wearing big smiles, walked into my office.

"Last time I saw you two, you were headed for Homestead, Florida, with four recap tires and a half a ham," I said. "You told me you were going to get a job delivering tombstones with the truck and would be there all winter. What happened?"

"Equipment failure," said The Pundit.

"The truck broke," said Lonzo.

"Yes, indeed," said The Pundit. "We did go to Homestead and we did get a job delivering tombstones for Lonzo's nephew, Luke. Then one afternoon we were wheeling across the causeway between Miami and Miami Beach, toting a truckload of tombstones, when disaster struck."

"Hit us right in the causeway," Lonzo said.

"What happened was," The Pundit said, "that the universal joint on the truck broke. The front end of the drive shaft fell onto the street and hooked up in a manhole cover. And us and the truck pole-vaulted all over the east half of Dade County, scattering tombstones like they were rose petals."

"Whee!" said Lonzo.

"Yes, indeed!" said the Pundit.

"So we run," said Lonzo.

"Why run?" I asked.

"Well," said The Pundit, "some of the cars coming along behind us sort of bumped into the tombstones scattered on the causeway and got bent up a little. And if we had stayed around we would have had to answer all sorts of questions about insurance and who really owns the truck and where did we get that license plate, and a lot

Philosophy on Wheels

of stuff like that. So we lit out of there."

"So the truck was gone," I said.

"And our jobs," said The Pundit. "When Luke heard about how his tombstones were strewn all over the Miami Beach Causeway, he got sort of mad. Said if we ever showed up at his place again, we'd need tombstones ourselves."

"So we come home," said Lonzo.

"But it wasn't all that easy," said The Pundit. "We didn't have bus fare back home. So we looked up Big Time Benny Biscayne, our summertime benefactor, and he arranged a plane ride to Asheville for us. Well, not exactly to Asheville, but close.

"Benny got us seats on a flight he called the "Colombian Express," The Pundit said. "It is operated by Now and Then Airline. Benny drove us out to a patch in the Everglades he said was Alligator International Airport to get the flight. We were the only passengers on the plane. The rest of the space was taken up by the bales of hay or something.

"The pilot said it was a new kind of insulation they were importing. Some people, he said, keep it in the walls of their houses. It was as dark as the inside of your hat when we took off," The Pundit said, "but I noticed they didn't turn on any lights. I asked the pilot about that and he said he was saving electricity. We never got more than twenty feet off the ground, either. And I asked the pilot about that. He said saving gasoline. Then I asked the pilot if he knew just where we wanted to get off, and he said if I didn't stop pestering him, he'd let me off right away.

"We finally landed, somewhere over in Tennessee, still in the dark. They headed us down a road and said to start walking. It was quite a ride," said The Pundit, "but I know it really was an airline we were on."

"How do you know?" I asked.

"They lost our luggage," he said.

At first I thought my car was on fire. The thick coils of greasy, gray smoke pouring out the windows made me wonder if I should get any closer or just find a phone and call the fire department.

Then I saw a pair of paint-spattered brogans sticking out the front window and I knew what the trouble was.

Inside, sprawled across the seats, were Lonzo and The Pundit, both puffing mightily at ropy black cigars.

It is not easy to sprawl in a 1964 Volkswagen bug. The configuration, as they say in the airline business, is against sprawling. But they were managing it in that limp, almost boneless way they adopt when they're resting. Which is most of the time.

When I opened the door on the driver's side, Lonzo almost fell out. The smoke made my eyes water. It smelled like burning electrical insulation. It was laced with a judicious dash of the bouquet of Thunderbird '81, a popular vintage, indeed.

It was a few days after the first of the month and Lonzo and The Pundit obviously had a little money left.

I coughed. "Where do you two find those terrible cigars?" I asked.

The Pundit smirked. "Havana," he said. "They're genuine Havanas."

"Havana, my foot," I said. "Fidel Castro has done a lot of rotten things to this country, but he never was responsible for those weeds you two are smoking. It's a wonder the air pollution people haven't run you out of town."

Lonzo looked hurt. "Them is genuine Wheeling Stogies," he said. "You can't get them just anywhere, you know. Them is tofers."

"Tofers?"

"Sure. Two fer a quarter."

I gasped for air and backed away from the car. "Open the windows some more and let that smoke blow out," I said. "Sooner or later I'm going to have to drive that thing home."

"We tried that earlier," said The Pundit, "but the smoke was eating the paint off the fenders. This isn't much of a car you got here. Couldn't you afford anything better? Why'd you get rid of the Honda if you couldn't get anything better for it than this?"

"We didn't get rid of the Honda," I said. "We still have it. We call it our 'heavy car.' This car is our second car. And it's a good car. It's the best 1964 Volkswagen that $500 can buy."

There was a long silence. Then The Pundit cleared his throat and

Philosophy on Wheels

said, "Oh, is it a Volkswagen? I didn't know they made them that early. I thought it was a Hupmobile."

Lonzo giggled. "That's what they yell at the football games," he said. "You hear them all the time saying Hup! Hup! Hup!"

"Listen," The Pundit said to me, "I been your social adviser since you moved here eight years ago and I feel sort of responsible. I tell you, you just can't go running all over town in a rust heap like this. It ain't fitting. For Pete's sake, you have a position to keep up. What is it they call you there in the newspaper now—a senior editor? Why, man, it just won't do to have you clanking around like an overage Mickey Rooney playing Andy Hardy in the Model A Ford all over again."

"Listen," I said to The Pundit, "I've heard about all the senior jokes I can swallow. It's not true that I'm now a senior editor because I'm the oldest guy in the building. There are two other people older than I am in there. And it's not true that if I get a few more credit hours I'll be able to graduate.

"And as far as that car being unfit for me, let me tell you just how well it does fit. I have been driving the thing all over town for about a week and a half. So this noontime after lunch I took it down to John Gasoline's place and had them fill the tank. It cost me the grand total of six dollars and ten cents, and I call that a very good fit."

There was another silence. Lonzo said, "I knew a fellow named Andy Hardy a few years back. He lived over in Johnson City and sold corks for a living—just to his friends, of course."

"That was a different Andy Hardy, Lonzo," said The Pundit. Then he crawled out of the car, brushed the cigar ashes off his vest, and said, "The real reason we come over here today wasn't to argue about your car. We wanted to see if we could borrow the spare tire and wheel from your Honda. You see, Lonzo was a little elevated the other night and he was driving the Honkerbus down Patton Avenue backwards when the curb got in the way—"

But I had started the Volkswagen engine and couldn't hear any more.

TWO ON THE SQUARE

The blue bus rumbled to a stop in front of the old library and the passenger doors swung open. Out of the bus came:

An old, rusty leaf spring from what obviously was an old, rusty automobile.

A battered strip of once-chrome auto bumper.

A tire as bald as a watermelon.

Four pieces of metal, all oil-covered but otherwise unidentifiable.

Lonzo, carrying a toolbox in one hand, a three-foot-long Stilson wrench in the other, and with a second bald tire hung around his neck like a horse collar.

The Pundit, wearing a broad smile and carrying a cylindrical object concealed in a brown paper bag.

The wind was blowing gently across the sidewalk from them to me, and it was immediately apparent that they both were in what could be called a high good humor.

It figured. It was the third day of the month and they always have a little money at the start of a month. The Pundit says it's his pension for military service in the Philippine Insurrection.

They both flopped down on the bench beside me. Lonzo dropped the wrench and the toolbox on the sidewalk, stripped the old tire off his neck, and reached out his hand to The Pundit who wordlessly handed him the brown paper bag.

While Lonzo gulped and belched, The Pundit beamed at me. "As you can see, we are getting ready for our annual winter retreat to Florida."

The Pundit grabbed the brown paper bag back from Lonzo. "We are getting the Honkerbus in shape for the long haul to Miami."

"What's wrong with the Honkerbus?" I asked.

Lonzo giggled. "A little of this and a little of that and a lot of bent metal after we drove it into a tree on the way back from a seminar we held up in Whiskey Cove. But don't worry. There ain't nothing wrong we can't fix . . . provided I can find a Honda with a good radiator that ain't being watched too closely."

"So you're going south for the season again," I said. "I certainly hope you do a better job of staying out of trouble than you have in the past. Remember the time you had to hire out to a farmer for stoop labor to get enough money to get home?"

"Don't you worry none about that," he said. "This time we got it all squared away down there. We're going to join the horsey set."

"I didn't know they were enlisting people in the cavalry again," I said.

"None of that, now," The Pundit said. "You know we ain't going to join no cavalry. No, what happened is that Big Time Benny Biscayne, our pal down there in Miami, has us all fixed up for a job."

I remembered Benny. The last time he fixed up a job for Lonzo and The Pundit, they were lucky to escape ten years in a federal slammer for transporting an illegal substance that Benny had sworn was talcum powder.

"What is it this time?" I asked. "Counterfeiting, maybe, or perhaps just a little gun-running?"

"Oh, it's nothing like that at all," said The Pundit. "Benny has it fixed up for us to become equine ecologists in the Sanitation Department at Gulfstream Park. It's an environmental-type job. We'll get to meet a lot of interesting people, Benny says, and have a chance to make a lot of money, too.

"We'll be right back there working with all those people who know all about horses," he continued. "All we have to do is keep our ears open and make a bet now and then on the right horses and we'll really rake in the money. We'll clean up."

"The part about cleaning up is the part I believe," I said.

The Pundit looked offended.

Lonzo took off his Caterpillar cap and scratched his head.

"Pundit," he said, "you been telling me that ever since we heard from Benny and it sounds great. But there's one thing I want to know. If all those people working back there know which horses are going to win, how come they're still back there working? Why ain't they out on the back deck of their 100-foot, twin-screw diesel yachts, smoking big cigars, sipping champagne, and eating cavyyar?"

"Well, Lonzo," said The Pundit, "I guess they just ain't got no horse sense."

"Oh," said Lonzo.

TWO ON THE SQUARE

The bus pulled up to the curb, stopped, and disgorged Lonzo and The Pundit.

The manner of their disembarkation was typical: The bus driver "assisted" them through the door onto the street and then hurled after them an assortment of rakes, hoes, pruning shears, hedge clippers, and a rusty power lawnmower.

The driver sped all of this paraphernalia on its way with a verbal salute that employed words and phrases I haven't heard since first sergeants started taking psychology courses.

The Pundit, his unshaven chin stuck out a mile, was answering in kind, while a giggling Lonzo weaved around, picking up their equipment.

The Pundit planked himself down on the bench, turned, recognized me, and said "Hah!"

His breath made my eyes water. It bleached my shirt. The aroma of very old grape juice wafted across the square, felling a stray dog turning the corner onto Patton Avenue.

Clearly, The Pundit and Lonzo were a little elevated.

"Hah! yourself," I said. "And why aren't you two still at the federal resort in Florida? Did you escape, or what?"

Lonzo, who had all of their tools clutched in his hands, sat down beside me with a thump and a clank.

"It was a open-and-shut case of the statue of imitations," he said with another giggle.

"If I told you once, I told you a thousand times, Lonzo, it ain't 'statue of imitations,' it's 'statute of limitations,'" said The Pundit.

"Whatever," said Lonzo amiably.

The Pundit turned to me. "What happened was," he said, "that box of money the Feds found on us that was given to us by Big Time Benny Biscayne, well, it turned out to be real money, not the homemade kind.

"That was a surprise," he said. "Must have been a huge surprise to Benny, too. He had to think the stuff was funny money. No way he'd have trusted us with real money if he knew. Anyway, when the Feds realized the money was all right, they got us to plead guilty to some ancient history involving some alcohol on which we had forgot to pay taxes.

"They had us all the way down to Eglin Field in Florida before they realized the statute of limitations had run out on that one. So

Philosophy on Wheels

they gave us bus tickets home. We cashed in the tickets, had a little celebration on the Red-Neck Riviera, and hitchhiked home on a truckload of watermelons."

"Why didn't you call me?" I asked.

"We didn't need nothing," said Lonzo.

"What did you do to get that bus driver so angry?" I asked.

"Nothing, really. The power mower has been giving us trouble, so Lonzo started it up for a minute to adjust the carburetor."

"He started a power mower on the bus?"

"Well, that's where we was at the time, wasn't it? Besides, it was just for a minute. There was no call for the passengers and that driver to get so put out."

Lonzo giggled again. "It wasn't running but a minute or two. Wasn't hardly long enough for the statue of imitations to take holt."

I was driving home when I saw them thumbing along I-40.

They looked hot, tired, footsore, and sweaty. Even at a distance I could see the rivulets of perspiration dripping off The Pundit's bald dome and running down under his collar.

Lonzo was wearing a gray T-shirt marked **Property of the Harvard Debating Team**. It was plastered to his body.

I pulled up and they collapsed into the back seat with grateful groans. Then I heard Lonzo's squeaky voice say, "If I owned this car, I'd shut the windows and turn on the air conditioning."

The Pundit's gravelly voice answered, "You forget, little chum, that we are riding with the last of the big-time spenders. This is probably the only automobile left in the entire state of North Carolina that doesn't have air conditioning."

We drove a while longer. It was hot. Then a peach pit whizzed past my ear and bounced across the roadway. I heard the crackling sound of a paper bag being crumpled up.

"Them peaches was delicious," said Lonzo. "Was that one sack all you had?"

We drove a while longer. Then I said, "All right, what happened? You two are supposed to be in Detroit, helping the Republicans with their convention. How come you're here instead?"

"Our vehicle was disabled," said The Pundit.

"We hitched our wagon to a disaster," said Lonzo.

"We were half-way across Tennessee on I-75," said The Pundit, "when the truck that was towing us pulled off and drove into a truck stop. So we unhitched our rope and drove over to another truck that seemed to be headed north. We tied up to that one and settled down to wait. Pretty soon the driver of the truck came out of the restaurant and started up his engine."

"We think he saw the rope, though," said Lonzo.

"In any event," said The Pundit, "he wasn't going north. We roared out of the truck stop back onto the interstate and down south we went, headed back to Knoxville at about 90 miles an hour. We was going so fast I couldn't get up on the front bumper of our Honkerbus to cut the rope."

"Indeed," said The Pundit, "it was a case of whither thou goest, so go I. We roared through Knoxville like a lightning bolt and ran out east on I-40, heading back toward Asheville. Finally, at a rest area near the state line, the truck pulling us stopped."

"Then we met the driver," said Lonzo.

"He is a big man," The Pundit continued, "with shoulders like the Golden Gate Bridge and a chest like Dolly Parton. Wherever he puts his feet he leaves footprints two inches deep in the concrete, and his voice would drown out the Ohio State Marching Band."

"And he was a little peeved," said Lonzo, "so he disabled our vehicle."

"Why didn't you stop him?" I asked.

"You haven't got the picture yet," said The Pundit. "He was holding up the front end of the Honkerbus with one hand while he used the other hand to tear the tires off the wheels. He said his name was Wheels McWallop," The Pundit continued, "and his mother was a Autocar and his father was a Kenworth and he was born in a Fruehauf trailer factory. He said he ate old cylinder heads and drank No. 2 diesel fuel. He said he could outrun any Smoky, outfight the Marine Corps, and outshout all the air horns on I-40. He said he was the belching, barging, barreling king of the interstate, and did we want to make anything out of it?"

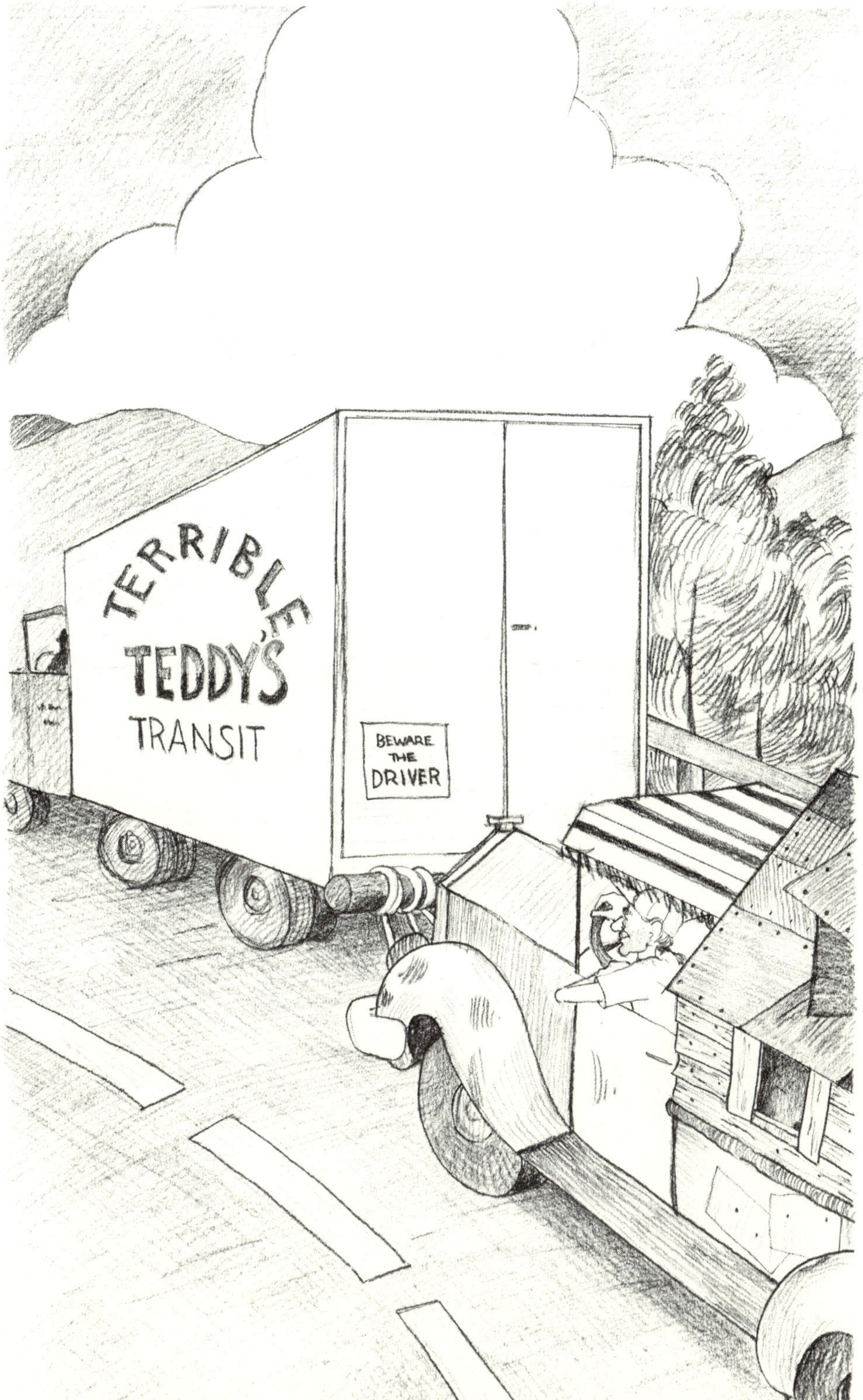

TERRIBLE TEDDY'S
TRANSIT
BEWARE THE DRIVER

"So now we are heading back to town, looking for two new tires," said The Pundit. "When we find them we'll get the Honkerbus running again."

"You still going to try to get to the convention?" I asked.

"No," The Pundit said, "it probably would be all over before we could get there."

"It was all over before it started," said Lonzo.

The Honkerbus pulled up in front of the house, and Lonzo and The Pundit climbed down from the flight deck.

The vehicle was covered with a newly applied coat of red barn paint. All four tires were holding air. All of the loose parts had been bolted back into place. Nothing was being held on with rope or baling wire.

The characteristic clatter of the engine had been replaced by a smooth purr of power. Clearly the Honkerbus had been revitalized.

Not so Lonzo or The Pundit. They resembled, as usual, two refugees from a great natural disaster.

The Pundit was wearing his usual rusty black suit with a vest but no tie. Lonzo was attired in greasy mechanic's coveralls and a cap proclaiming the virtues of a certain brand of auto parts.

"We come by to say goodbye," said The Pundit. "We are on our way south for our annual sojourn in the Sun State."

"Yeah," said Lonzo with a vacant smile.

"Yes," said The Pundit, "it has been a long, hard job getting our transportation ready for the trip, but thanks to Lonzo's nephew Junior we are finally ready to go."

"What did Lonzo's nephew Junior have to do with it?"

"Well," said The Pundit, "the Honkerbus had been laid up for a long time and we sort of let the registration expire. When we went to renew the registration we discovered that the mice in the Widder Lady's barn had destroyed the title."

"Just et that sucker right up," said Lonzo.

Philosophy on Wheels

"Someone said the best thing to do would be to go to Raleigh and get a replacement title," The Pundit said. "So last week we took the bus to Raleigh. What a waste of time!"

"Why?" I asked.

"Raleigh," said The Pundit, "is a city of the living dead. Everyone down there is out looking for a new job, now that the Republicans got in. They ought to hang a big sign over the city limits saying 'No decisions until after January 5.'"

"That's the nauguration," said Lonzo helpfully.

"Anyway," said The Pundit, "we didn't get a replacement title. The one person there who would listen to us wouldn't listen no more after we described the vehicle to him. He said it was more like we was describing a three-car crash. So, no title and no registration plates. Then we went to see Junior."

"How did Junior help?" I asked.

"Junior knows all about making license plates," said The Pundit. "He learned the trade at a place called Joliet, in Illinois, and took post-graduate studies at Raiford, in Florida. He whomped us up a plate in no time at all."

I looked at the license plate on the back of the vehicle. It looked all right except that it said "First In Fright." The state motto is "First In Flight." I pointed out the discrepancy.

"Junior is a little weak in spelling," said The Pundit, "but nobody but an editor would have noticed that. And so we're off. By the way, we are going to need change for the turnpike. Can you cash a twenty?"

I gave him change. He handed me a twenty-dollar bill. They both leaped back into the Honkerbus and, with hardly a parting wave, drove off down the hill.

Then, as I stood there in the cold, deepening darkness, I began to wonder. I didn't recall any turnpike toll booths between Asheville and Florida.

I went back into the house, turned on a light, and looked at the bill.

It looked fine, except for a slight discrepancy. Both the back and the front of the bill proclaimed that it was the property of the United Skates of America.

TWO ON THE SQUARE

They made a fuss getting on the bus; they usually do.

Lonzo was carrying a battered toolbox. He managed to fetch the bus driver a sharp rap on the knee with the box as he maneuvered his way to the back of the bus where I was sitting.

The Pundit was carrying an eight-foot piece of bent, battered, and rusty auto exhaust pipe. When he turned his body to fish the bus fare out of his pocket, he almost decapitated three people sitting in a front seat.

With sighs of relief, they flopped down onto a seat next to mine. Both of them were blue with cold. Lonzo's lower jaw was vibrating. Had he had two teeth that met, they would have been chattering. The Pundit pulled an incredibly soiled red bandanna from his pocket, applied it to his red nose, and made a noise like a moose call.

A lady who had been sitting in front of him hurriedly pulled the cord to signal the bus driver that she wanted to get off.

I asked them what they were up to.

The Pundit smiled broadly.

"We are preparing," he said, "to make our annual journey to warmer climes. In case you haven't noticed, winter is upon us and it is getting too cold to sleep under the bridge. So we are pulling out for the land of eternal sunshine."

"We are going to the dogs," said Lonzo, leering at a lady across the aisle. She, too, got off the bus.

"What my little companion means," said The Pundit, "is that we have been promised employment in Florida for the season. We are going to consort with the sporting set down there."

"You're dern tootin'," said Lonzo, still leering. "We been promised jobs cleaning out the kennels at the dog track in Hialeah."

"Well, what about this business with the exhaust pipe and the tools?" I asked.

"Transportation is our problem," The Pundit said. "You will recall that owing to a slight miscalculation a few weeks ago, our vehicle, the Honkerbus, got all bent out of shape in a collision with a fire hydrant that had no business at all being where it was."

I said I recalled the incident.

"Well," said The Pundit, "we attempted to get some compensation from the city. It was, after all, the city's hydrant."

"Yeah," said Lonzo, "but that city manager down there at City Hall, why he wouldn't pay us a dime. Not a dime. He said if we didn't

Philosophy on Wheels

stop bothering them, they was going to make us pay for the hydrant."

"That's a hard way to treat a lifelong Democrat, I tell you. So," said The Pundit, "we decided to repair the Honkerbus and drive that to Florida. And we've been going here and there lately, just picking up this and that to get the thing back on the road. We are pretty nearly ready to set sail again for the palm trees and the oranges. We just lack a few more parts."

"What we lack most," Lonzo said, "is the drive shaft off a 1964 Volkswagen bus. You got any idea where we can get a drive shaft off a 1964 Volkswagen bus?"

I said I didn't have any idea at all about who might be able to sell them a drive shaft off a 1964 Volkswagen bus.

There was a significant pause. The Pundit looked at Lonzo; Lonzo looked at The Pundit. Finally, The Pundit cleared his throat, delicately, and said, "I guess you misunderstood the question. We didn't ask you anything about buying a drive shaft; we just want to know where one is."

Then I grabbed the cord and signaled the bus driver I wanted to get off.

It was some night before Christmas and all through the house things were pretty quiet. Suddenly, out on the lawn, there arose such a clatter, I dashed from my chair to see what was the matter.

There was no Dancer, no Prancer, no Donder, no Blizten, and certainly no St. Nick.

What there was, was the Honkerbus, clacking and wheezing, emitting stray wisps of steam from up front and wreaths of blue oil smoke from out back.

Instead of St. Nick there was The Pundit, his ratty old overcoat held together with a huge safety pin, his bottle nose gleaming redly in the twilight. I thought of Rudolph, but even The Pundit's nose wasn't bright enough to guide a sleigh that night.

TWO ON THE SQUARE

He was ensconced in the elevated, open-air driver's seat. Beside him sat Lonzo, attired in a Russian-style karakul hat and a running suit that at one time had been the property of the Athletic Department at St. Olaf College.

Lonzo was giggling; The Pundit was smiling broadly.

My heart jumped into my throat; I streaked across the street to my car and counted the wheels.

Lonzo and The Pundit learned long ago that the wheels on my Volkswagen also fit the Honkerbus, and the sudden appearance of the Honkerbus too often has signaled the sudden disappearance of one of my wheels.

This time, however, I counted four wheels on the ground and one securely in the trunk, so I relaxed.

"You seem to be bound somewhere," I said to The Pundit.

"Yes," said The Pundit, "I finally convinced Lonzo that the state of Florida is not going to vanish under the Atlantic Ocean, not this year at least, and we are headed for sunshine and orange juice. It is a great relief to me, I can tell you. Nights are mighty cold in that Dempsey Dumpster now."

"That's fine," I said. "Is Lonzo going to wrestle alligators again this season?"

"No," said The Pundit, "the Charles Barnum of Weekiewatchee Springs already has engaged an alligator wrestler for the season. We have been assured, however, that if the new man makes the slightest mistake, Lonzo can have the job."

As we talked, I noticed that there was something subtly different about The Pundit. His eyes were clear. His speech was distinct. He appeared, well . . . almost healthy.

"I know what it is about you that's different," I blurted. "You're sober! For the first time I can remember, you're sober! What happened?"

"I'm sober because I'm driving," said The Pundit. "Listen, son, when people live like me and Lonzo live, they got to go along to get along. It's getting to be pretty plain that nobody thinks there's anything funny about drinking and driving anymore.

"And every blue coat and brass button between here and Miami Beach is on the lookout for us at this time of year—we know them all. This time, if we get caught driving with a snootful, they are going to put us under the courthouse—way under. So we are going to stay

Philosophy on Wheels

sober as two judges . . . until we get there."

"That's the smartest thing you've done since you deserted from the Philippine Constabulary in 1908," I said.

"A man's got to go with the flow," said The Pundit.

Lonzo and The Pundit wheeled around the corner and strode into my office. The Pundit was wearing his customary rusty black suit, a greasy gray fedora, a once-white shirt, and a black string tie.

Lonzo was attired tastefully in spotted painter's pants, a torn T-shirt a la Marlon Brando, and a red-and-white baseball cap advertising the Knoxville World's Fair.

It was shortly after the first of the month and they obviously were in the money and in good spirits. Especially the spirits.

Lonzo was carrying the wheel and tire that had mysteriously disappeared from my old Volkswagen when they started out for Knoxville a while back.

"We come here," said Lonzo, "to return this here wheel we borrowed from you a while ago. But we looked all over the parking lot and we can't find that old car to put this here wheel into. What have you done with it?"

"Forget that old car and keep the wheel," I said. "I just turned that old Volkswagen in on a brand new kamikase special."

Lonzo's jaw dropped. The Pundit appeared stricken.

"My Lord," said The Pundit. "You shouldn't have done that!"

"For the love of mud!" said Lonzo. "Now where are we going to go when we want to borrow a wheel to keep the Honkerbus running after we have sold a wheel or two for refreshment?"

"Why would you want to go and sell a fine old car like that?" asked The Pundit. "Why, that car was a true friend of mankind. For all those years it faithfully carried people all over the place in all kinds of weather. It was tried and true blue, a good and faithful servant."

Lonzo, always easily moved by sentiment, sobbed.

"The only thing about that old car that was true blue was me in the winter," I said. "There just wasn't any way to get any heat into the thing, and last winter I like to died of frostbite."

"Sissy!" said The Pundit. "What did they give you for the old car?"

TWO ON THE SQUARE

"None of your business," I said. "But when I brought it in to be appraised, it gave the people at the auto agency the biggest laugh they've had since the interest rate went to 16 percent.

"The man who did the actual appraising told me he was happy to have a chance to appraise a car like that. He said he might never get another chance to appraise a 1964 Volkswagen. He said he wasn't even born when that car was made."

"See!" said The Pundit. "It's like I said. You sold an old friend for a few paltry dollars."

"For a pot of message," said Lonzo.

A solid body interposed itself between me and the sun, and the odor of mothballs started to make my eyes water.

I looked over my shoulder. There stood The Pundit and Lonzo, The Pundit puffing on an evil-looking cigar, Lonzo wearing a gap-toothed grin.

Lonzo was worth a second look. He was swathed in a huge raccoon coat that obviously had seen better days. The raccoon skins had become bald in spots, making the garment look like a molting animal. Every time Lonzo moved, a cloud of raccoon hairs drifted off in the wind. The odor of moth balls was so strong it wiped out Lonzo's usual ripe aroma.

"Where did you get that coat?" I asked.

Lonzo grinned again. "I found it in an alley down back of Lexington Avenue," he said. "It must have fallen out the window of one of those places where they sell second-hand stuff."

"It's not second-hand," I said. "It's more like fifty-second hand. And it didn't fall out of any window. It more likely escaped and then died of old age in the alley."

"Whatever," said Lonzo. "It keeps me warm, in any event."

"Doesn't matter much," said The Pundit in his gravelly baritone. "In a couple of weeks we'll be back in the orange groves at Weekiewatchee Springs for the winter season, basking in the warm Florida sun."

"Lovely," I said, "but how are you going to get there?"

88

Philosophy on Wheels

"True, the Honkerbus has rolled its last mile," said The Pundit. "It was a fitting end for a truly noble machine," he added, wiping away a furtive tear. Lonzo sobbed softly.

"But," said The Pundit, "life goes on. Just the other day Lonzo and me ran across an acquaintance who offered to help with our transportation problem. He is a sidewalk entrepreneur called Hotwheels Harry, and he sometimes sells slightly used cars.

"We told him we were looking for something like the Honkerbus and he said he might have the answer, that there's a vehicle he's had his eye on for some time."

"It's Japanesey, too," said Lonzo.

"Yes," said The Pundit. "Harry described it as a Mitsumushi Arigoto, a sort of pickup truck manufactured by the Banzai Motor Car Company. Harry says if he can make the right kind of a deal with the truck's present owner, he will be able to let us have this vehicle at a very attractive price."

"Harry says it will be a steal," said Lonzo.

"That's probably true," I said. "What does the word *Arigoto* mean?"

"Harry says that translates out to 'thundering peach blossom,'" Lonzo said.

"What does a Japanese pickup truck pick up?" I asked.

"Anything its new owners can get their hands on," said The Pundit.

"And that brings up a small problem," he added. "Harry says he'll give us a break on the purchase price if we promise to get the truck out of town as soon as he turns it over to us. That means we got to start putting together some money fast. Would you like to invest?"

"I never buy things from people named 'Hotwheels,'" I said.

"Well, how about a classy fur coat?" countered The Pundit.

"I never invest in molting raccoons, either," I said.

"What size wheels you got on that new Japanese car of yours?" asked The Pundit.

"Don't even think of it," I said. "The trunk on this car locks. There's no way you two can 'borrow' a wheel from it."

"You might be surprised," said The Pundit.

"Remember Pearl Harbor?" said Lonzo.

TWO ON THE SQUARE

The bus driver suggested politely that it would be a good idea to pay their fares.

Lonzo blinked. The Pundit cleared his throat thunderously and asked the bus driver if he had change for a $50 bill.

The driver said, certainly, he could change any $50 bill The Pundit could produce, but unless he saw a $50 bill or the right coins for the fare, the bus wasn't moving and neither were Lonzo and The Pundit.

The Pundit cleared his throat again, excavated a wrinkled black leather coin purse from his pocket and reluctantly counted out the change.

The Pundit was carrying a rusty bumper jack. Lonzo was clutching an auto wheel with tire attached.

For a second I felt worried. Then I recalled that I sold my Volkswagen two years ago. I now drive a Rising Sun sedan, and wheels from that car won't fit the Honkerbus.

As the last lingering nickel dropped into the fare box, the driver thanked The Pundit and let out the clutch. The bus lurched forward. Lonzo, holding the auto wheel with both hands, lurched backward. He dropped the wheel and grabbed the back of a seat.

The wheel rolled down the aisle of the bus, stopping with a thump against the back seat, right next to a little old lady wearing tennis shoes and carrying a furled umbrella.

The little old lady looked at the wheel, looked at Lonzo, took a firm grip on her umbrella, and advanced on Lonzo with murder in her eyes.

When order was restored, The Pundit dropped his bulky frame on the seat next to me.

"You are getting ready," I said.

The Pundit nodded. "Yes, indeed, Florida calls," he said.

"It's getting too cold to sleep in a Dempsey Dumpster or the Widder Lady's barn," I said.

"Afraid so," said The Pundit. "Even when we wrap ourselves up in newspaper, we get cold. There used to be more heat in newspapers than there is nowadays. What are you people doing to them?

"Well, never mind that," he continued. "I guess there used to be more heat in Lonzo and me, too.

"And you guessed right. We are preparing our vehicle for our annual journey to the Sunny South. Lonzo has been offered his old

Philosophy on Wheels

winter job as the premiere alligator wrestler south of Orlando, and I have a promise of employment as a dog walker at the Weekiewatchee Springs greyhound race track and gambling emporium."

"Sounds like a high-class winter in the entertainment business to me," I said.

"It will be in a lot of ways," said The Pundit. "But I wish the race track attracted a better class of contestants. Some of the dogs they run there are real dogs, if you know what I mean.

"But," he said with a sigh, "that's show biz, I guess."

"Are you having any trouble getting the Honkerbus ready to run?" I asked.

"No more than usual," he said. "It's a matter of replacing a part here and there and finding things that fall off the back of trucks or are accidentally left not nailed down."

"I guess you and Lonzo are really sorry that I sold my Volkswagen bug," I said. "Now you can't come around and make off with my wheels."

The Pundit yawned elaborately and smiled.

"That's right," he said. "But we did happen to run into a guy who has a lot of old wheels but who was looking for a front seat for a Rising Sun sedan.

"Well, this is our stop. We get off here. Come on, Lonzo."

And they disappeared into the night.

When I got home a few minutes later I discovered that one of the front seats from my car had disappeared into the night, too.

I'll have to do something about that. The Chief of Staff says the orange crate I used to replace the seat is too uncomfortable.

It was one of those days we get around the first week in May in which Old Mother Nature isn't content to merely smile on Asheville; she slobbers all over the place.

The sun was beating down warmly. The sky was a high, clear, brilliant blue. The green, green mountains marched out as far as the eye could see. So when The Pundit called and asked me to meet him and Lonzo for lunch at the Pisgah Inn on the Blue Ridge Parkway, I was delighted to go.

TWO ON THE SQUARE

A few minutes later, after a stop at the deli to get fixings for a picnic lunch (I was reasonably certain The Pundit was not contemplating picking up a lunch check at the restaurant there), I was rolling up the Parkway in Hirohito's Revenge savoring the weather, the flowers, and the spectacular scenery.

The Blue Ridge Parkway, in my opinion, is one of the few really good things the federal government has done with our tax money. I don't know how much it cost and I don't care. Whatever the bill came to, the result was worth the money.

The car hummed along contentedly and I played the hold-your-breath game in the six tunnels between Asheville and the Mount Pisgah motel. The idea is to see if you can hold your breath for as long as it takes the car in which you're riding to traverse the tunnel. It helps if you also are doing the driving because a driver who isn't playing the game tends to slow down a lot in the tunnels, just to make life interesting for passengers who are playing.

The Pisgah Inn is a motel and restaurant owned by the U.S. Park Service and leased on an annual basis to commercial operators. It is located near one of the highest stretches on the Parkway and is above 6,000 feet in altitude. The motel rooms and the restaurant dining room look out over a huge green, high valley, over rolling mountain ranges, and on a clear day, almost, it seems, to the sea at Charleston. The scenery is spectacular and the Pisgah Inn is one of my favorite places in the mountains.

As I pulled into the parking area, a bowl that holds about seventy-five cars comfortably, I looked for the Honkerbus, but Lonzo and The Pundit had not yet arrived.

I got out of my car, stretched luxuriously in the sunlight, squatted on the back bumper, and waited.

In a few minutes I began to hear a high-pitched, screaming sound. It was very faint at first, but it rapidly grew louder. A couple of minutes later it was deafening. Then the Honkerbus, black smoke rolling from its smokestack and a spurt of steam jetting out from underneath, rolled into the parking area and, with a hideous grating of metal on metal, braked to a stop.

Lonzo and The Pundit leaped down from the front seat and ran around to the front of the vehicle. Lonzo lifted the engine cover and instantly he, The Pundit, and the entire Honkerbus were enveloped in a dense and expanding cloud of steam. I heard The Pundit roar,

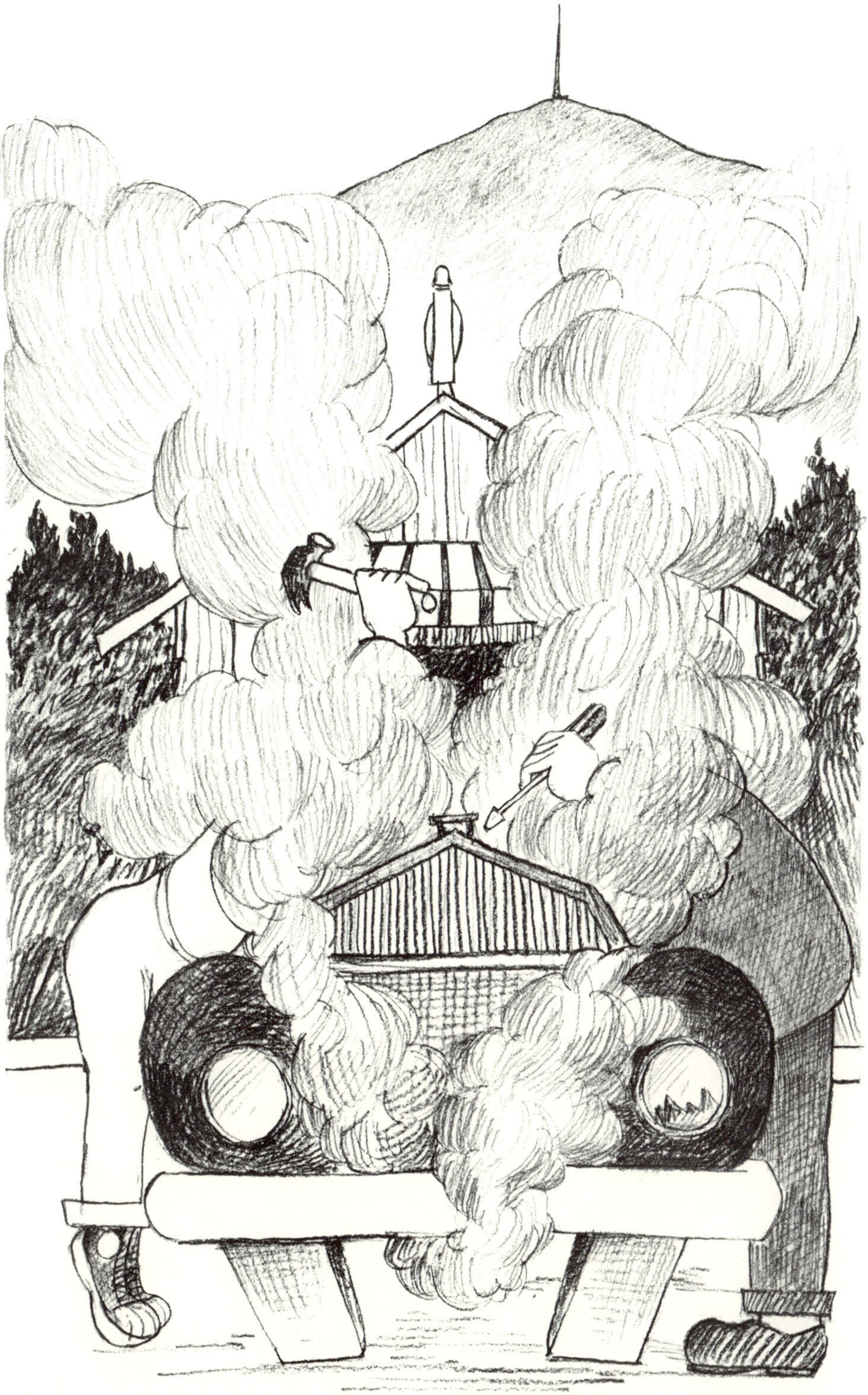

"Turn off the blagstaggering, rumbustuous engine, Lonzo, we got a bad leak up here in the radiator!"

And I heard Lonzo scream back in his reedy voice, "We dassent do that, Pundit. If we turn it off, it'll seize up and we'll never get it started again."

There was silence for a moment, silence, that is, except for the steady scream of escaping steam.

Then The Pundit asked, "Where are the flabjabbering, whipper-jawed pliers, Lonzo?"

"Right where you left them after you fished that cork out of the wine bottle last night, Pundit."

More sounds of escaping steam.

A heavy-set man driving a big, black car with New York license plates cruised slowly by, stopped, then said to me, "Now I know why they're called the Smoky Mountains," and drove away.

More sounds of escaping steam. Then a spanking clean green-and-white Park Service cruiser drove to the edge of the steam cloud and a spanking clean new park ranger got out, looking curiously at the steam cloud. His stiff new Smoky Bear hat was plunked squarely on his head. He was young, tall, handsome, and scrubbed all pink and white. He looked as though he had that morning been taken out of the carton in which he had been packed by the manufacturer.

Then there came from inside the cloud a scream of anguish from Lonzo. "Confound it, Pundit," he yelled, "you're standing on my hand!"

The scream galvanized the ranger. He raced to the back of his cruiser, already almost hidden in the mist, opened the trunk, pulled out a big red fire extinguisher and a first-aid kit, and plunged into the steam cloud shouting, "Hang on in there. I'm coming with help!"

An awed voice behind me said, "I swear, I haven't seen anything like that since they stopped making Nelson Eddy movies!"

The voice belonged to one of two slightly overweight, reasonably middle-aged women attired in Hawaiian shirts, running shorts, and cameras. They were getting out of a big sedan bearing Cuyahoga County, Ohio, license plates.

By now the cruiser, the Honkerbus, and Lonzo, The Pundit, and the ranger all were invisible in the steam cloud. From within the cloud we could hear occasional statements, such as, "Hold that dadgummed thing steady, dadgum ye!" and "That rowerbazzle stuff is hot; don't

Philosophy on Wheels

let it drip down on my fergoozelin sneakers that-away," and, "If you two gentlemen would just let me handle this problem, I'm sure I could have it under control in no time at all, and please, please, gentlemen, watch your language!"

There were more clanking noises, more wet, hydraulic sounds. Finally Lonzo's voice said, "Here, this hunk of hose will fix it. Get that cowboy hat out of my face and give me room to work, will ye?"

In a minute or two the screaming, hissing sound stopped. Then Lonzo said, "Here, Pundit, you pour this into the radiator whilst I race the motor so's we don't crack the block."

There was the sound of the Honkerbus engine revving up, and gradually the steam cloud dissipated, revealing Lonzo lolling in the front seat of the machine, The Pundit pouring something out of an old jerrican into the radiator, and the ranger leaning limply against the front fender of his cruiser.

His clean new uniform was soaking wet and filthy dirty. His tie was wound around the back of his neck. His polished shoes were sodden. The steam had taken all the starch out of his campaign hat. It drooped off his head like the ears of a discouraged rabbit.

One of the women said to the other, "I think it's some sort of a display, Gert. I bet that's supposed to be one of those old-time whiskey stills they used to make moonshine. I hear the parks people had some historical-type exhibits up here along the Parkway."

"I don't know, Myrt," said the other woman. "Those dummies aren't nearly as lifelike as what we saw at Disney World."

The Pundit snorted. Lonzo hiccuped. The ranger straightened up, said something about getting himself cleaned up, and went off toward the back door of the restaurant.

Gert, or maybe it was Myrt, went over to The Pundit and said, "I saw where you put the water into this thing, mister, but where does the whiskey come out?"

The Pundit eyed their big, shiny car and the rings on Gert's, or maybe it was Myrt's, fingers. With almost an old-world gesture he whipped off his soggy black fedora, smiled, and said he and Lonzo would be happy to explain the whole thing to the ladies if they would care to join us for lunch.

Unfortunately, he said, it would have to be lunch somewhere else. He and Lonzo couldn't remain in that vicinity for very long.

The second woman looked at Lonzo and said to her companion,

"Say, the skinny one is kinda cute." Lonzo reddened, gulped, wiggled his Adam's apple, and dove under the car, murmuring something about checking the differential.

I grabbed The Pundit by the elbow. "I didn't bring enough lunch for five people," I whispered.

"Just give me the bag and get lost," The Pundit hissed. I handed him the sack from the deli, he dragged Lonzo out from under the car, and the four of them climbed into the Honkerbus. Lonzo put the thing in gear and let out the clutch, but the Honkerbus didn't move an inch.

There was general pandemonium. Then I noticed that the left rear wheel of the Honkerbus had been chained to the frame with a heavy chain. The chain was secured with a big padlock marked **Property of the U.S. Park Service.** I called it to their attention. There was some terrible language from The Pundit. Myrt and Gert were giggling. Lonzo was still blushing.

Then the ranger came back. He was hatless, but otherwise he was all pink and clean and spic and span and ship-shape and Bristol fashion.

"None of you is going anywhere until you two return my fire extinguisher and my first-aid kit," he said, a little smugly. "I think you ought to know that they are teaching a new course now at the Ranger Academy. It's called, 'How to Contend with Lonzo, The Pundit, and Other Unmitigated Public Nuisances.' So cough up the extinguisher and the kit."

Grumbling and muttering mutinously, The Pundit rummaged around in the back of the Honkerbus, came up with the two articles, and gave them to the ranger. The ranger carefully stowed them in the trunk of his cruiser. Then he took the lock and chain off the Honkerbus and put them in his cruiser. Then he said, "I'm going back to the restaurant now. They are still baking my hat."

And off he went. So, too, did Myrt and Gert. "They told us we'd run into a lot of local color up here on the Parkway," said Myrt, or maybe it was Gert, "but you two are a little more colorful than we figure we can handle. Look us up if you ever get to Rocky River."

Watched by a crestfallen Pundit, they got into their car and drove off.

"Well, we might as well sit down and have lunch," I said.

"Are you crazy?" said The Pundit. "We got to get out of here

Philosophy on Wheels

pronto. The hose we used to fix the Honkerbus come off the radiator in Nelson Eddy's cruiser. And the antifreeze we used to fill up our radiator came out of his car, too.

"In about three minutes Dudley Doright is going out to go get his hat blocked, and he very quickly is going to discover that, new course or no new course, they didn't teach him everything he ought to know at that ranger academy.

"Drive on, Lonzo," he said. "I detest scenes of violence, and they's going to be one here if we aren't gone when that ranger realizes what's happened."

Lonzo let in the clutch and this time the Honkerbus rolled. As they pulled out of the parking area, I remembered that they still had the lunch with them.

As I walked toward the restaurant to buy a second lunch, I consoled myself with the thought that the day was still beautiful, I was smack in the middle of some of the most beautiful scenery in the country, and I probably could have a park ranger as company for lunch.

They came into the office Saturday and asked for a ride downtown.
"Where's the Honkerbus?"
There was a long pause.
"We sold it," said Lonzo.
"We got an offer we couldn't refuse," said The Pundit.
"What happened?" I asked.
"Well," said The Pundit, "you know we been living in the barn on the Widder's farm up in Whiskey Cove. It's warm enough in the summertime, and we meet a nicer class of people there than we do in the Dempsey Dumpsters uptown.

"We been using the Honkerbus to get back and forth between the cove and town. And sometimes we get back there pretty late. Well, the other night we was steaming up the road into the cove, when some people waved flashlights at us and made us stop.

"They said they was representing the Whiskey Cove Improvement Association and they wanted to buy the Honkerbus. They said they couldn't think of a better way to improve the cove than to get rid of the Honkerbus. They offered us fifty bucks."

"Highway robbery," I said.

"Of course," said The Pundit. "And we naturally spurned their offer with indignation. Then one of the representatives took me aside. He pulled a card from his wallet and showed it to me. The card said he was a licensed explosives technician, qualified to explode things in twenty-four states and the District of Columbia.

"He said that he just wanted to explain that if we didn't sell the Honkerbus to the improvement association, it might be necessary to fire a Youngstown Salute.

"I asked him what in the world was a Youngstown Salute and he said some morning when we came out and started up the car we would find out. We would get quite a bang out of it, he said.

"That sort of thing makes us nervous, me and Lonzo, so we took the fifty bucks and gave them the car. They didn't even try to drive it. They made us walk up the road a way and in about ten minutes there was a flash and a roar and the Honkerbus went to glory."

A fat, glistening tear made a white streak down Lonzo's grimy cheek.

"So now," said The Pundit, with a deep sigh, "we are living back in town. No more suburban life for us. It's probably just as well," he said. "The hay fever season is about to start and there's a lot of goldenrod up there in Whiskey Cove."

The Chief of Staff was in the kitchen, getting supper ready. I was in the living room, trading yawns with the basset hounds.

Outside the early winter twilight was deepening fast. A cold wind was wrenching the few remaining leaves from the big oak tree in the front yard. It was a good night to be indoors near a warm fire.

The I heard a sound I had come to think I'd never hear again. It was an unsyncopated rattle of loosely connected metal parts clashing together violently, the shrill whine of a turbine, and the whistle of escaping steam.

It sounded unmistakably like the Honkerbus. But that noble machine had met a violent end up in Whiskey Cove. Or had it?

Then I heard, too, Lonzo's looney laughter and the deep, gravelly voice of The Pundit.

I ran out on the porch and there it was, steam leaking from every

Philosophy on Wheels

joint, the red glare from the firebox lighting up the night, its amber headlights boring down Buckingham Court!

It was, indeed, the Honkerbus, somehow resurrected from the junkyard.

It was, indeed, also Lonzo and The Pundit. Lonzo still was attired in the ratty raccoon coat he had worn when last I saw him. The Pundit had traded in his greasy fedora for a naval officer's uniform cap. With a white scarf around his throat and a long, black leather overcoat over his shoulders, he looked like Hollywood's version of a World War II U-boat captain.

"Greetings and farewell," said The Pundit, climbing down from the "bridge" of the Honkerbus.

"We have come to make our adoos. We are off to Weekiewatchee Springs for our annual sojourn in the land of sunshine, oranges, and slow greyhounds."

"That," I said, pointing to the vehicle, "looks a lot like the Honkerbus. But it can't be. You told me that the Honkerbus had been blown apart up in Whiskey Cove."

"Well," said The Pundit, "it was a very dark night and some members of the Whiskey Cove Beautification Committee probably got confused that night. Me and Lonzo had been tipped off that they was planning to destroy the Honkerbus, so that afternoon we hid the Honkerbus. When we was stopped that night we was riding an old tractor we had sort of borrowed earlier.

"But the committee had gone to a lot of trouble getting the dynamite and staying up late and all, and they felt they was entitled to blow up something. So they blew up the tractor. It wasn't until the pieces stopped falling that they realized the tractor belonged to the guy who bought the dynamite. Well, goodbye, and good luck. And by the way, take a look in the trunk of that new car of yours."

So saying, The Pundit climbed back up behind the wheel and the Honkerbus took off down the court with a scream of steam and a grinding of metal.

In fear and trembling, I opened the trunk lid on my new car. The spare wheel, miraculously, was still there. On top of it was a piece of notepaper. And, standing there in the cold under the street light, I read it. It said:

> This truck lid, we suppose,
> Is locked to keep out those

TWO ON THE SQUARE

>Who would steal your wheel.
>But Lonzo can get in
>By using just a pin;
>Your wheel he could steal.
>But though we'll travel far,
>And though we'll need a tire,
>Your wheel we won't steal.
>To tell the truth of it,
>Your wheel just won't fit;
>And that's a sorry deal.
>A wheel we will filch
>From another poor Joe Zilch,
>So keep your $%!!.* wheel!

From far down the hill, almost to Biltmore Avenue, I still could hear the whine of the Honkerbus turbine and over it the high-pitched, slightly looney cackle of Lonzo's laughter.

The Honkerbus, trailing a wisp of thin, blue smoke from a rear wheel and making an infernal racket, rounded the corner and came to a stop.

Lonzo, wearing grease-stiff coveralls, once-white tennis shoes, and a black cap advertising a brand of tractor, debarked and approached. He was carrying a black tin toolbox. The Pundit, also in coveralls, followed him.

"Hello," I said, as Lonzo plunked his skinny body down on the bench beside me.

"Never mind that," said Lonzo. "Tell us about Hurley's Comet. Where is it? Does Hurley park it in the street? Can we get it started without a key?"

"Wait a minute," I said. "I really don't know where that comet is right now, and furthermore I don't think you can start it."

Lonzo looked irritated. "I can start anything," he snarled, "with a paper clip and sixty seconds uninterrupted."

Philosophy on Wheels

The Pundit grinned. "You ought to see what he can do with jumper cables," he said.

"Why all this fuss about the comet?" I asked.

"Maybe I better explain," said The Pundit, fanning himself with his battered black fedora.

"When we put the Honkerbus together a few years ago, we used some parts from a '54 comet in the back end. Now the right rear axle is going bad and making a lot of noise. We need the rear axle from a Comet to put in the Honkerbus."

"Yes, indeedy," said Lonzo, "but they don't have any Comets to tear down over at the Last Chance Auto Parts Emporium. But one of the people over there said you wrote a column a while back about some geezer named Hurley who owns a Comet.

"And we want to see him. Well, we ain't so anxious to see him maybe, but we sure want to get our hands on his Comet."

"I'm pretty sure Hurley wouldn't mind if you monkeyed around with that comet," I said, "but you're going to need a very tall stepladder to get the back axle out of that comet. Like about forty million miles."

Lonzo sneered, but the light of comprehension began to break over The Pundit's face.

"Let's go, Lonzo," he said. "This comet's a dud."

"I can get the rear axle out of anything," said Lonzo.

"Not this time, Lonzo," I said. "This is not an auto comet, it is a comet comet. It is the real thing. It is a celestial body."

Lonzo blinked and blushed. Talk about stuff like bodies always makes him uncomfortable.

The Pundit chuckled.

"Let's go, Lonzo," he said.

"Furthermore," I said, "it's not Hurley's Comet."

Lonzo looked shocked. "You mean it's hot?"

"No, not at all," I said. "What I mean is that Hurley doesn't own this comet. The comet is Halley's Comet. It is named after Sir Edmund Halley, an English astronomer who discovered it back in 1759."

"That really is the wrong year," said Lonzo. "I mean, what we want is a '54 Comet, not something out of a museum. I didn't know they made Comets that old.

"Gee," he said, "sometimes if you got a car part that's the wrong year, you can lathe it down to fit or shim it up or something, anything, to make it work. But one that's off by 205 years . . . well, I just don't think I can rig that one. How in the everlasting world did this Hurley ever get a license for a Comet that's 200 years old, anyway?"

"I don't know," I said, "and Hurley won't tell you."

5
Some Civics Lessons

When The Pundit joined us on the bench beneath the yellowing plane tree leaves, his expression was grave, his demeanor solemn.

"I have had some unsettling news about my grandnephew Cletus," he said, settling himself comfortably in his favorite end of the bench.

"I don't think you ever met Cletus, Lonzo," he said. "Cletus is the son of my niece Ethelburga. She's the one who ran away to Georgia with the sewing machine salesman."

Lonzo blinked.

"Anyhow," said The Pundit, "she wrote me a letter the other day. It seems that Cletus opened a hardware store in the town of Pineslash down there in Turpentine County. He prospered and is now running for mayor of the town.

"But if what Ethelburga says is correct, I fear his political career is finished almost before it got started.

"Ethelburga said Cletus was detected in the act of discussing an issue the other day, right out there in the open before a crowd of people."

"Mercy!" said Lonzo.

"Mercy, indeed!" said The Pundit, pulling the stub of a ropy black cigar from his pocket and applying a match to it.

"I mean," he said, "if candidates are going to go around actually discussing issues, well, what is a voter to think? This sort of thing could destablize our whole political system.

"What's more," said The Pundit, "when this graceless scamp was caught discussing an issue, he shamelessly refused to claim he was misquoted."

"I don't think they do that anymore," said Lonzo, his brow furrowed by concentration. "I think that now they just claim that what they said was taken out of contracts."

"Whatever," said The Pundit, puffing vigorously on the cigar stub and sending great clouds of oily gray smoke to join the black diesel smoke from the buses.

"But that," he continued, "is only part of the story. There's more and it's worse. Ethelburga said that only a few days after the issue scandal, Cletus had the gall to make a positive statement during a candidates' night meeting."

"Unbelievable!" said Lonzo.

"I'm afraid that Cletus has really blotted his copy book as they used to say back when I served in the Coldstream Guards," said The Pundit. "Just imagine a candidate daring to make a positive statement!

"Of course, that happened in Georgia," The Pundit said, "and anything goes in politics down there. Nothing like that could happen here in North Carolina."

Lonzo's eyes glazed over. He scratched his head. He blinked. He sniffled. His mouth opened. But finally he appeared to have decided to say nothing.

"But the worst part happened just last week," said The Pundit. "Ethelburga said Cletus was overheard saying that his opponent wasn't really a villain and that if he, Cletus, wasn't a candidate himself, he'd probably vote for the man."

"That did it. He's dead," said Lonzo.

"Ethelburga said Cletus now has been disowned by the Democrats, ostracized by the Republicans, denounced by the Socialist Workers party, and has been getting nasty letters from the Klan."

"I wonder what Americans think of him?" I said.

"That's irrelevant," said The Pundit.

"To add to Cletus's troubles," The Pundit continued, "there's a rumor going around that he's being investigated by the Fair Elections Commission."

"That's the least of his troubles," said Lonzo.

"Yes," said The Pundit. "I doubt if any of us will live long enough to hear how that comes out."

Some Civics Lessons

The summer sun was warm on Pack Square.

Lonzo, wearing dilapidated black tennis shoes, paint-spattered blue jeans, and a T-shirt marked **I Lost It In Atlantic City**, was slouched comfortably across half the bench. The Pundit and I shared the other half.

"Where in the Sam Hill have you been, anyway?" asked The Pundit as I sat down. "You've been harder to find these days than a pickpocket at the policemen's ball."

"Oh, I've been away," I said. "I won a contest and got an all-expense, six-day visit to glamorous Circleville, Ohio.

"That was second prize. First prize was three days in Circleville."

"Well, never mind that," The Pundit said. "I've been looking for you because I need some advice.

"I have been mulling it over and discussing it with Lonzo here, and I have about come to the conclusion that I ought to run for governor, now that that fellow—what's his name?—oh yeah, Hunt—looks like he's going to give up the job—finally."

Lonzo turned to me, smiled, and nodded gravely. "Why not?" he asked in his reedy voice. "Half the people in the state are running. And The Pundit's certainly got the time to run."

When I got my hat back out of the tree over the bench, I said, "There's no question that The Pundit is available. He's been available for the last forty years. I just sort of wonder if one of the political parties will consider him suitable."

"Never mind all that political party stuff," said The Pundit in his gravelly growl. "I plan to run as a independent."

"You certainly are," I agreed.

"So what is the first thing I do?" said The Pundit. "Do I get my picture taken?"

"Well," I answered, "I guess the first thing you do is get your fingerprints taken."

"Fingerprints?"

"Yes, fingerprints," I said. "I guess you haven't been following the news very carefully. Congress just passed a new law saying that anyone who wants to run for public office has got to have his fingerprints taken and cleared with the FBI first.

"It's a reaction, I guess. There's been too much Watergate and Abscam and Colcor and all of those funny-sounding things involving politicians."

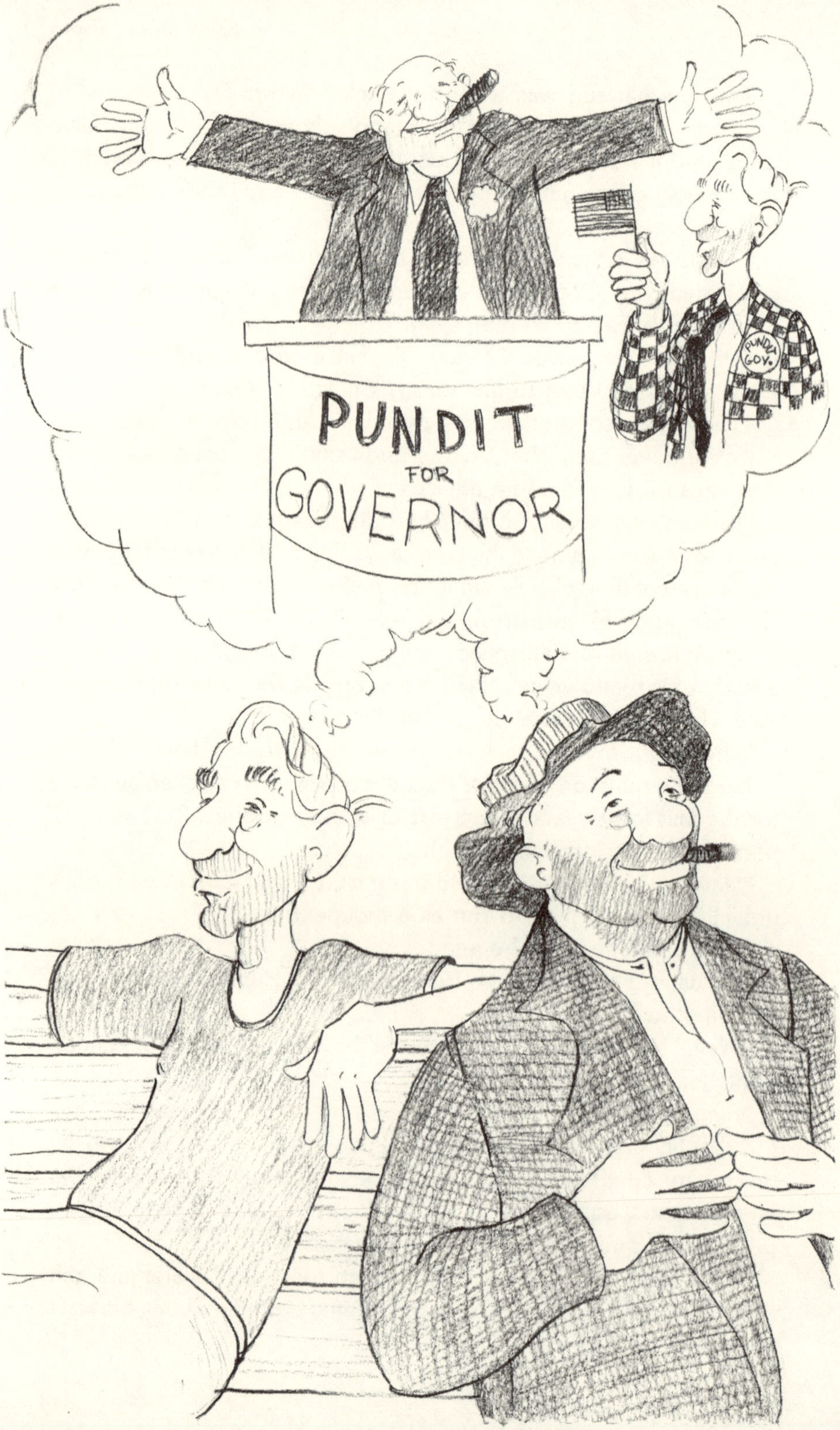
PUNDIT
FOR
GOVERNOR
PUNDIT
GOV.

Some Civics Lessons

Lonzo made a noise like a dog with a bone in his throat. The Pundit's eyebrows rose so far they disappeared under his greasy black hat.

"Fingerprints," he said, thoughtfully chewing on the end of his cigar. "Fingerprints! Funny I never heard that."

Lonzo appeared alarmed. "The FBI!" he said squeakily.

The Pundit pulled his hat down lower over his eyes.

"Fingerprints!" he said. "Why, shucks, a thing like that could change politics all over this state."

"Any state," I said.

"Lessee," said The Pundit, still thoughtful. "There's no felonies there, leastwise none that anybody can prove . . . but there are a few pretty colorful misdemeanors. There was that trifling scam in south Georgia and a few little misunderstandings in Florida. They might make interesting reading for someone.

"Hummm! Fingerprints! What is this world coming to?

"Well," he said, heaving himself up from the bench, "let's just put that governor thing on hold."

I watched them as they trudged up the hill from the courthouse.

Every few feet The Pundit would turn and say something to Lonzo, waving a long finger under Lonzo's nose as he did so. Lonzo would stare blankly at the finger, shrug, and shuffle along for a few feet more.

They were not exactly dressed for success. The Pundit's rusty black business suit was rustier than ever. He wore a once-white shirt without a tie and a greasy gray felt fedora. His salt-and-pepper hair stuck out through a hole in the hat.

Lonzo was wearing his customary paint-spattered tennis shoes and slacks, a cotton sweatshirt that once had been the property of the Rollins College Athletic Department, and a black yachting cap.

"You two seem upset," I said, as they flumped down on the bench beside me.

The Pundit vented an exasperated snort.

"Once again, Lonzo's levity has resulted in a financial crisis for us," he said.

Lonzo grinned sheepishly. "Shucks," he said, "it warn't nothing."

"I had heard on the under-the-bridge telegraph that the Board of Elections was looking for some poll-watchers," The Pundit said.

Lonzo leered. "It's a political job," he said, "you don't have to do nothing."

"It sounded like the sort of part-time work that's ideal for us, particularly since Lonzo got us fired from Kelly Girl," The Pundit said.

"And this month is just the same old story for us. There's too much month and not enough money, and if we don't find some income soon we're going to be sleeping in the elevator shaft at the parking garage again, and that's too hard on my old bones. So we went down to the courthouse to apply for a poll-watcher job. Finally we found the Board of Elections," The Pundit said, "around the corner in an old funeral parlor. We went in and asked to talk to someone in charge. There was some whispering in the back room. Finally out came an attractive woman with freckles who said she ran the place, and what did we want."

"Pretty as a speckled pup, she was," said Lonzo with a dreamy smile.

"I told her we wanted jobs watching some polls," The Pundit said.

"So first off she wanted to know if we had been registered," he continued. "But before I could answer that one, Lonzo told her he couldn't remember if he'd been registered, but he was mighty certain he'd been baptized.

"She looked like she didn't know whether to laugh or cry.

"Finally she said that poll-watching was a serious business and that a lot of people wanted to do it and there weren't any poll-watcher jobs vacant at the time. So Lonzo said that was perfectly all right, that we weren't particular. If we couldn't watch any polls he'd just as soon watch some Lithuanians or maybe some Ukranians. Lonzo told her we'd be happy to watch just whatever they had in stock.

"Lonzo told her that he remembered watching some Hungarians once. It was at a circus. They were acrobats. Two of them were ladies and they wore the tightest clothes he ever did see. If we could just be hired to watch Hungarian acrobats, Lonzo told the lady at the Board of Elections, he'd be happy to work for half pay. Or less, even.

"Well, the lady in charge there got that look on her face again; the don't-know-whether-to-laugh-or-cry look.

"She said she didn't have anybody of any denomination for us to watch, that she had a lot of work to do, and she wanted us out of her office before it became public knowledge that we had been there and it got into the newspapers, maybe. So she shooed us out.

"As we were going out the door, Lonzo looked back over his shoulder and said, 'Does this mean we don't get the job?'"

The Pundit sighed. "That's what it meant, all right. We didn't get the job." He sighed again. "In the meantime there is the matter of lunch which we haven't had yet. Do you care to spring?"

Then I sighed, and the three of us started across Pack Square in search of a little kielbasa.

The Pundit popped like the white rabbit out the door of a bank on Pack Square, veered across the street toward the other bank, spotted me, and tacked across in my direction.

"This is what they call a fortuitous meeting," he said as he subsided on the bench next to me.

"I was pretty sure it was you sitting here when I saw that hat," he said. "No one else in town would have the guts to wear a hat like that."

"What's the matter with this hat?" I asked indignantly. "This is a perfectly good hat. I got this hat in Toledo, Ohio. It is all the style these days. It is a genuine Irish walking hat."

"And you have a genuine Irish head for it," he said. "There's really nothing wrong with the hat, I suppose, except that it makes you look like Grandpa Joad in *The Grapes of Wrath*.

"Anyway, hat or no hat, I'm glad I met you. I need your help."

I sighed. The Pundit operates his own, highly personalized version of the United Way, and he has me down as a frequent contributor.

"What is it this time, and if it's more than fifty cents, count me out," I replied.

He looked at me coldly. "You better watch your mouth," he said. "Remember, I'm a subscriber. What I'm doing is, I'm taking up a collection for Lonzo."

"I see," I said. "You are planning to enter him for next year's Rhododendron Ball?"

"You really are mouthy today. No, I'm getting up what I call the Free Lonzo Fund. He is a civil-rights martyr now."

"I'm having a little trouble placing Lonzo there with the Wilmington 10," I said. "Tell me what happened."

"Well, the problem was that Lonzo went to vote in the primary election last Tuesday," said The Pundit. "And when he finally got into the voting booth, he couldn't find the name of his candidate. Oh, there were plenty of other names. My Lord, on that top line there it looked like they reprinted the Charlotte telephone directory. Why they even had a fellow named Napoleon Lashamore running for something or other.

"He's probably a fine man, but who ever heard of Napoleon Lashamore?"

"Probably his mother did," I murmured.

"Please don't interrupt," said The Pundit. "Anyhow, there was Lonzo, looking and looking but not finding the name he was looking for. Now it may have been that Lonzo had been sampling a new shipment of refreshments we just got from up north. Whatever. But Lonzo figured maybe the machine was broken. So he got out his Swiss army knife and started to take the front off the machine.

"That's when someone violated the sanctity of the polling place," said The Pundit.

"They peeked.

"And in no time at all, Lonzo was looking over the metropolis from a suite in the Chateau Morrissey, the local lockup.

"And I'm collecting the Free Lonzo Fund to bail him out. It isn't that he minds being cooped up so much," said The Pundit, "as it is the fact that he has some books out from the library that will be overdue if he can't get out to return them soon."

"As a veteran library fine-payer I can sympathize with that," I said. "By the way, who is Lonzo's candidate?"

"A fellow named Noneoftheabove," said The Pundit.

I paid up promptly.

Some Civics Lessons

Lonzo and The Pundit were draped more or less artistically over their favorite bench. Lonzo wore a bright yellow oilskin slicker and his usual vacant smile. The Pundit was chewing industriously on the last inch of an evil-smelling black cigar.

"We have been unvoting," said Lonzo.

"It was very pleasant," said The Pundit.

I circled upwind of them and sat down uneasily.

"Explain, please," I said.

"Well, the acorns are popping off car roofs already," said The Pundit.

"And the brown leaves are starting to fly," said Lonzo.

"And we need money to get the Honkerbus in shape for our annual winter sojourn in Florida," said The Pundit. "So we went up Kenilworth and started knocking on doors to line up leaf-raking customers. We have noticed in the past that there's always a bumper crop of leaves in Kenilworth."

"It is a phenomenon with which I am intimately acquainted," I said.

"Anyhow," The Pundit continued, "we were working our way along when we come to this big brick building. They wasn't many leaves out front, but we went in anyway. And, good grief, it turned out to be a voting place! I had forgotten that today is an election day."

"Didn't matter," said Lonzo. "They wasn't anyone there but the people running the thing. But they was nice people."

"Indeed, they were," said The Pundit. "They offered us chairs and coffee. The six of them and Lonzo and me, we chatted about this and that. The weather, you know, and the best route to get to Weekiewatchee Springs. We signed up four of them for leaf-raking jobs.

"One of them wanted to know if we could carry a load of truck tires down to Florida with us to be dropped off at the Port Saint Lucie Surfboard and Hang Glider Supply Company."

"The thing of it was," said Lonzo, "was that they was just plain bored. There wasn't nothing to do. They couldn't play cards, they couldn't sing or dance or play the ukulele. All they could do was wait for customers. And the customers was mighty thin on the ground."

"That's true," said The Pundit. "Me and Lonzo offered to have each of us vote so's they could get a little practice. But they said it would never do, that we wasn't registered."

Lonzo grinned. "Shucks," he said, "we been registered in a whole hatful of government institutions at one time or another. We told them that, but it didn't make no difference. Sticklers, that's what!"

"But nice people, though."

"It almost got embarrassing," said The Pundit. "They was pitifully grateful to have someone to talk to. And they was all dressed up in clean clothes and shirts and such, just sort of sitting around.

"I said I wondered why half of them couldn't go home or someplace and let the other half mind the precinct, but they said it was against the rules. Sometimes the rules don't quite fit the occasion," The Pundit said with the sad smile of a man who has been up against rules before.

We all sighed.

"By the way," I said. "I have work for you two. I need someone to clean out the gutters on my house and get them nailed back in place."

The Pundit eyed Lonzo. "You mean up on the roof of your house?" he asked. "We get there with a ladder and climb around and all like that?"

I nodded.

"Sorry," he said. "Lonzo and me are strictly ground-floor men. The last time we climbed a ladder it took us thirty days to get over it."

"You were that frightened?"

"No, we was that sentenced."

The Pundit's tanned, bald head sweated shinily in the afternoon sun. He was busy making notes on a piece of paper on a clipboard he held on his knee.

Lonzo was half asleep under a big, floppy, biscuit-colored straw hat sporting a red cloth band with the word **Venezia** printed on it in black. He told me later that it was his gondolier's hat.

The Honkerbus was parked at the curb, quietly leaking radiator water into the gutter.

"I see you made it back up the hill from Myrtle Beach," I said.

"No," said The Pundit, gravely. "No, we really didn't make it back. We drowned in the Waccamaw River and our bodies are still there. What you are seeing is our astral spirit."

Some Civics Lessons

"It smells like some kind of spirit," I agreed. "But I'm really surprised that that refugee from a junk yard you two ride around in made it all the way back up the hill from the beach."

"I told you before that we'd think of something," said The Pundit. "And we did."

"What was it?" I asked.

"Thirty feet of good rope and an unsuspecting truck driver," said The Pundit. "With that combination we can go anywhere in the country."

"Long as we travel at night," said Lonzo with a giggle.

"Well, enough travel news," said The Pundit. "We are listing some odd jobs we want to do for people. We need money. What can we do for you?"

"Nothing doing," I said with a shudder. "The last time I hired you two, one of you connected the 220-volt house current to the telephone line, and Alexander Graham Bell isn't speaking to me anymore."

"Them confounded little wires all look alike anyway," said Lonzo.

"Let's let bygones be gonebys," said The Pundit. "We really do need money. We got to get new tires for the Honkerbus because we are planning another trip."

"Where are you going this time?" I asked.

"All the way to Atlantic City," said Lonzo proudly.

"Why Atlantic City?"

"We want to attend the convention," said The Pundit.

"What convention?"

"Why the national political convention," said Lonzo. "Say," he added, "for a geezer that works for a newspaper, you don't know much about what's going on."

I thought that one over for a minute. Then I said, "You can go to Atlantic City if you want. I suppose lots of trucks go there, even at night. But you won't find any national political convention there. Not this year."

Lonzo's face sagged.

"It's in Chicago?" he asked.

"Nope," I said. "The Republican convention starts in Detroit next week. Maybe you can go there."

Lonzo scowled. "Who wants to go to Detroit?" he said. "Everyone is out of work there."

Then he scrabbled over to the Honkerbus, drew back his foot, and kicked the tire. The tire blew out with a bang and Lonzo sat down hard with another bang.

The language was shocking.

I turned to The Pundit who was grinning.

"I expect we'll go Detroit," he said. "I understand the Purple Gang is no longer in business."

"You realize that the convention there is a Republican convention," I said. "Somehow I had you and Lonzo figured for the other party."

"No," said The Pundit. "They're all the same to us."

"Sometimes I feel that way, too," I said.

Lonzo sat huddled on the bench in Pack Square, shoulders hunched against a cold, autumn rain, head bowed, staring glumly at his paint-spattered sneakers.

"Where's The Pundit?" I asked.

Lonzo raised a none-too-clean forefinger in the air. "Over there," he said, pointing to the top of the courthouse where the jail is located.

"And it's all your fault," he said. "You and those dad-burned columns you are forever writing about The Pundit and me. That and The Pundit's confounded Frencheyes. Those are the things what done it."

I thought that one over for a minute. "Maybe you better tell me about it," I said.

"We was setting under the bridge the other day, The Pundit and me, sipping a little import from Madison County, when Ol' Stepandahalf came hitching along the river bank in a big hurry. We asked him where the fire was. He said it was election day and he was in a hurry to go vote.

"Well, me and The Pundit didn't have nothing pressing on our social calendar, so we decided we'd go vote, too. We should have knowed better."

"Seems to me I recall that the last time you two tried to vote, Lonzo, you got thrown in jail," I said.

Some Civics Lessons

"Like I said, we should have knowed better," Lonzo repeated, "but we didn't. We walked all the way over to the school and, let me tell you, that's a long walk.

"Right away a feisty, black-haired guy wearing a three-piece suit come over and told us he wanted us to do three things that he said would help matters along.

"We asked what the three things was.

"The feisty guy said it was simple: He wanted us to shut up, get up, and get out.

"The Pundit reared back and said, 'Now just wait a minute here! Hold the phone! You got no call to throw us out! We are two freeborn American citizens, and we come here to to exercise our Frencheyes, just as was guaranteed to us in Millard Filmore's second inaugural address.'

"But that didn't stop the feisty guy. He said he knew exactly who we was. He said he reads about us all the time in your columns. He said we couldn't vote, that we wasn't even registered. He said according to you we live in Dempsey Dumpsters and don't have no address and so we couldn't be registered.

"He said you got to have a address to get registered, and he said Dempsey Dumpsters didn't signify as bonus fidey residences. He also said something about where The Pundit could put his Frencheyes. I never knew The Pundit had any Frencheyes. Come to think of it, I don't know what Frencheyes are anyway."

"I think it has something to do with the fast food business," I said.

"Interesting," said Lonzo. "Anyway, The Pundit got sort of red in the face. He asked the feisty guy who did he think he was to be going against the words of Millard Filmore?

"'By grannies,' The Pundit said, 'We are getting mighty persnickety about technical things like registrations, ain't we? I tell you, nothing like this ever happened around here when Fletcher T. Bowron was mayor.'"

Lonzo giggled. "That one," he said, "really stopped the feisty guy. Finally the feisty guy sort of shook his head and said old Fletcher T. Bowron one time was mayor of Los Angeles but never of Asheville. Then The Pundit sort of shook *his* head and said, 'Oh, I guess that's why there ain't any palm trees around here no more.'

"That's when the feisty guy called the boys in blue, and that's how your columns and The Pundit's dag-nabbed Frencheyes got him in

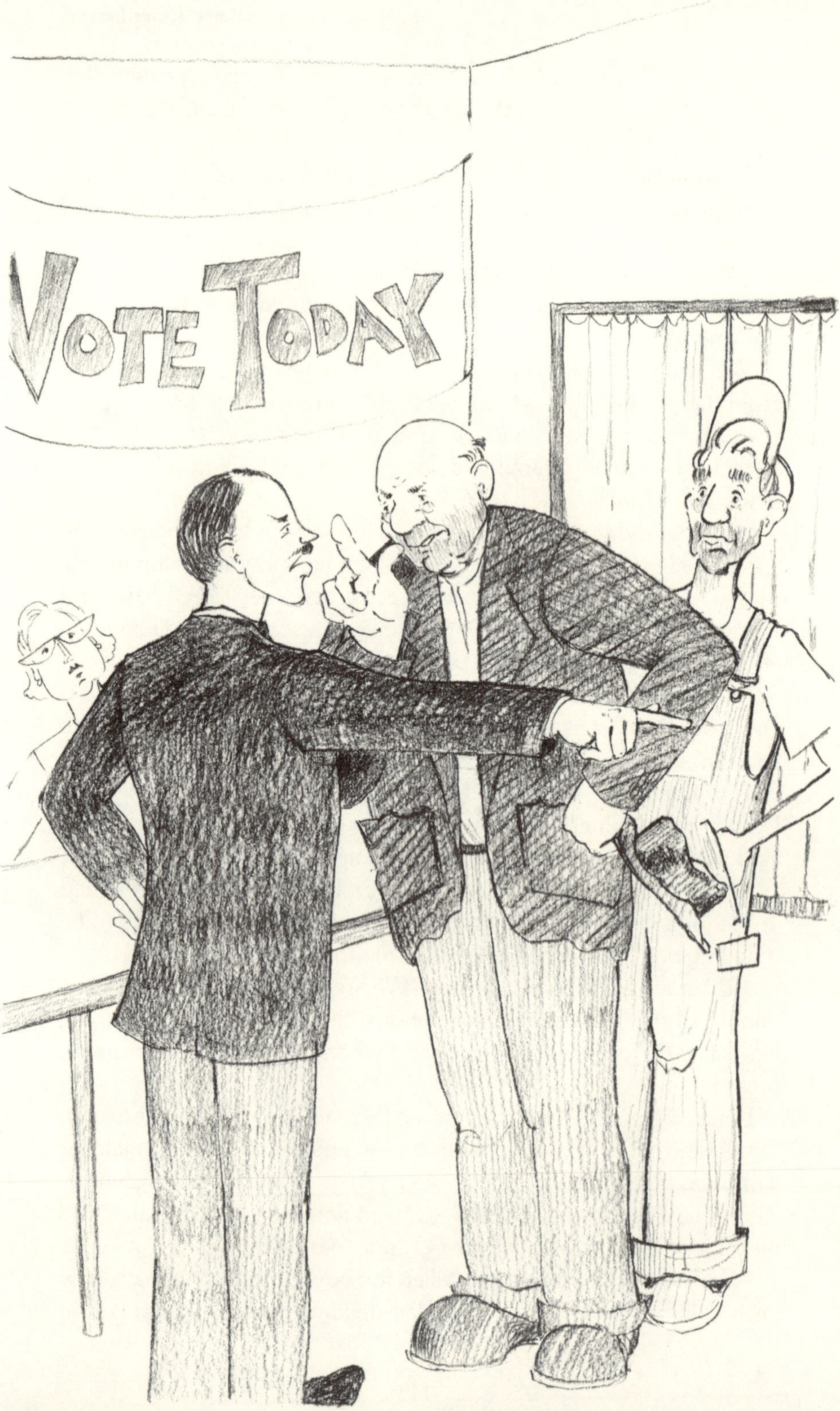
VOTE TODAY

Some Civics Lessons

jail. Maybe if we used Millard Filmore's address we could get registered in time for the next election. Did he live in Asheville, do you know?"

I said, well, no, but he never lived in Los Angeles, either.

I saw them as they rounded the corner.

It was immediately apparent that they were, as The Pundit once put it, "exhilarated." They were, in fact, as limp as two boiled owls.

The Pundit was progressing in a series of swooping ellipses, each one leading to a collision with a store front, then proceeding along the sidewalk to the curb, then swinging back to hit a store front again.

Lonzo was stumping along with one foot on the curb and one foot in the gutter, grumbling loudly about how slanty the sidewalk was at that point.

Somehow they worked their way across the street and sat down beside me.

The Pundit peered at me from under eyelids at half-mast.

"You probably are going to make some snide comment about our condition," he said.

"Not me," I said. "I'm not my brother's keeper, and even if I was, neither of you is my brother.

"It does seem to me, however," I continued, "that you both are so high you ought to be on oxygen."

"I knew I could rely on you to bring in some gas," said The Pundit.

"What has happened here," he said, "is simply that we have been attending a session of the Smith Bridge Institute for Metaphysical Studies. We were having a lively debate on several topics of great public interest," he said.

Then he yawned. The effect was like a scene from *Jaws*. "It might be, however," he said, "that we partook too liberally of the refreshments." He stopped talking. His eyes closed. His head sank.

"What was the Smith Bridge Institute talking about?" I asked.

"Well," The Pundit said, opening his eyes with an effort, "we discussed the election, for one thing. Do you know that this Republican fellow from California stands a very good chance of getting elected president?"

I admitted that I had heard something of the sort. "Might have picked it up at the newspaper office," I said.

"Well, believe me, it's true," said The Pundit. "The man stands an excellent chance. There's a good chance that a lot of surprising things might happen this time around.

"Come on, old friend," The Pundit said, turning to Lonzo, "we got to go down to the school and vote."

Lonzo himself yawned. The effect was like *Jaws*—without teeth. Then he smiled amiably and slowly elevated himself off the bench.

For a second they stood face-to-face, sort of steadying each other. Then they turned and started to totter away.

"By the way," I said, "I think that meeting of the Metaphysical Institute ran longer than you think. Today is Wednesday. Yesterday was Tuesday. That was election day."

They stared at me for a minute. Then The Pundit said, "By grannies, maybe we really did partook too much. Who won?"

"That Republican fellow from California," I said.

"You mean Mr. Hoover?"

"There's something I want you to write about," said The Pundit, scowling. "It's about the legal system. It's all wrong and I think something ought to be done about it. If it isn't fixed, we'll never go back to Arkansas."

Lonzo nodded gravely.

Almost any newspaperman hears a lot of this kind of talk from people outside the profession, and I wasn't impressed.

"You had another run-in with the law?" I asked offhandedly.

"No, no," said The Pundit, "confound it, this has nothing to do with me or Lonzo. It's about Lonzo's nephew, Lucifer, and the great state of Arkansas, that's what it's about. We just got back from a visit to some of Lonzo's kinfolks in Hayseed, Arkansas, and all they was able to talk about was Lucifer."

"They're that proud of him?" I asked.

"No, dang it! It's just the opposite," said Lonzo. "He's in the penitentiary in Little Rock and they are fixing to hang him for murder. But Abel Pettifog is trying to get him off and that ain't right."

"You really want Lucifer to hang?" I asked, amazed.

"You bet your bottom dollar," said The Pundit. "And so does everyone else who ever knew Lucifer. Hanging Lucifer would be the best thing to happen in the state of Arkansas since that Rockefeller guy rented the place a few years back.

"This Lucifer is bad, bad news," said The Pundit. "He has been in three reforms schools in Arkansas and one each in Oklahoma, Texas, and Louisiana. He has been in and out of the Arkansas State Penitentiary so many times the warden calls him 'Boomerang.'

"He has been picked up, paroled, probated, and prayed over a hundred times, at least, and none of it has done a bit of good, not a bit. He has been psychoanalyzed, psychologized, rehabilitated, and restored to society a dozen times. But he's still as dangerous as a rattlesnake."

"My mama always said he was no damned good," said Lonzo, "and she knew him as well as anybody."

"The thing that last got Lucifer into the clutches of the law was that he tried to hold up the biggest motel in western Arkansas while the Arkansas Sheriffs Association was holding a convention there," said The Pundit. "In addition to his other problems, Lucifer ain't too smart. In the course of the robbery he shot and killed a desk clerk. No reason, he just shot the man."

"Lucifer likes to shoot people," said Lonzo.

"Sixteen sheriffs arrested him while he was trying to get his car started and make a getaway," said The Pundit. "He had forgot to turn off his headlights and his battery had run down."

"Well," I said, "ordinarily I am sort of opposed to capital punishment, but in Lucifer's case I'm willing to make an exception."

"That's the way just about everybody in the great state of Arkansas thinks," said The Pundit. "Everybody, that is, except Lawyer Pettifog."

The Pundit angrily threw his greasy black felt hat on the sidewalk and stomped on it. Lonzo walked over and kicked the daylights out of one of the tires on the Honkerbus.

The Pundit collapsed back on the bench. "This Lawyer Pettifog," he said, "has developed an appeal and is trying to get Lucifer off. He says that the state has no right to execute Lucifer, because the state failed to help Lucifer when it had him in its custody.

"It was obvious, that lawyer says, that Lucifer was a wrong number from the days when he was a kid, but the state failed to do whatever it would have taken to straighten him out. Lucifer had a constitutional right to have the state make him stop robbing and stealing and shooting and killing, but the state deprived Lucifer of that right," The Pundit said.

"Absurd," I said.

"My mama always said Lucifer was no damned good," said Lonzo.

"But, my Lord," I said, "Lawyer Pettifog's theory makes failures of everyone in the state of Arkansas. In fact, we are all wrong, all of society, if he's right."

"Precisely," said The Pundit. "Me and Lonzo were in Arkansas when Pettifog filed his appeal with the supreme court there. I thought the sound of legal laughter would be deafening in Little Rock. But—hold on there—at least one judge took Pettifog's case seriously and they've scheduled a hearing on the thing!

"I have a sneaking suspicion," said The Pundit, "that the people of Arkansas are going to get another chance to rehabilitate Lucifer. And I don't want me and Lonzo to be there when it happens."

"Mercy, no!" said Lonzo.

"It's gotta be mercy," said The Pundit. "It certainly isn't justice."

6
Philosophy Almost Anywhere

The Pundit burst through the office door, threw his hat and coat on the table, and raced out again. His usual ponderous shuffle had changed to a bounding, antelope-like series of springs. He was moving faster than I ever had seen him move before.

A few minutes later he reappeared, shuffling again, his face wreathed with a contented grin. He sighed deeply as he sank into the luxurious chair I keep on hand for visitors.

"Phew!" he said. "I'm sure glad I was able to get back on the American Standard up here. I couldn't have held out much longer. I tell you, son, for a while there I felt as though I was wanted and couldn't come, and when I did come was found wanting."

I abandoned thoughts of writing another editorial and asked him what had caused him so much discomfort.

"Well, I was down in the Pack Library and my visit took longer than I figured. Now don't get me wrong. Those folks who work at the library are fine people, but sometimes I just don't think they're up to it. I wanted a copy of a novel called *The Forty Days of Musa Dagh,* by a fellow named Franz Werfel, and all I got was a book called *Forty Ways to Amuse a Dog.*

"Must be a matter of regional accent, or something. Anyway, all this literary palaver at the front desk took so long that I was caught short and had to find the men's room."

His face pictured irritation. "You know it takes a nickel to get into the men's room at the library?

"Imagine that! A nickel-grabber in a public building!"

I murmured something soothing about a nickel being only a nickel.

The Pundit's face grew red. "Dog bite it," he said. "I can afford the nickel. But I had just put my last nickel in the parking meter on the square so the meter maids wouldn't leave a $5 greeting card on my car."

"Maybe," I said, "the city shouldn't have closed that comfort station under Pack Square."

He looked thoughtful for a minute. "Maybe you're right," he said. "But I've been around here longer than you have, and I can remember times when that comfort station was downright uncomfortable."

We talked at random for a while. He told me about his latest attempt to get a pension from the Veterans' Administration.

The Pundit, while serving in World War II in a messkit repair battalion, was bitten on the arm by a first sergeant who had gotten into the lemon extract in the cookhouse.

He has claimed ever since that the experience so unnerved him that he should have been declared eligible for a pension.

"I went over to the VA again just the other day, but it's still no soap and no pension. Those people just don't understand the suffering and anguish I went through. I did find one doctor over there who admitted there was something wrong with me, though," he said.

"That doctor said I had the worst case of the TAL syndrome he ever saw."

"What in the world is the TAL syndrome?" I asked.

"The doctor said it stands for 'Totalium Averso Laborium,'" said The Pundit.

"I told the doctor I don't talk Latin, but he said I should just kick it around a while and it would come to me. Do you know what it means?"

"Sorry," I said. "It's Greek to me."

"It has got so that the words 'Madison County' are like a signal around here," said The Pundit. "People hear just those two words and begin to laugh. It's ridiculous. It's like an automatic reaction, a knee-jerk. You don't have to be funny—just say 'Madison County' and people fall apart.

"It's like Bob Hope saying 'Brooklyn,' or Jack Benny using that ridiculous business about 'Anaheim, Azusa and Cucamonga, and the

Philosophy Almost Anywhere

La Brea Tar Pits.' No jokes—just say the words and get a hee-haw. People are strange."

"What's a La Brea Carpet?" Lonzo asked.

"That's a sticky question," said Montrose Calhoun, adjusting the black bold tie that adorned his stringy neck.

"But you're right, Pundit," he continued. "Madison County has become the butt of a lot of local jokes, and it really isn't funny. It's most unjust, really."

Monty Calhoun, formerly a jewel in the faculty of one of the oldest and most respected universities in the South and now a member in good standing of the Pack Square School of Applied Philosophy and People Watching, lifted his gleaming white Panama hat from his head, mopped the sweat band with an immaculate white handkerchief, and grinned.

"I have occasion to visit friends in Madison County about once a week," he said, "and I never have seen anything there that would justify the jokes that are sometimes made about the place. It's just a normal, ordinary mountain county with some fine, normal mountain people living there. Nothing to laugh about at all."

"Of course," said The Pundit.

"Naturally," said Lonzo.

"However," said Monty, "I did eavesdrop on one conversation up there recently that struck me as being faintly humorous.

"I was sitting on one of those benches in front of the courthouse in Marshall one morning. On the other bench was an elderly man clad in overalls and a baseball cap. He was sitting and whistling and spitting, just the picture of contentment on a warm October morning.

"Suddenly another elderly gentleman turned the corner and walked right briskly up to the first overall. 'Say, Zeb,' said the second overall to the first overall, 'have you heard Congressman Gudger's last speech?'

"'By God, I hope so,' said the first overall."

Lonzo giggled. The Pundit guffawed.

"That reminds me of one time I was up in Madison County," The Pundit said, "and I was sitting on a bench in front of the courthouse. Probably the same bench you was sitting on, Monty.

"And there was the same overall guy sitting there whittling and spitting. And maybe the same second guy in overalls wheels around the corner and sits down next to the first guy. 'Zeb,' says the second

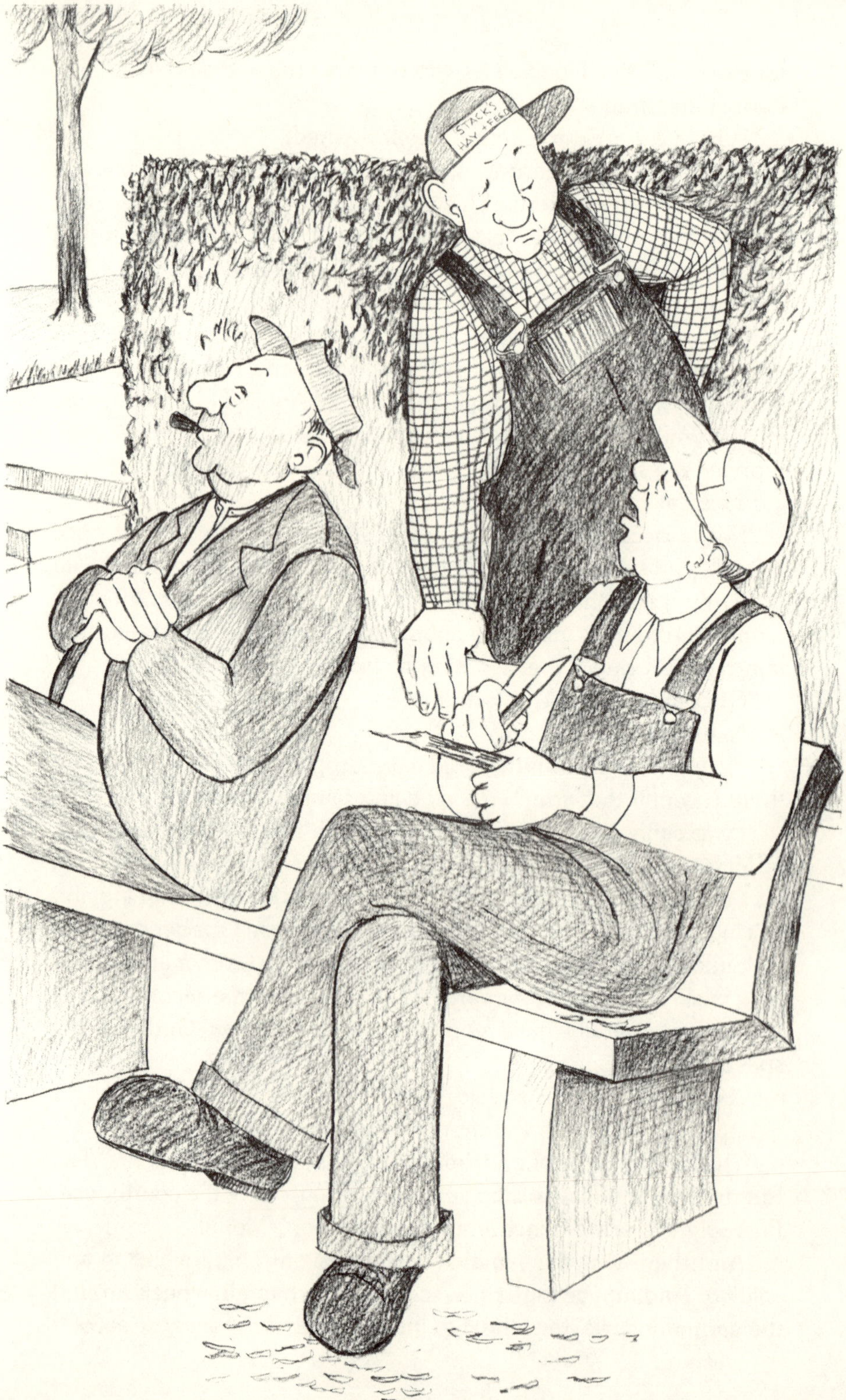
STACK'S
HAY + FEED

overall, 'didn't your mule get sick with the glanders last year?'

"'Yep,' said the first overall. 'Well,' said the second overall, 'my mule has them glanders this year; terrible sick it is. What did you do for your mule when it was sick that time?'

"'Gave it a pint of kerosene,' says the first overall, never missing a whittle.

"'Hum . . . Well, I might try that,' says the second overall, walking away.

"The next morning I was back on the same bench," The Pundit continued. "And the same first overall was sitting there just like the day before. And, sure enough, the second guy in overalls comes around the corner and sits down, too. But this time he looks sort of sad.

"'Zeb,' says the second overall, 'you remember I talked to you yesterday morning about the time your mule had the glanders and you told me you gave it a pint of kerosene?'

"'Yep,' said the first overall, whittling away.

"'Well,' says the second overall, 'Zeb, I did the same thing to my mule yesterday and, Zeb, that kerosene killed my mule!'

"'Killed my mule, too,' said the first overall, never missing a whittle."

"Of course," said Monty.

"Naturally," said Lonzo.

"That brings to mind the time I had a job with Ol' Ketchum, the Madison County undertaker," said Lonzo. "I was hired as a sort of handyman, relief driver, and for lifting and hauling.

"This was during the Korean War. A young man from Madison County had got killed, and the government was sending his body back by airplane. The soldier's parents hired Ol' Ketchum to handle the funeral. Well, the next day Ol' Ketchum sent a hearse down to the Asheville Airport to pick up the casket and bring it back to Hot Springs. Ketchum's son, Soulful, was driving, and Ol' Ketchum sent me along to help.

"That was before we got the freeway and a drive from Hot Springs to the Asheville Airport was a two-hour affair or maybe more. Anyway, Soulful and I got to the airport about noon. The plane with the casket was due in about 1 p.m., so we waited and we waited and we waited and we waited.

"That confounded plane didn't get there until after 8 p.m., and by the time we got the casket off the plane and aboard the hearse, it was dark. We left the airport finally, and started driving back to Hot Springs.

"Somewhere up on Merrimon Avenue, Soulful said we was getting low on gas, so he pulled into a service station. While the guy at the station was filling the tank, Soulful went into the station to buy some cigarettes. I was sitting in the shotgun seat, just sort of resting, when a young man in a soldier suit came up to the hearse. He was stationed at some fort in Kentucky, he said, and he was on furlough. He was hitchhiking home to Marshall, and could we give him a ride?

"Well, I didn't see no harm in it, so I told him if he didn't mind riding with a dead body, sure, he could get in the back of the hearse. He said he'd ride with the Devil to get back home that night, so he picked up his bag and climbed in the back and shut the door.

"Well, there was a pretty girl in the gas station and Soulful stayed a while to talk to her. It had been a long day and I was tired, so I sort of went off to sleep. I vaguely remember feeling the car bounce when Soulful finally got back into it and the motor starting up. Then I dozed off again.

"Soulful pulled out onto the highway and started toward Madison County again. He had been driving for about twenty minutes when the little trap door between the back of the hearse and the front seat slid back, a hand came out and tapped him on the shoulder, and a voice said, 'Say, is it all right if I smoke back here?'

"And that's when I learned how to get a Cadillac hearse out of a six-foot ditch."

There was a respectful silence there on the bench in Pack Square.

Finally Monty cleared his throat and said, "Could have happened anywhere, of course."

"Of course," said The Pundit.

"Naturally," said Lonzo.

"It could even happen in Cucamonga," I said, and they all burst out laughing.

Philosophy Almost Anywhere

"I just can't figure out why a body would want to send somebody else a cartridge and a bare tree. It just don't seem friendly or Christmasy-like. And what about all that other stuff, like those mades of millican and that stuff? What in tarnation is that all about?"

As the plaintive voice whined through the quiet of the library, I looked up.

It was, of course, Lonzo, wearing a puzzled frown and weaving slightly. Behind him stood The Pundit, his bottle-shaped nose redder than ever.

"Now you just stop fretting, Lonzo," said The Pundit. "We've found the man and he'll soon set you straight."

So they sat down at the reading desk beside me.

Lonzo smiled dreamily, blinked, and belched in my general direction. My eyes watered. It was obvious that he had gotten into the Christmas spirit.

"All right," I said, "what is this about cartridges and millicans?"

"Well," said The Pundit, "me and Lonzo was just holding a happy hour over in a warm corner of the stairwell at the garage. We was sipping a little and enjoying the Muzak. Then Lonzo made the mistake of actually listening to the words of one of those Christmas carols."

"Yeah," said Lonzo, "and I want to know why that fellow sent his friend a cartridge and a bare tree."

"Well," I said, "this sounds like a difficult case. I believe you also mentioned something about mades of millican."

"Right," said Lonzo. "That don't figure either. What was it they made out of millican, and what's millican? Now I got the part about turtle doves. That's as plain as day. But I can't decide how in the world they can tell a French hen from a German hen or a Chinese hen or even a ordinary old American hen. And what in the blue-eyed world is a calling-bird?"

The Pundit grinned and hiccuped. He, too, was into the spirit of the thing.

"Can't say as I ever did see Lonzo so worked up about anything before," he said. "I sure hope you can help him."

"I got the part about the golden rings," Lonzo said. "That's pretty easy. And the ladies dancing isn't so tough. But what about them tin lords a-sleeping? Shouldn't someone wake them up? And those bummers bumming worry me, too. What's that got to do with Christmas?"

TWO ON THE SQUARE

"Hmmm," I said. "This sounds like a very difficult problem to me.

"And to explain it all properly to you, I am going to give a quote from a book. *Okeefenokee Abracadabra,* written by the late Sir Walter of Kelly.

"Yes," I said, "I'm confident that will clear up the mystery."

"Saywhat?" said Lonzo.

"Howzat?" said The Pundit.

"Certainly," I said. "Sir Walter had it all down cold. Don't either of you remember the great passage in which he wrote, 'Deck Us All With Boston Charlie, Walla Walla Wash and Kalamazoo'?"

Lonzo blinked.

The Pundit edged away from me a little.

"Well," I said, "if that doesn't clear things up for you, how about the next version in which he said, 'Nora's Freezin' on the Trolley, Swaller Dollar Cauliflower Alleygaroo'? Surely that will end the mystery!"

I paused a minute, overcome by the sheer beauty of Sir Walter's poesy.

I noticed Lonzo peering cautiously at me out of the corner of his eye.

The Pundit had his feet pulled out from under the reading desk, sort of getting ready for a quick getaway.

"Do you understand it now?" I asked Lonzo.

"Not exactly," said Lonzo.

"Darn it, man, you just haven't been listening," I said. "Now I am going to recite the last, the greatest couplet in Sir Walter's book. Surely that will do the trick. It goes, 'Good King Sauerkraut Looked Out on His Feets Uneven.'

"There, now," I said, "that is the be-all and end-all. It explains your problem right down to the ground."

Lonzo looked at The Pundit.

"Maybe he reads too much," said Lonzo.

"Naw," said The Pundit. "That's not it. I just think the man is drunk."

With that, they both got up and went away, in the general direction of the information desk.

And I wondered how the man on that desk was going to explain the mades of millican.

Philosophy Almost Anywhere

"Talk softly," The Pundit half-whispered. "Lonzo's resting comfortably and he needs it. He's had a tough week."

Lonzo was indeed resting comfortably. He was sprawled across the bench with his feet splayed out and his head tilted back. His eyes were closed and he was emitting rhythmical grinding sounds I classified as snores.

"He seems to be tireder than usual," I said. "What happened this time?"

"Poor critter is a victim of medical science," said The Pundit.

"It all started about ten days ago," he continued. "Lonzo developed a sore spot inside his mouth, what we used to call a canker spot when we were kids. He put up with it for a while, trying to eat around it, you know. But then it got so bad he couldn't stand to have alcohol in his mouth. Well, when things got that bad, we knew something had to be done."

The Pundit said they had been visiting the Widder Lady of Whiskey Cove at the time, and she arranged for them to see Old Doc Nostrum, her family doctor.

That interview, according to The Pundit, went something like this:

Lonzo: I got this here sore spot in my mouth, like a canker spot.

The Doc: Now, you just hold on there a minute! I don't want to hear a durn thing about your canker spot, see. Instead, I want to tell you about my canker spot. My canker spot is bigger, I bet, than your canker spot, and it hurts a lot more than yours does, and if I could cure yours, don't you think I'd cure mine first?

Lonzo: You telling me there's nothing can be done?

The Doc: Not at all. It can be treated. If we treat it, it will go away in about seven days. If we don't treat it, it will go away in about a week.

Lonzo: What causes these dang things, anyway?

The Doc: I went to medical school, not divinity school.

Lonzo: You going to charge me for this call?

The Doc: No. I don't expect miracles, either. But I am going to write a prescription for some mouthwash. Get the stuff and use it. It will help . . . a little . . . maybe.

"As we was leaving the doctor's office," said The Pundit, "I got a good look at the framed diploma he had hanging on the wall. It said he had graduated with honors from the Fred Harvey School of Restaurant Management.

"Well, anyway, about the stuff he prescribed . . . we got a little bottle at the drugstore and Lonzo squooshed some around in his mouth every two or three hours. Well, sir, yesterday Lonzo woke up and the canker spot had vanished—just disappeared entirely. We decided to go out and celebrate, but as we was climbing out of the Dempsey Dumpster where we spent the night, we discovered that the pain had just sort of slud from Lonzo's head to his hip.

"It took him something terrible, just under his wallet. He had a gimp in his gait, a hitch in his haunch. The whole livelong day he sort of slunk around looking for all the world like a rural version of Groucho Marx. He walked past a woman waiting for a bus yesterday afternoon, and she took one look at him and belted him with her umbrella. Never said a word, just walloped him.

"Between the pain and the prospects of getting belted again, poor Lonzo's plumb wore out."

"Does Lonzo have any of that mouthwash left?" I asked.

"About a half a bottle," said The Pundit.

"Then it's simple. Tell him to start rubbing the mouthwash over the sore place on his hip. He ought to recover in a flash."

"Do you think so?" The Pundit asked.

"Certainly," I said. "I've eaten in a lot of Fred Harvey Restaurants."

"Then it's a piece of cake," said The Pundit.

I heard a scuffle in the hall outside the office and The Pundit's gravelly voice saying, "Confound it, man, keep your hands to yourself!"

As an undertone I heard the excited whining sound Lonzo makes whenever there's a rumpus.

In the face of physical violence, Lonzo has adopted the perfect defense. He falls on the ground, rolls up in a ball, and makes a noise like a frightened pony.

Lonzo doesn't win any fights that way, but he doesn't lose any, either. It's hard to beat up a man who flops down, rolls up, and whinnies. By the time Lonzo's opponents have stopped laughing, most of them have forgotten why they wanted to hit him in the first place.

Out in the hall I discovered one of our maintenance men, wearing a shocked expression and trying hard to get Lonzo and The Pundit into the elevator shaft.

I promised the maintenance man that I'd make them leave soon, then I shoved the two of them into my office.

"Did you see that?" said The Pundit indignantly. "That man was trying to shove us into the elevator shaft!"

"Yeah," said Lonzo, "and the elevator wasn't even on this floor, neither!"

"I have told you two before to stay out of here," I said. "It takes too long to air the place out after you visit, and there's something about you that makes people automatically want to throw you out."

"We came here in response to your invitation to look at your new stuff here and admire the carpet on the floor in the newsroom and enjoy some refreshments, just like you people wrote in the paper," The Pundit said.

"Yeah," said Lonzo. "Where are those refreshments, anyway? We heard they was punch and cookies. Anything in the punch?"

"Not even a Hawaiian's socks," I said. "The open house was held a week ago."

"You mean this ain't October the eleventh?" asked The Pundit.

"That was a week ago," I repeated.

"Does that mean we don't get no punch?" asked Lonzo.

"That newspaper we found in the Dempsey Dumpster must of been older than it looked," said The Pundit.

"Are you sure there ain't no punch left at all?" said Lonzo.

"Not a drop," I said. "We had so many people in here for the open house the place looked like Napoleon's retreat from Moscow. We had people waiting in line to look at the janitor's broom. It was great to be able to meet so many friendly, interested people and to show them our building.

"They came and they talked and they looked and they drank the punch and they ate the cookies, and we just barely had enough to supply the demand.

"One time the punch supply got so low the business manager was going to dump a bottle of red ink into a bucket of ice water and call it a Depression Cocktail."

Lonzo sobbed softly.

The Pundit grinned and said, "Come on, Lonzo, there's nothing

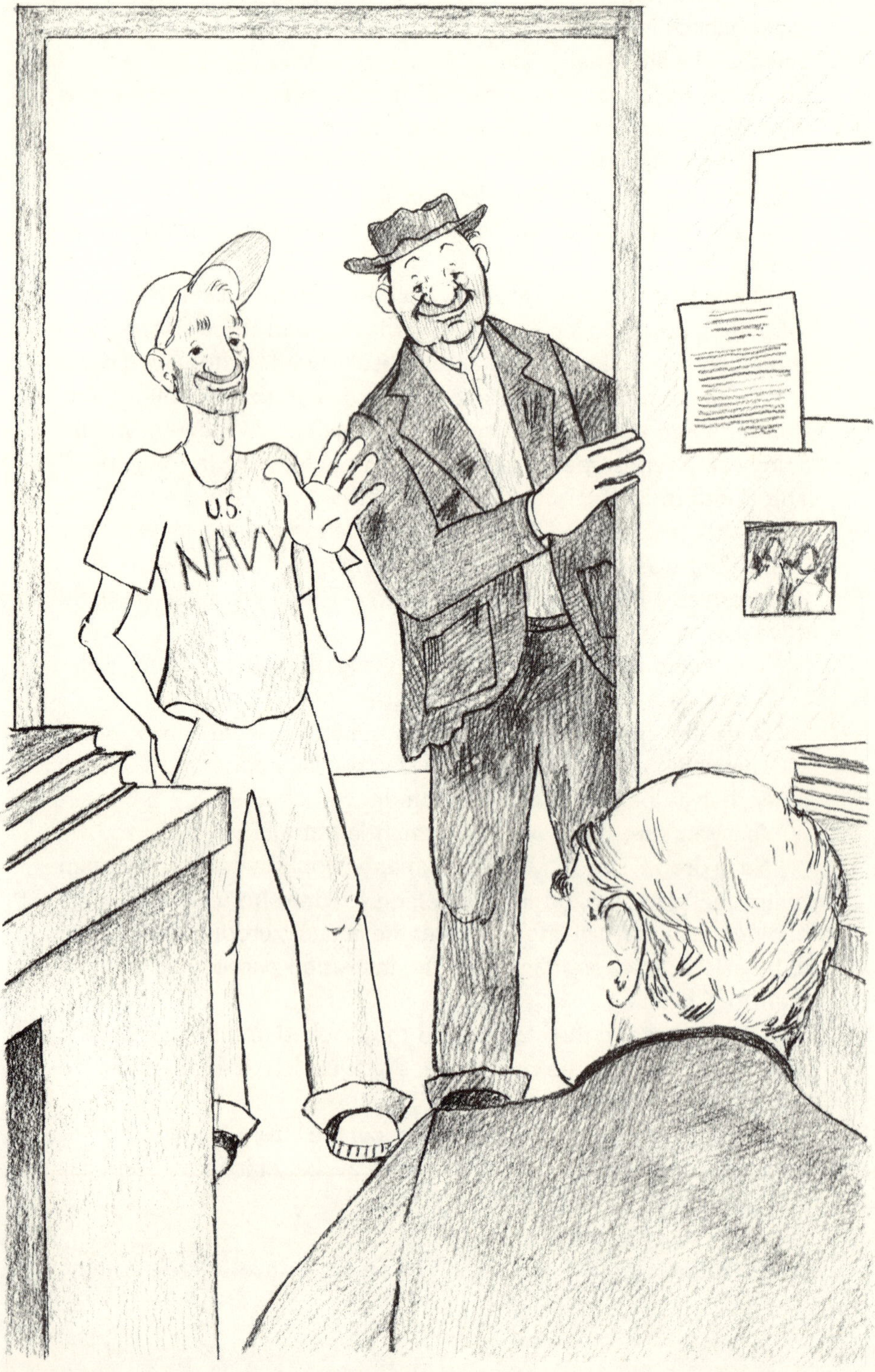
U.S.
NAVY

Philosophy Almost Anywhere

doing here. We might as well get down to City Hall."

"What's going on at the hall?" I asked.

"Well," said The Pundit, "in that same newspaper we found in the Dempsey Dumpster, we saw a story about how the people at City Hall want everyone in Asheville to save water.

"And Lonzo and me, we're experts at saving water. We haven't used any since the flood back in '77 and we couldn't avoid that. When it comes to saving water, Lonzo and me are the people to talk to, believe me."

"Maybe they'll give you some punch at City Hall," I said.

"I didn't know they had any Hawaiians at City Hall," said The Pundit.

"We took the Honkerbus, the poor man's Greyhound, out for a trial run yesterday," said The Pundit.

"How did it go?" I asked.

"All right, I guess," said The Pundit. "The two front wheels don't match and that makes driving a little difficult, and a few parts fell off, but they were nothing important."

"We flew along," said Lonzo. "Just went like 60! Went like a bird! Beautiful, beautiful!"

"We was coming down the road from Mine Hole Gap," said The Pundit, "when we saw a sign by the side of the road that puzzled Lonzo. It said, 'This way to the educational complex.' He couldn't figure that out."

"Last time I knew, there was a school there," said Lonzo. "What in the world ever happened to that?"

"There's still a school there," I said. "You are simply victims of modern-day improvements in the nomenclature of educational adjuncts."

Lonzo blinked.

Then he said, "Well, that explains it perfectly." Then he blinked again.

"What he means, Lonzo," said The Pundit, "is that they call things in schools by different names now from what they did when we were kids. It's just a way to make getting an education harder, is all.

"And it's exactly the right thing to do, too. Education ought to be painful. If getting an education don't make you sweat, it probably isn't worth getting. If it's easy, people get uneasy about it. They start wondering where the tax money is going. There's got to be some struggle and some tears or it just don't ring true."

Lonzo blinked again.

"Talkin' about tears puts me in mind of Miz Bull, the lady who ran the second grade class I was in," he said.

"She ran that class her way, and no mistake. She didn't weigh but about ninety pounds, but she could hit like Joe Louis. She could whale the tar out of a room full of farm boys and never muss her hair. I recall one time she clouted Junior Reavis with a piece of stovewood, and it was three days before he stopped hearing bells ringing. You talk about tears! But I tell you, Pundit, Junior Reavis never gave her no more lip after that! No, sir!"

"You and me, Lonzo," said The Pundit, "had the advantage of going to school when the term 'board of education' meant a two-by-four cut to a handy length. That was in the days before all the teachers had to go to college and learn how to motivate their pupils. In the old days they motivated them with a rap on the skull. The taxpayers really thought they were getting their money's worth from education in those days. It sort of reassured parents, don't you know. There was plenty of struggle connected with it.

"But they don't do things like that no more. Nowadays, if a teacher gives one of the kids a hard look, the kid's parents show up in school the next day with a lawyer in tow, reciting the Constitution and the Bill of Rights. So there's no more of that, and maybe it's a good thing.

"But, Lonzo, they done all sorts of things to keep education difficult. As soon as it looked like kids was learning to read easier, they changed the way they teach reading, and that had everything nicely confused for a few years. Then they come up with something called the new math and that kept the struggle department running for a while.

"But as soon as the kids start catching on to that wrinkle, they'll come up with something else. They're smart people, those educators, and they understand the need for struggle."

"True," I said, "but I still can't swallow terms like 'educational media distribution center.'"

"What's that?" asked Lonzo.

"It's what we used to call the school library," said I.
"Glory be!" said Lonzo.

"Butter," said The Pundit.
"Fingers!" said Lonzo.
"Unavoidable," said The Pundit.
"For sure!" said Lonzo.
"It's the butter they give you in restaurants these days," said The Pundit.
"They give you the stuff all done up in little plastic tubs about the size of a man's thumbnail. On one corner of the thing it says 'Pull here' and you pull there and not a blasted thing happens."
"Not a solitary thing," said Lonzo, nodding in agreement.
"And," said The Pundit, "when you finally do get the thing open, then the fun has just started. No one, I don't care who he is, can dig that butter out of there without getting it all over his fingers. You can have the dexterity of a brain surgeon and the cool nerves of a test pilot, and you're still going to end up buttered from wrist to elbow like a breakfast biscuit."
"I'm hungry," said Lonzo.
"Listen," said The Pundit, "I knew we were in trouble thirty years ago when they first started serving coffee cream in those little cardboard buckets with the paper stretched across the top. You remember them. You had to turn them upside down to see where your fingernail could get a purchase. And you invariably ended up with coffee cream all over your trousers."
"Disgusting," said Lonzo, burping gently.
"Then they 'improved' things," said The Pundit, his red knob of a nose wiggling with indignation. "They started putting the coffee cream in those three-cornered thingumbobs made of damp paper with a little blue patch over the hole. Now there's a real challenge for a man of the world who has enjoyed a convivial night and is perhaps a little shaky in the morning. You squeeze one of those things just a shade too hard and you have cream all down your wrist and making a puddle inside the elbow of your jacket.

"Those things have been the biggest boost for the dry cleaning industry since the invention of carbon tetrachloride."

"I sure could go for some grits and gravy," said Lonzo wistfully.

"And, son, you got to watch the contents, too. More often than not, the cream that spatters all over your blazer sleeve never saw a cow. It's something that started in a soybean field," said The Pundit.

"Awful," said Lonzo, licking his lips.

"And it is not simply a matter of coffee cream or butter that bedevils the diner these days," said The Pundit. "There is the affair of the mustard and catsup served in little plastic bags. You're supposed to tear off one corner, squeeze the opposite end and, Voila! out comes the mustard.

"Well, Voila! nothing. You can't tear the corner off with a pair of pliers. I use my teeth whenever I am forced to deal with these satanic devices. Poor Old Lonzo doesn't even have that going for him, do you, Lonzo?"

"No teeth," said Lonzo. Then he grinned. Sure enough, no teeth, or none that met, in any case.

"And, listen," said The Pundit, "if you finally are able to get one of those things open, there's no telling which way that mustard is going to go. You could just as well wind up putting the stuff on a stranger's hot dog.

"Furthermore, they are encasing jelly and apple butter in plastic. Have you ever seen the mess grape jelly can make on a beige jacket?"

"Hold it," I said. "I give up. I was going to invite you both to step around the corner to Pigear's Place and have a bite of lunch with me, but you obviously are never ever going to enter a restaurant again."

"Whatever," replied The Pundit, "gave you such an outlandish notion? We are quite capable of overlooking trifles."

"Let's go," said Lonzo.

And we went.

"I swear," said The Pundit, "I haven't been so cold since the last time me and Admiral Byrd went to Little America.

"The man who managed the winter up here did a fine job, but the idiot who's running the spring must have flunked kindergarten."

"I haven't seen either of you for a while," I said. "Where have you been?"

"Well, we come back from Florida too soon, that's for sure," said The Pundit. "And then we found ourselves with a subsistence problem.

"We had fifteen days of eating money in a thirty-day month. And the confounded weather has been too cold to stay nights in a Dempsey Dumpster, and the Widder Lady of Whiskey Cove hasn't been the All-American hostess lately, not since we set her barn on fire.

"So," The Pundit continued, "we declared an emergency. Lonzo resurrected his Medicare card and checked into the hospital so the doctors there could install a blowout patch in him."

Lonzo smiled dreamily. "They fixed my hisnia," he said.

"Hisnia?"

"He means *hernia*," said The Pundit.

"I don't neither, confound it," snapped Lonzo. "Hernias happen to females. I'm a male and I had a hisnia."

The Pundit shrugged. "Anyway," he said, "that took care of Lonzo's problem. I decided to check into the local lockup until things warmed up. So I went and fortified myself. In fact I got so fortified I could have defended the United States, Canada, Mexico, and most of the Western Hemisphere. Bare-handed.

"Then I laid around Pritchard Park looking pretty fortified. But nothing happened. You got to do more than just get fortified these days to get arrested. It was getting colder out there and I was hungry, so I went behind the music store, got a packing box, and dragged it down to Pack Square. Then I stripped down to my BVDs, climbed on the box, and struck a pose. Pretty soon here comes one of Asheville's finest, swinging his stick.

"He sees me and says I should get down and cover up immediately or he'll run me in. I says I'm a piece of sculpture, that I'm fine art, and there's nothing a Philistine like him can do about it. He says he's not a Philistine, that's he's been a registered Democrat all his life. Then he gives me a lesson in art appreciation and runs me in.

"Lonzo spent a couple of weeks at the hospital. They wanted to send him home earlier, but how could they send a guy home who's got no home? They finally couldn't stand it no longer so they gave him a bus transfer and threw him out the front door."

"About time, too," Lonzo growled. "They kept giving me baths. And some of those nurses have the coldest hands."

"That was yesterday," said The Pundit. "And this morning the high sheriff handed me my walking papers. So we're back in circulation."

"Where are you going to stay?" I asked.

"Oh, that's no problem now," said The Pundit. "When the Widder Lady heard Lonzo was in the hospital, she came hotfootin' it to make up. Everything's lovey-dovey now, and me and Lonzo is welcome to sleep in what's left of her barn any time.

"There is one thing that's bothering me, though."

"What's that?"

"Well, when I was up there on that box in Pack Square posing like a statue, well, it felt just fine! It felt great! A little chilly, but exhilarating. I got a urge to do it again. You suppose I'm all right?"

"Don't ask me, I'm a Philistine," I said.

"Hoo! Boy!" The Pundit wheezed, pulling up his left trouser leg, "lookie there!"

I looked. He had a neat plaster walking cast that stretched from just below his knee to down below his ankle.

"You're too old for those touch football games, and I've told you that before," I said.

The Pundit looked annoyed. "It wasn't nothing like touch football," he said. "It was those confounded tourists. There isn't a doggone one of them that understands the rule of the ripened red light.

"You know what I mean. It's a plain and simple fact that a lot of drivers in Asheville don't pay any attention at all to a red traffic light after it has turned red. They let it ripen a little, like, say, thirty or forty-five seconds, before they start to do anything about it. Long as everyone on the street understands this, it goes along all right. But someone from out of town can really cause a panic at an intersection."

"And that," I said, staring at the Pundit's cast, "is what happened to you?"

Philosophy Almost Anywhere

"Precisely," said The Pundit.

"Me and Lonzo were headed up north the other morning. We were going to make some arrangements for the punch to be served at an upcoming summer festival to be sponsored by the River Bank Philosophical and Four-Part Harmony Society.

"We came to an intersection and an amber traffic light. I was driving, so naturally, I speeded up. Well, sir, the light changed to red and it hadn't been red more than five or ten seconds when he did it.

"This pilgrim from Pennsyltucky or Michohio or Wisdiana or some place was going crosstown at the time. He saw a green light and, like a tourist, didn't wait for the red to ripen. He just sailed out into the intersection wearing nothing more substantial than a Japanese car and a smile of righteousness."

"Good Lord!!" I said. "How many were killed?"

"You really are a crepe-hanger," said The Pundit. "Wasn't nobody killed; I told you I was driving. I just slid that old Honkerbus up on the sidewalk and skinned it between a stone wall on one hand and a light pole on the other. Never touched that tourist.

"It was a tight fit, though. The Honkerbus is two feet longer and two feet narrower than it was before, and it's bent like a boomerang. And I have enough surgical metal in my leg to open up my own hardware store."

"Well, at least you spared the tourist," I said.

"Yes, I did," said The Pundit. "Heaven knows we need all of them we can get. But I sure wish they'd stop going around charging green lights all the time."

"It's the nature of those Northerners," I said. "They see a green light and they get impatient. They just want to go."

"Perhaps," said The Pundit, "but how do you explain all the trouble we have with people from Florida?"

"Nobody's really from Florida," I said. "Everyone who comes up here from Florida really started someplace else. Like Pennsyltucky. Like those other places. Where they go on a green light."

"Gosh," said The Pundit.

7
Getaway Days

"On our way back from Weekiewatchee Springs this time," said The Pundit, "me and Lonzo stopped off in Savannah to visit Lonzo's Uncle Doro."

"Doro!" I said. "Now there's an unusual name."

"Yeah," said Lonzo. "It's short for Alcindoro. Just before Doro was born, his mother had been reading a book called *The Stories of the Great Operas*. She found that name Alcindoro in there and insisted on giving it to the new baby.

"Later, at the baptizing, the preacher forgot the real name and sort of shortened it to Doro, and that's what he's been called ever since. His mother wasn't too pleased about that, let me tell you, and that preacher got an earful afterward, but it was too late by then."

"Doro has a railroad job," Lonzo added.

"That's right," said The Pundit. "He's engineer, fireman, brakeman, and conductor of the little train that runs up and down the riverfront there in Savannah.

"It's a mighty good job," The Pundit said. "But Doro's kind of bored with it. He says he feels he really isn't getting anywhere."

"Well, he isn't," said Lonzo, reasonably. "All he does is run up the river bank and then back down again all day long. Course, he gets to blow the whistle a lot, and I reckon that counts for something."

"What it counts for is occupational deafness, if you ask me," said The Pundit, lighting up the stub of one of the evil-smelling black cigars to which he is addicted.

"I liked Savannah all right," he continued, "but we had trouble getting accustomed to the Girl Scouts."

"Lord!" said Lonzo. "They were all over the place. Everywhere you go they's packs and swarms of little gigglers, all decked out in

TWO ON THE SQUARE

green dresses and funny hats and all talking a mile a minute. I swear, it's downright uncomfortable."

"There's a lot of Girl Scouts there," I said, "because Savannah was the home of Juliette Gordon Low, the woman who founded the Girl Scout movement. Her home is there, and Girl Scouts come from all over the country to visit the place. It's like a pilgrimage."

"Well, there's too much movement in that movement and too many pilgrims on that pilgrimage," said Lonzo grumpily.

"It did kind of bother Lonzo," said The Pundit with a grin. "Every time we started to walk across the street, a bunch of them grabbed us by the elbows to steer us safely across."

"Dang it, I can get across a street by my own self," said Lonzo. Then a grin split his leathery face. "By doggies, Pundit, they got to you, too."

Turning to me, he said, "The Pundit finished smoking one of those old ropes of his whilst we was strollin' down Abercorn Street and threw the butt in the gutter. Well, in about three seconds, they was a whole school of them little green fishes around him, just giving him fits about littering. One of them picked up the butt and put it back into his hand.

"The Pundit was standing there with the burning butt in his hand, wondering what to do with it, when a full-sized lady dressed in one of those green uniforms come up and give him a lecture about air pollution. She was the leader of those Girl Scouts, she said, and she wanted him to know that he was setting a terrible example for them.

"By this time, the butt was starting to burn The Pundit's fingers, and he's standing there, switching from one foot to the other and breaking out in a sweat, while this lady reads the riot act to him.

"Oh, it was beautiful! Old Pundit didn't know whether to swallow the butt or climb a tree.

"Finally, about the time the lady starts lecturing on the impact he's having on the environment, The Pundit says something in Spanish, drops the burning butt in his pocket, tips his hat, and walks away.

"He won't tell me what it was he said in Spanish, but it shut up the lady pretty good."

"You're too young to know," said The Pundit. "And I really didn't think that woman would understand it, but she did, all right. It had something to do with the fact that we were right around the corner from Bull Street. Thank heaven there was a public fountain on Bull

Street and we used that to put out the fire in my coat pocket.

"Things, however, didn't get any better the next day when Doro and his wife, Dora, took us to lunch at a place called The Pirate's Cave."

"Humph," said Lonzo, indignantly.

"Yas," said The Pundit. "They was some trouble. First was they sent Lonzo back to the car to get some shoes on. Then the guy at the door looks at the cigars in my pocket and says if I light up one of those, they're going to throw us out. Doro and Dora by this time are some embarrassed. Doro said something about he really ought to get back to his train. Dora said if he cut out then, she wasn't going to let him into the house that night.

"Well, when we finally did get into the place it was real nice. It was all little dark rooms and big pretty waitresses, and I went to the men's room and got lost on the way back. I needed assistance from about six waitresses to find my bearings, sort of.

"Anyway, I finally located the others and we had lunch. It was very nice. Lonzo even used a fork. The dessert was just outstanding. Finally the waitress brought the check.

"Lonzo grabbed it and I almost had a heart attack because I thought for the first time in his life he was going to pay a check. But I had underestimated him. He looked at the thing twice, then lit a match so he could see it better. By this time the waitress and everyone else around us was watching carefully.

"Finally Lonzo looked up, screamed loudly, and said that it was a fine meal, all right, but that a bill for $314.02 for lunch for four people seemed a little steep to him.

"Then I thought the waitress was going to have a heart attack. She grabbed the check back, walked over to the front desk, and came back in a couple of minutes with two men.

" 'Sir,' one of them says to Lonzo, 'I have to tell you that this check is not a demand for $312.02. The figure you have been reading really is the Zip Code for downtown Savannah. And what we want you to do is zip right out of this restaurant. Don't worry about paying and don't show us a credit card. I don't think we could stand it. We are writing you four up as a bad investment. Just leave and never, never come back.'

"Well, we left, naturally, before they could change their minds and make us pay. Lonzo and me climbed into the Honkerbus and said

TWO ON THE SQUARE

goodbye to Doro and Dora before we drove away.

"Lonzo said we really enjoyed our visit to Savannah and we would like to come back a lot if we could just hit on some times when they wasn't so many confounded Girl Scouts cluttering up the place.

"Doro sort of sighed and Dora winced and Doro said he'd think about it, but it didn't seem like we would be able to visit very often. There wasn't that many restaurants in Savannah, he said.

"So we drove back up to the mountains. Maybe we'll let Savannah get along without us for a while. But Lonzo, I recall, has another cousin who lives at a place called Thunderbolt, right close to Savannah. Maybe we'll visit him on our way back next spring.

"A place with a name like that ought to take Lonzo in stride."

"I have never been so insulted in my whole life," said The Pundit through gritted teeth.

"Never," said Lonzo, looking more forlorn than usual.

"We have been kicked out of the whole state of South Carolina," said The Pundit.

"They said we was trash," said Lonzo as a couple of big tears trailed down his face and soaked the grimy sweatshirt he was wearing.

"It wasn't trash, exactly," said The Pundit. "We was classified as hazardous waste. If I get a choice I think I'd rather be called trash."

"It happened this way," said The Pundit.

"Lonzo and me have been down in Charleston in the oyster business. We had a deal with a guy who has a boat. He found the oysters, and we were using the Honkerbus to truck them to market in Charleston. Things was going along all right until one day about a week ago. That morning the guy with the boat got back early with a full load. That put us ahead of schedule, so on the way back me and Lonzo stopped for refreshments.

"Well, with one thing and another, we didn't get to the Cooper River bridge until about 4:30 in the afternoon."

"You must have been very well refreshed," I said.

"Oh, we certainly was," said Lonzo, sincerely.

"We was crossing over the bridge," said The Pundit, "when we had a slight mechanical problem."

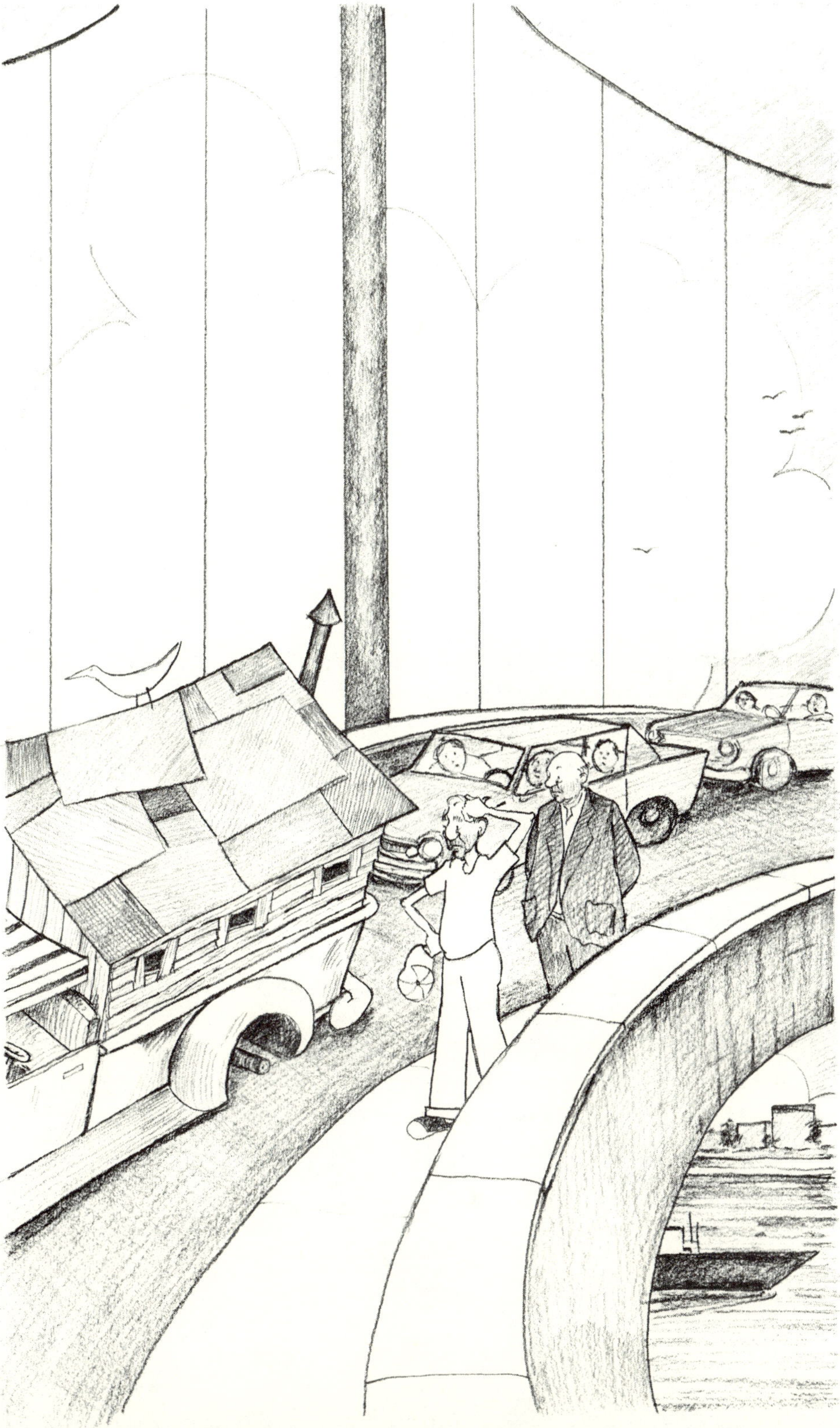

"The only thing that happened was a wheel came off, that's all," said Lonzo. "It wasn't nothing serious."

"Anyway, we had to stop," said The Pundit. "And so did a whole lot of people behind us who were mighty anxious to get to Charleston. We was starting to jack up the Honkerbus when a couple of cops came running up.

"They was hollering about getting the Honkerbus moving. One of them opened the back door of the Honkerbus and took a deep breath. He like to fell down. The Honkerbus had been sitting in the sun for a long time and was a very hot day. Them oysters was ripe.

"He started screaming about getting rid of the oysters, so Lonzo grabbed a basketful and threw it off the bridge. Unfortunately there was a navy destroyer under the bridge and the oysters landed on the destroyer's deck. The destroyer started blowing its siren and aiming its gun at the bridge. My, them sailors was agitated!

"Well, there was a lot more screaming from the cops, this time about starting World War III. Then a wrecker arrived and pulled us off the bridge."

"When we got to the far side," said Lonzo, "the wrecker operator said we owed him twenty bucks for the tow. The Pundit told the man to get it from the cops. The Pundit said we didn't call for no wrecker and we wasn't going to pay no money. Then there was some more screaming."

"Finally," said The Pundit, "here comes a civilian who said he was with the state health department. He took one look at us and another at the Honkerbus and another at the oysters and said we was hazardous waste and that South Carolina was tired of getting hazardous waste from North Carolina and we should be run out of the state. Otherwise, he said, they could bury us down near Barnwell with the rest of the hazardous waste.

"While all this was going on, Lonzo eased away, borrowed a wheel from a Good Samaritan who hadn't locked his car, and put it on the Honkerbus. The state police escorted us all the way up I-26 and out of the state.

"I guess it's a distinction, in a way."

Getaway Days

They obviously had come in to get out of the weather. Lonzo's teeth were clattering and The Pundit's face was blue with cold.

"You came back from the sunny south too soon," I said.

"Had to," said The Pundit.

"Things got kinda warm down there," said Lonzo.

"Tell me," I said.

"Well," said The Pundit, "on our trip back from Florida we stopped off in Wayback, Georgia, to visit Lonzo's nephew, Clydie."

"Clydie lives there in Wayback," said Lonzo.

"Anyhow," said The Pundit, "it rained a lot and all the rivers and cricks come up out their banks whilst we was down there.

"One afternoon Clydie's mama told him to go fetch her sister, Clydie's Ant Min. Ant Min had been visiting some folks who live out on Fourflusher Crick, and she had got to feeling poorly and wanted to come back.

"So we took Clydie's old Volkswagen bug and started out there. Clydie is a fisherman and he has a rack on top of the bug and on the rack he always carries a ten-foot Johnboat. We drove for about fifteen miles, then come to some high water. So we took the Johnboat down, got into it, and paddled about a half mile to the cabin where Ant Min had been staying.

"When we paddled up to the front porch, they told us Ant Min wasn't feeling poorly no more. In fact, they said, she wasn't feeling nothing. We went inside and, sure enough, there was Ant Min, all four hundred pounds of her, laid out on a rickety brass bedstead, dead as four o'clock in the morning.

"Well, Clydie carried on some for a while, then he sort of calmed down, borrowed the phone, and called the undertaker in town. The undertaker said he didn't know when he could get around to coming and collecting Ant Min, and besides, he'd have to rent a boat and it would cost a pile of money. Clydie told him to forget it, that the three of us would carry Ant Min back into town. We wrapped her in a blanket, laid her out in the boat, and the three of us, all barefoot, waded the boat back to the car. My, but that water was cold!

"When we got to the car, we discovered we couldn't get Ant Min into that bug. No kind of pushing or shoving or squeezing would work. She was a big woman. So we put her back in the Johnboat and lifted the boat and Ant Min back up to the top of the car, strapped the boat in place, and started back.

"By now we were all three of us exhausted, cold, and hungry. On the edge of town Clydie pulled into the parking lot of a place called Junior Odom's Blue Hawaii Bar and Friday Night Fish Fry. We had earned a little refreshment, Clydie said, and the drinks was on him. So we parked the car and went in.

"Some little refreshment later, Clydie decided we had better get on into town, so we went back out into the parking lot. We could not find the car; we could not find the Johnboat; we could not find Ant Min. Somebody had stole the whole thing.

"When we left, Clydie was trying to explain the situation to a deputy sheriff who thought he was taking down a routine stolen car report and couldn't understand why Ant Min went along with the thief.

"He was getting more exasperated by the minute. And Lonzo and me get uneasy around exasperated deputies.

"And we certainly didn't want to be around when Clydie tried to explain how come Ant Min was dead in the Johnboat. So we left, sudden like."

They came out to Folly Beach to "borrow" twenty dollars for gas to get back to Asheville. I needed to get to downtown Charleston, but the Chief of Staff had the car, so I "loaned" them the money in exchange for a lift.

On the way downtown we saw him standing on the downtown side of the bridge over the Folly River, not waving a thumb, not even appearing to watch traffic, but supremely confident that someone would stop and give him a ride.

The Pundit did.

He was just a tad over five feet high, slim as a pool cue, and erect as a Marine drill instructor. He wore a neatly trimmed white beard and moustache. A lime-colored ascot topped a blue blazer with brass buttons and sharply creased white deck pants. The whole thing was underpinned by large blue-and-white Adidas.

His bright, blue eyes gleamed with interest as he climbed aboard the Honkerbus.

"This," he said, "is a quaint vehicle, indeed. Some imported car, I take it. An Isotta-Fraschini, perhaps?"

Lonzo's eyebrows lifted at the word "quaint."

"Not exactly," I said. "It's really a modified Huff-Daland."

"Then it must be an antique," he said. I nodded. He continued, "My name is Morris I. Light. I have been staying with Sidney and Carol for a few weeks aboard their boat over at the Folly Beach Marina.

"Lovely people, Sidney and Carol. Not Charlestonians, of course, but lovely, nevertheless."

By now The Pundit had gotten the Honkerbus up to its maximum velocity of 36 miles per hour, and we were rolling comfortably along Folly Beach Road in the bright sunlight.

Mr. Light licked his thin lips. "I am so grateful for the lift, you know. I promised Pinckney—that's my cousin—that I'd get into town today to look in on his art exhibition at the museum. Pinckney would be so hurt if I failed to appear. He's going through a Da-Da phase, you know, and it makes him so sensitive.

"Lord, that sun is hot. You wouldn't happen to have any refreshments in this car, would you? A little chilled sauterne? Chateau Yquem '45 would be too much to hope for, I suppose?"

Lonzo said, "You're dead right about that Chateau whatever '45, Morris, but we got some supermarket '86 aboard if you want a snort."

"It's Mr. Light to you," said our passenger, "and hand me the bottle."

Grinning, Lonzo fished a half-gallon of Thunderbird out from under the back seat and handed it to Mr. Light. Mr. Light, in turn, fished around in a jacket pocket and produced a small silver cup and a clean handkerchief. He wiped the cup with the handkerchief, filled it with wine, drank the wine, and refilled the cup.

Then he rode a while, sitting at ease and sipping.

"It's always pleasant to meet visitors to Charleston," he said, "even though the city isn't what it once was. No, I'm afraid that many of the fine old Charleston traditions are gone. Change has left a mark, and in spite of all we can do to stop it, Charleston is not the same."

He took another sip. "No," he said, "the old ways are going, even though we try hard to preserve the past. I have the honor to be a member of a preservation group here in Charleston, and we do what we can to keep the standards high. We have a goal and strive to reach it."

"Where were you when they put a piano bar in my favorite seafood restaurant?" I asked.

Mr. Light winced. "That's just what I mean," he said.

We were by then passing over the bascule bridge across the Ashley River.

"The preservation group of which I am a member is seeking to restore Charleston to the way it appeared in the 70s. But, despite what we do, this sort of thing keeps taking place," he said, waving at a high-rise motel. He waved with the hand that held the silver cup, but he didn't spill a drop.

Lonzo goggled at him with the fish-eyed stare Lonzo uses when he doesn't understand something.

"Just the 70s?" he asked. "Shucks, that was only ten years or so ago. That don't signify much."

Mr. Light stared back with the demeanor of Marie Antoinette confronted by a particularly troublesome peasant. "I'm talking about the 1870s, you oaf," he said, through gritted teeth.

Then he took a final swallow of wine, handed the bottle back to me, and said to The Pundit, "Stop here, driver. This is where I get off."

The Honkerbus ground to a halt and Mr. Light descended nimbly, surefootedly to the sidewalk.

"By the way," he said, "if you plan to stay in Charleston long, you'll have to repaint this vehicle. We have a list of approved colors for historic artifacts. And if this thing is a historic artifact, the color is definitely nonconforming.

"Just thought I'd mention it. Have a nice day."

And he walked down the street, headed, doubtless, for Pinckney's art exhibit.

"Da-Da," said The Pundit.

"Ga-Ga," said Lonzo.

"Ta-Ta," I said, alighting from the Honkerbus myself.

Getaway Days

The Honkerbus slid up to the curb at Pack Square so silently it almost decked an unwary pedestrian.

I stared at the transformation it had undergone. Gone was the smoke-belching steam boiler and the whining, wheezing steam turbine. Gone was the rust, the corrosion, the general dilapidation. The more loosely fitting parts of the vehicle had been welded or wired back into place, and a gleaming coat of screaming orange enamel had been brushed all over the thing.

Topside, over the driver's bench, was a snowy white awning, replete with a fringe all around.

New tires with broad whitewalls graced all four wheels, and the sounds of gospel music rolled from a tape deck and amplifier located under what would be called the dash in most automobiles. From under the hood came the soft purr of a contented engine.

Lonzo, his skinny face twisted in concentration, was driving. He wore a white linen laboratory coat, a white straw hat tied around his scrawny neck by a black shoestring, his usual black tennis sneakers, and aviator's goggles.

Beside him, her back as straight as a ramrod, sat the Little Old Lady, her white sneakers planted firmly on the dashboard, one hand holding down a huge hat trimmed with mauve orchids, the other holding down her skirt.

The Pundit lolled elegantly in the back seat, his greasy collar unbuttoned in the heat, a ropy black cigar fuming in his right hand.

"Holy Toledo! You birds really put a fortune into fixing up that wreck. Where on earth did you get the money?" I asked.

"Fortitude, industry, and sobriety," said The Pundit. "Lonzo and me have been saving our lunch money in a little tin box."

"Well, the old clunker looks great," I said. "Where did you get that outstanding shade of orange paint?"

"Oh, it sort of fell off the back of a truck," said The Pundit.

The Little Old Lady glanced around exasperatedly. "Let's go," she screeched. "I paid my ticket. Let's go!"

"What's with her?" I said.

"We're going to the beach," said The Pundit.

"Come on!" roared the Little Old Lady. "It's been a long time. Myrtle was just a baby then."

"Myrtle Beach?" I asked.

"That's what she thinks," said The Pundit.

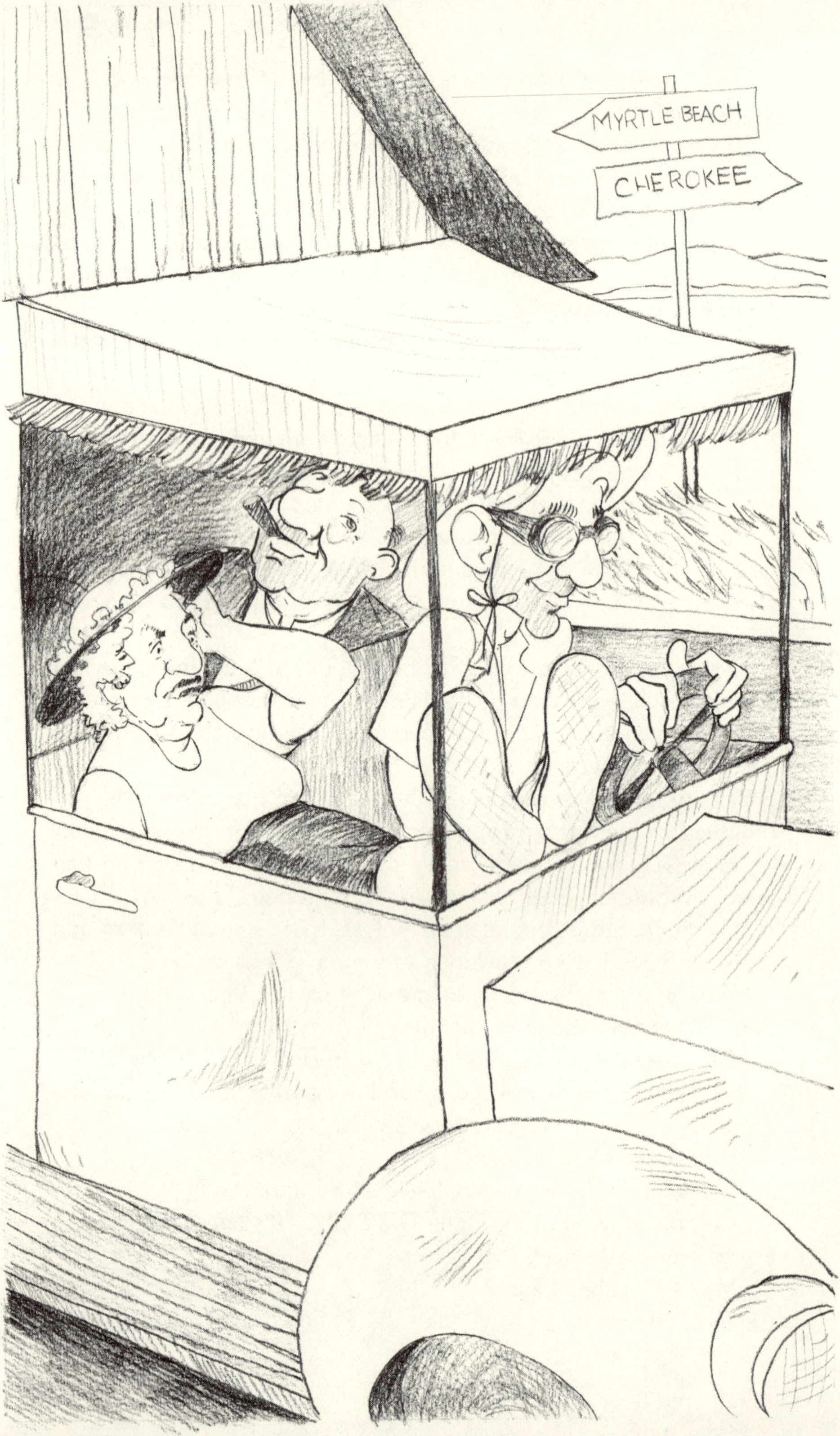
MYRTLE BEACH
CHEROKEE

"Come on, come on!" said the Little Old Lady. "By thunder, we never had delays like this when Old Harry C. was sheriff. Let's get going."

"Simmer down, Maud," said The Pundit. "We'll get down there on the Grand Strand soon enough. And don't forget, before we can go to the beach we got to head out west to Cherokee and pick up the right route numbers."

The Little Old Lady petuantly kicked the dashboard.

"Route numbers?" I asked.

"Yeah, you know," said The Pundit quietly, "numbers like B-9 and I-23 and N-32. Them kind of numbers."

"So that's where you got the money to repair the Honkerbus!" I said. "You've been playing Cherokee Bingo!"

"Industry, fortitude, sobriety," said The Pundit. "And a few lucky numbers."

"I never heard of going to the Grand Strand by way of Cherokee before," snarled the Little Old Lady. "By thunder, we didn't do things this way when Old Harry S. was in the White House."

"Never mind, Maud," said The Pundit as Lonzo let out the clutch and they all slid smoothly out into traffic.

As they started down Patton Avenue, I heard the Little Old Lady ask, "And whatever happened to I-26?"

"It's not on our card," said The Pundit.

TWO ON THE SQUARE

I hadn't seen them for a while, but they looked the same as ever, just lounging on the bench in the late winter sunlight.

There was one notable difference. Lonzo was wearing a Carolina blue and white T-shirt that carried the seal of the University of North Carolina at Chapel Hill on the front and a message implying something awful about North Carolina State University students on the back.

"Going back to school?" I asked, sitting down.

Lonzo grinned. The Pundit lit one of his evil-looking black cigars and said, "None of your sass, scribbler. We could go back if we wanted, I guess, but the fact is we been down enjoying the deep-sea fishing in Morehead City and on the way back we stopped off in Chapel Hill to visit Lonzo's nephew, Peachy. He's a bird, that Peachy!"

"Lonzo has more nephews than a banker has ways of saying no," I said, ignoring the invitation to ask how two flat-broke transients had been able to finance deep-sea fishing at Morehead City.

"Yes, he has," said The Pundit, "and some of them are respectable. You take Peachy, for instance. He's really respectable. He did twenty years in the navy, retired, and then got a job in Chapel Hill with the university. He has a good job, too. He's in charge of dispensing rare gasses."

"It figures," said Lonzo. "Peachy's a gasser himself."

"Peachy's been there ever since he retired twenty years ago. He lives in a little house down at the end of Rosemary Street. But he has problems with Chapel Hill," said The Pundit.

"How so?" I asked. "Most people I know seem to love Chapel Hill. A couple of years ago I was watching a football game on TV and the announcer, who had never been to Chapel Hill before, said, 'This isn't a town; it's a move set.'"

"Well, I know that," said The Pundit, "but Peachy still has problems."

"Like, for instance, parking," said Lonzo. "We wanted to take Peachy down to Franklin Street to get some hamburgers, but he didn't want to drive there.

"He said they's 20,000 students at the university and each one of them owns three cars which they all park around Franklin Street. And they's 10,000 faculty members and they all own bicycles and ride around on the things all the time, generally not watching where they are going. They all wear what he used to call in the navy a 'ten-thousand yard stare,' Peachy said.

"The only safe way to go downtown in Chapel Hill for lunch, Peachy told us, is to park in Carrboro and take a bus into Chapel Hill.

"Well, I suggested maybe we could cut through the university grounds and sort of sneak up on the golden arches place. But Peachy said that wouldn't work. They keep changing the rules on the university grounds. One day a street is two-way traffic, the next day it's one-way traffic, and the third day it's all torn up to replace a sewer pipe.

"He thinks the university trustees do it just to keep the faculty and students on their toes. He knows thirteen ways to get from his house to the university's rare gasses building, Peachy says, and some days twelve of them don't work. He has a dear woman friend who works at the Carolina Inn, Peachy said, but the relationship is falling apart because he hasn't been able to get to the Carolina Inn for three months."

"Wow," I said. "Things are really bad down there now, I guess. It must really tax Peachy's patience to put up with all that inconvenience."

"Tax? Did you say 'Tax?'" The Pundit asked. "There's another of Peachy's problems. You ought to hear Peachy talk about taxes there. Peachy said he only owns that little shotgun bungalow way down there at the wrong end of Rosemary Street, but when he looks at his tax bill he feels like the proprietor and sole owner of the Taj Mahal.

"He doesn't mind paying reasonable taxes, Peachy said, but the tax rate in Chapel Hill has him looking for two guys named Gramm and Rudman. I tell you, Peachy is hot about taxes."

"Then there's those kids with the blue faces," said Lonzo with a shudder.

"Horrible!" said The Pundit. "We was still there last Saturday and we had walked from Peachy's house to down in front of the university. But there wasn't a soul around. Not a soul. It was uncanny. We opened the door of a student saloon down there and found it was jam-packed with students, sitting there elbow-to-elbow in a darkened room, all drinking beer and watching a big TV screen.

"We started to walk back to the house when all of a sudden the doors of all the saloons on Franklin Street busted open and out came all the students, yelling and screaming like a pack of Indians. In no time at all there were about sixty million of them out there, jumping up and down. They was singing and screaming something about Number 1. They had traffic stopped cold.

"Most of them had six-packs or big pitchers of beer. Some of the older ones (seniors probably, Peachy told us) had jugs of more sophisticated stuff. And they proceeded to get well and truly ossified right there in the street.

"And most of them, including some girls, had their faces painted a disgusting shade of blue. And most of them, but not the girls, were mother-naked to the waist."

"It was awful," said Lonzo, with another shudder.

"All Lonzo and me wanted to do was get out of there, but it took us twenty minutes to work and wiggle our way across Franklin Street and out of that mob," said The Pundit.

"That wasn't so bad," said Lonzo with a knowing leer.

"Anyway," said The Pundit, "when we got back to Peachy's place we asked him about it. He said the North Carolinas had won some sort of a basketball tournament and that's what the riot was all about. They do that all the time, Peachy said. He said working for the university would be a great job if the students and faculty would just go away and leave him alone, but they wouldn't."

"So," said The Pundit, "we left. But before we left I couldn't help saying to Peachy that me and Lonzo wondered why he stayed. We said he had told us all about how tough life was in Chapel Hill with the parking problem and the street problem and the crazy professors and the loony students and the taxes and all, and we just didn't understand why he didn't pull up stakes and go someplace he liked better.

"And Peachy rared back and looked me in the eye and said, 'Leave? Leave Chapel Hill? Are you crazy? I love this place. This isn't just the greatest place in the world; it's the only place in the world. You and Lonzo been living too long at too high an altitude or something. What an idea! Leave Chapel Hill! Well, I never . . .'

"And, still talking to himself, Peachy went back into his bungalow, and we started up the Honkerbus and came home," The Pundit said.

8
A Little Work

We were sprawling on the back porch of the Widder's farmhouse up in Whiskey Cove.

It was high summer in the mountains. The air was warm and sweet. The sun shone down like a benediction. The hum of hard-working bees was hypnotic in the late afternoon stillness.

Off to the south, the perfect cone of Mount Pisgah rose elegantly against the horizon. To the west, across the Haywood Gap, the Smokies made a serrate pattern against the high blue sky. And around the other side of the house, unseen but always present, the Black Mountains loomed huge and threatening, their tops wreathed in cumulus clouds trying to form a thunderhead.

The Pundit had removed his dingy black suit coat and half-sat, half-lay on the porch steps with his back against one of the two-by-fours that hold up the porch roof. He was puffing meditatively on one of the Wheeling Stogies to which he is addicted.

Lonzo sat in the shade, propped up by the wall of the house. He was sipping meditatively at something contained in a bottle concealed in a brown paper bag.

I was flat out on a swing seat suspended from the porch roof, about half asleep.

We sat for a while, just enjoying the heat and the peace.

"Where," I asked, "is the Widder?"

"Gone," said Lonzo, sipping again.

"Gone where?"

"She and Ella-Ella Quistleberry went to Raleigh," said The Pundit. "Ella-Ella got the Widder interested in jeanylogy. Ella-Ella is big on that stuff and she talked the Widder into going to Raleigh with her to a convention of jeanylogists."

"I think the word is genealogy," I said.

"That's what he said . . . jeanylogy," said Lonzo. "And we're farm-sitting until they get back. They left us in charge of the farm and the house and everything. They even left us in charge of Richard."

"Who's Richard?" I asked.

On cue, the screen door swung slowly open and from the shadowy kitchen emerged, an inch at a time, a lemon-colored hound dog. Its head was about nine sizes too large for the size of its body and it wasn't a small body. Its coat was rough and appeared to have worn off in some spots. Its ribs protruded, its eyes were almost closed, and it had more sharp angles and elbows than a church designed by a modern architect. It moved with painful slowness.

"That," said The Pundit, "is Richard. He's Ella-Ella Quistleberry's dog. And since Ella-Ella is hung up on the history of the English kings, that confounded flea bag's full name is Richard the Lion-Hearted."

I watched in fascination as Richard the Lion-Hearted oozed across the porch to a dish full of water. A long, pink tongue uncoiled from his open mouth. He lapped up some water.

Then he appeared to have forgotten what he was doing. His eyes closed entirely. His body swayed, sagged, and descended by degrees.

Finally he was stretched out on the porch floor, his head half in the water dish, out of this world. I noticed that the worn spots in his hide coincided with the places where his body came in contact with the floor.

"What kind of a dog is that?" I asked.

"A pot hound," said Lonzo.

"Come on," I said. "Plott hounds are fine hunting dogs. This animal doesn't appear to have enough git-up to chase a three-legged rabbit."

"I didn't say Plott," said Lonzo. "I said pot. This thing doesn't hunt anything. All he does is pot around all day."

Richard the Lion-Hearted started to snore.

I watched him for a while more. "My word," I said, "that dog sleeps soundly. He doesn't even scratch in his sleep."

"Course not," said The Pundit. "It's not Monday. See, he rests up real good over the weekend, so he'll have enough pep to scratch on Monday. The rest of the week he's simply too tired to scratch."

"Astounding," I said.

"Yep," said Lonzo, almost proudly, "that there is a inert hound. When Ella-Ella left him with us she told us that neither snow nor sleet

A Little Work

nor rain nor food nor water nor sex nor thunderstorms nor brass bands nor Sears-Roebuck catalogs nor circus parades got Richard the Lion-Hearted excited. She said he was a dog king and always kept his cool.

"She told us something else about the dog, too, but I disremember what it was. Do you remember, Pundit?"

His reply was a snore in an entirely different pitch from that emitted by Richard. The Pundit, ropy cigar smoldering in the flower bed beside the porch steps, had succumbed to the magic of the day.

"There's something else that always keep his cool," said Lonzo, taking another swig. "But I sure wish I could remember the rest of what Ella-Ella said about that dog. As I recall, it was something important."

In seconds he, too, was asleep.

I watched long shadows stretch across the yard as the sun slid down behind the ramparts of the Smokies. The day cooled and Lonzo, The Pundit, and Richard the Lion-Hearted slept.

I was beginning to think about driving back to town when the chicken house down in back of the barn erupted into a cacophony of noisy squawking.

Richard the Lion-Hearted raised his head a reluctant inch. He fought his eyes open a crack. He audibly sniffed the air. Then, with a mighty scrabbling of elbows, knees, and paws, he hurled himself upright and shot like a rocket off the porch.

Howling like a wolf, he raced across the back yard, down around the chicken house, and then up to the back of the barn.

The Widder's barn is built up against a hill. The front of the barn is level with the ground, but the back of the barn is up in the air, supported by rock pillars. The space under the barn is used to store machinery and farm supplies.

The dog was racing back and forth excitedly across the opening to the space under the barn. It was alternately roaring and barking and howling. It was clearly beside itself with emotion. And clearly it was disturbed by something in the space under the barn.

The dog's antics and the furious cackling from the chicken house woke both Lonzo and The Pundit.

The Pundit looked at the dog ricocheting back and forth behind the barn. Lonzo looked, too.

"My stars!" said The Pundit. "I never saw that hound move like that before. He must have something cornered in there. I'll get the shotgun!"

Lonzo was yawning, blinking, and shaking his head. The Pundit disappeared into the kitchen and emerged a minute later carrying a .12-gauge, double-barreled shotgun with old-fashioned exposed hammers.

"I wish I could remember what else Ella-Ella told us," Lonzo said as The Pundit cocked both hammers.

The dog continued to have a fit; the chickens still were yelling bloody murder. The Pundit shuffled down off the porch. Lonzo, still muttering under his breath, fell in behind him. I brought up the rear. As we approached the space under the barn, the dog, encouraged by the reinforcements, took the lead, and we all plunged into the darkness.

The dog sniffed and snuffled. Lonzo barked his shin on a hay rake and said something terrible. We pushed further on into the darkness.

"Look!" said The Pundit and there, far in the back of the storage area were two green spots, eyes peering at us in the blackness. Swiftly The Pundit raised the shotgun to his shoulder.

"Wait!" screamed Lonzo, "I remember—"

The gun roared like a cannon in the confined space. My eardrums rang. The recoil hurled The Pundit flat on his back. Richard the Lion-Hearted fainted.

"I remember, I remember," screamed Lonzo again. "Ella-Ella said the only thing that agitates him is a skunk."

The Pundit's collarbone knitted nicely in a couple of months. He said later he, too, forgot something. He said the Widder Lady long before had warned him that if he pulled the right trigger on the gun, both barrels would fire simultaneously.

"I don't know how anyone in a situation like that could be expected to remember to pull the left trigger first," he said in aggrieved tones. The Widder replied tartly that her late husband had managed it all right.

I buried the clothes I was wearing, took a half-hour shower, and drove home in a bath towel. My wife promptly shaved all the hair off my head and graciously allowed me to sleep on the back porch— for a month.

Lonzo and The Pundit were not welcome at the regular meetings of the River Bank Philosophical and Outdoor Cooking Society for a long time. Richard the Lion-Hearted was revived and dunked in tomato juice which, despite folklore to the contrary, utterly failed to

A Little Work

remove the odor of skunk from his mangy hide. He had to sleep outside until Christmas.

Ella-Ella Quistleberry blamed The Pundit. She said she was sure that The Pundit was a direct descendant of the other Richard, the one who had the kids in the tower strangled. Or may it was one of the Henrys. I never did get the Plantagenets straight.

At any rate Ella-Ella got so nasty about having her dog skunked she managed to offend the Widder who told her what she could do with her old jeanylogy, anyway.

Caused no end of excitement at that particular Grange meeting up in Whiskey Cove, I hear.

Lonzo started to climb aboard the bus.

His progress was slow. He was carrying a mop, a broom, two buckets, a leaf rake, a dust pan, an old upright electric vacuum sweeper, and an enormous feather duster.

As he struggled up the steps, I heard the gravelly voice of The Pundit behind him say, "Tilt a little to the left, Lonzo. That's it! That's just fine! Now, up one more step, old friend! Good! Now pay the fare."

Lonzo didn't have a hand free to pay the fare, however. So he blinked owlishly, then let go of everything. Buckets, mops, dusters, rake, and the rest cascaded all over the front of the bus. The bus driver neatly fielded a bucket.

One of the springy tines on the leaf rake snagged the hat worn by a little old lady sitting on the fore-and-aft seat next to the front door of the bus. The little old lady wore Adidas, blue jeans, a cotton sweat shirt, and a huge, flowered hat that would have graced a Gibson Girl.

In one hand she held an overflowing oilcloth shopping bag. In the other she clutched an oak cane the size of a small tree. Her eyebrows were reminiscent of the late John L. Lewis of labor union fame. She had a Benito Mussolini chin and snapping blue eyes.

Irritatedly, she reached up and tried to pull the rake loose from her hat. But her hat came off instead. So did her wig. Then she really got angry.

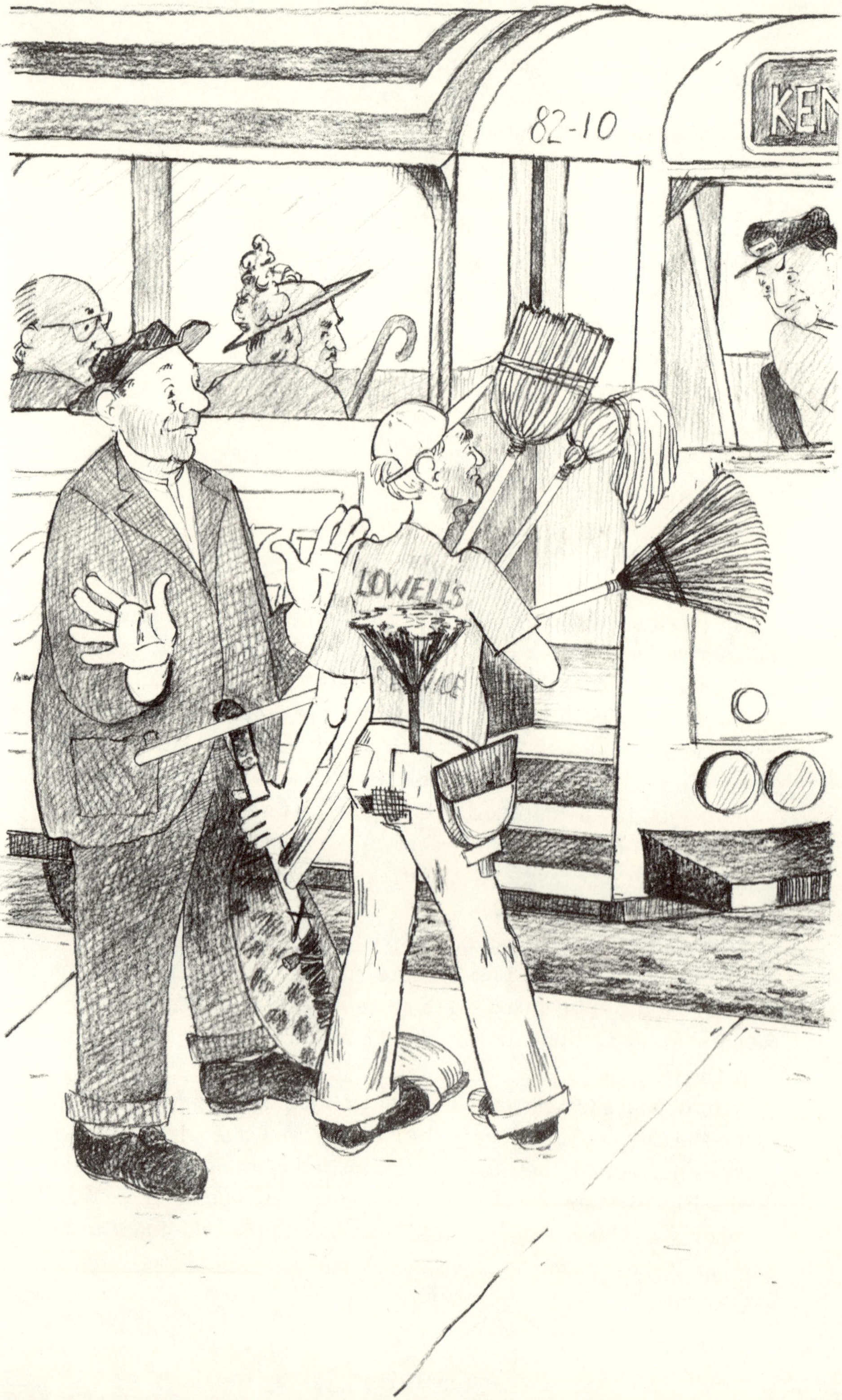
82-10
KEN
LOWELL'S

A Little Work

Jamming her hat back on her head and muttering furiously, she grabbed the rake handle and yanked it toward her.

Lonzo was standing with his back to her. Out of the corner of his eye he saw his rake start to disappear. Automatically he grabbed the other end and pulled his way. There was a brief tug-of-war. Then Lonzo let go of his end of the rake. The little old lady reeled backwards, caromed off a seat, and sat down in the aisle.

She scrabbled up again, took a good grip on her cane, and dealt Lonzo a sharp rap on the shin. Lonzo sat down in the aisle, hugged his leg, and moaned softly.

"Dastard," snarled the little old lady. "Masher! Molester! That will teach you to leave decent girls alone!"

The Pundit by this time also had gotten aboard the bus. Wearing an oily smile, he approached the little old lady. "My dear lady," he said in syrupy tones, "I assure you that my colleague had no—"

"Another dastard!" said the little old lady. "Take that, you dastard! And that! And that!"

Every time she used the word "that," she smacked The Pundit on the shins with the cane.

"Let me out of here," said the little old lady. "A decent girl isn't safe at all on a public bus any more! Nothing like this happened when Jesse James Bailey was sheriff, let me tell you!" she shouted as she picked up her shopping bag.

She hopped across Lonzo, did an arabesque over The Pundit, waggled her cane threateningly at the bus driver, and bolted off the bus.

The bus driver sighed and drove on.

As soon as they were able to walk, Lonzo and The Pundit got up and limped over to the seat across the aisle from me. Every time the bus lurched, Lonzo's bucket rolled and clanked across the floor.

"Just what do you two dastards think you're doing?" I asked.

"It ought to be perfectly evident," said The Pundit. "We're working. We have started a domestic engineering service."

"Domestic engineering?"

"We clean people's houses," said Lonzo.

"It's a big thing these days," said The Pundit.

"We just go out and clean people's houses. We provide a service; they pay a fee. And, boy, do we need a few fees! I'm sure you've heard of the kind of service," he said. "They call themselves Helping Hand or Modern Maid or Mr. Clean or something like that."

"I guess I have," I said. "By the way, what do you two call your particular service?"

"Elbowgrease," said The Pundit.

"Pretty slick, ain't it?" said Lonzo.

"You two always were pretty slippery," I said. "And if you keep tangling with people like that little old lady, you'll have to invent a name with the words Blue Cross in it."

"Something tells me we'll see her again," said Lonzo. "Look!" He pulled the business end of the leaf rake from under a seat. There, still tangled in one of the tines, was the little old lady's wig.

"Things were tough down there in Florida this year," said Lonzo, attired in dingy canvas pants, out-at-the-toes tennis shoes, a T-shirt bearing words in Spanish that are better left untranslated, and a deep tan.

"Me and The Pundit lost our jobs in November," he said in his reedy voice. "The state wouldn't let me rassle alligators no more, and The Pundit was hounded off the dog track. The oranges all froze so there wasn't none to pick. It was terrible and I was hungry."

"Yes," said The Pundit, "we had some financial difficulties there this year.

"We had a job for a few weeks working for a man named Luther Burgerbank. He told us he was a botanist and he had an idea about freeze-proof citrus fruit. He said the trouble is that citrus fruit just hangs there from the trees, all out in the open. When the air temperature falls too low, the fruit freezes.

"Luther's idea was to cross a grapefruit tree with Irish potatoes. He wanted to get a tree that would bear grapefruit underground. It was just a matter of changing around some genes, he said."

"Did it work?" I asked.

"Well, after a few days, Luther's older brother came out to the farm and got Luther back on his medication. And Luther went back to being a lawyer. As far as I know all he got from crossing the two plants was some cross-eyed potatoes.

A Little Work

"But his brother paid us enough to buy gas for the Honkerbus to get us back here."

"What are you two going to do now that you're back in Asheville?" I asked.

"Well," said The Pundit, "we've been thinking about public service. How about we run Lonzo for Congress? You can handle the public relations, as a public service, naturally."

Lonzo gave me that vacant smile, the one that makes people think his porch light is not on.

I shuddered.

"No soap," I said. "There already are two guys around town who are full-time candidates for Congress. They have the job sewed up. The district couldn't stand much more of that."

The Pundit coughed, pulled the collar of his shabby black suit coat tighter around his frayed shirt, and said, "Then we'll go to college. We been reading about all those people defaulting on student loans. Me and Lonzo maybe could get a couple to default on for our own selves."

For a fleeting, frightful moment I pictured Lonzo as a freshman on campus and in a class I was teaching. Then sanity reasserted itself.

"You and Lonzo have about as much chance of getting into a college as I have of becoming a brain surgeon," I said. "And that's no chance at all. Unless Lonzo can play basketball.

"Can you play basketball, Lonzo?"

Lonzo's eyes, at half-mast, snapped wide open. "Sure," he said, "at shortstop."

"Well, dribble on out of here, then," I said. "I have work to do. My first patient of the day is due in ten minutes. It's a guy who wants to talk to me about inventing a martini that doesn't use alcohol."

"I thought you said you wasn't a surgeon," Lonzo said.

"I'm not," I replied. "I'm a psychiatrist."

TWO ON THE SQUARE

There was a cool breeze blowing away from us across the river and the sunlight felt good on my shoulders.

The Pundit was propped up against a bridge pier, his greasy black fedora pushed back off his face, a plume of evil-looking gray smoke swirling away from the ropy cigar in his mouth.

Lonzo was flat on his back on the concrete apron under the bridge, bleary eyes fixed on a propped-up fishing pole.

From time to time he took a sip of amber fluid from a bottle bearing the label "Mother MacCready's Killarney Balm."

For a while none of us said a word. I gazed at the flowing water of the river until it almost had me hypnotized. Time passed, marked only by an occasional gurgle from Lonzo's direction.

Finally Lonzo, in his thin, high-pitched voice, asked, "Don't you have to go back to the paragraph ranch today?"

"No," I said. "It's a holiday. It's Labor Day."

"Oh," said Lonzo.

"You probably wouldn't know much about that," I said. "It's a national holiday for people who work."

"I know all about Labor Day, dang it," Lonzo snapped. "And I know all about work, too. Me and The Pundit there, we been working hard for the past couple months. Painting houses, mowing lawns, and like that.

"It's been hard. The way we do it is, The Pundit finds the work and I do the work and we split the money. The Pundit says that's a fair exhange, but I just finished doing two houses in eight days and I ain't so sure."

"Course it's fair," said The Pundit. "Why, shoot, without me to find the houses and talk the owners into having them painted, you wouldn't have no houses to paint. And you'd be paying three kinds of prices for paint, too. And there would go your profit margin," added The Pundit with the air of a man holding a master's degree in business administration.

"You're right about that," Lonzo admitted. "I swear, I never heard of house paint that sells for two dollars a gallon, and I'd like to know where you're getting that stuff."

"Don't bother your head about that, old friend," said The Pundit. "I'll keep getting it and you keep slapping it on, and pretty soon we'll have enough saved up to buy a replacement for the Honkerbus."

The Honkerbus was a mongrel, steam-driven old wreck of a vehicle that a few weeks ago was blown to Kingdom Come as part of an informal rural renewal program. The folks who lit the fuse have nominated themselves for a national beautification award.

"And, don't forget," The Pundit added, "winter's coming and we got to have some way to get back down to Wackahoola Springs for the tarpon fishing season."

Lonzo shuddered. "All right," he said, "but this time, I swear I ain't going to wrestle no alligators. No matter what happens, I done retired from the alligator wrestling business."

"Of course you don't have to wrestle no alligators," said The Pundit. "I'd never ask you to wrestle no alligators, Lonzo."

"Like heck you wouldn't," said Lonzo.

"Well, maybe a few small ones," said The Pundit. "But, I tell you the truth, if we don't get enough money to get away from here before the autumn rains wash that water-color paint off them houses, wrestling alligators is going to look easy."

It was quiet there under the bridge. The only sound was the subdued snoring of a diesel switching engine languidly bunting boxcars around in the freight yard on the far side of the river.

Then Lonzo hacked, wheezed, and woke up.

The Pundit grandly motioned for me to seat myself beside him.

"It is always a pleasure to have an expert come to help us watch this river," he said. "I've been reading in the newspaper about how you have been telling the peasants the history of the river."

"Aw, shucks! It wasn't anything like that," I said. "I'm no expert. I just did a little work for the friends of the river and the regionals, is all."

From over in the grass where Lonzo was recumbent, I heard a wheezing, gasping, half-choking sound. For a second I was alarmed. Then I realized that the sound was what passes for laughter with Lonzo.

"Haw!" said Lonzo, sitting up and wiping a tear of mirth from the corner of his eye with the back of a grimy hand. "Haw! He calls that work!

TWO ON THE SQUARE

"Come on, we seen you work down there at your office. You sit there in the stuffed jaybird seat and push on those little buttons on the typewriting machine. I swear, it looks like a backbreaking way to make a living. It's a good thing you got electricity to help you get those little buttons pushed down.

"Work, you call it! Haw!"

So saying, Lonzo lay back down again.

I sighed.

"Lonzo," I said, "you have just added your name to a long list of people, including two wives, a passel of children, a mother-in-law, several neighbors, and hundreds of visitors to the newspaper office who just don't understand how hard I really do work."

Lonzo said "Haw!" again.

"I certainly understand the travail and turmoil that you intellectuals experience in the daily practice of your profession," The Pundit said. "But you got to admit, to proletarians like Lonzo, it doesn't exactly look like you're lifting that barge or toting that bale.

"Anyway," said The Pundit, "what brings you down here to the Elysian Fields?"

"Well, the Widder Lady from Whiskey Cove asked me to find you two," I said.

Lonzo sat bolt upright. The Pundit looked at me as though he feared I might pull a snake out of my pocket.

"What about the Widder Lady?" he asked.

"She says you two owe her money," I said. "She paid your room rent the last time you were guests at the sheriff's lockup."

Lonzo looked mournful. "We ain't got the money so she flat can't have it," he said.

"She doesn't want the money, she wants some work," I said. "The highway people just cut down two oak trees on her property. She wants them cut up for firewood. It'll make about four, five cords."

There was a long, long silence. Lonzo and The Pundit stared out over the darkening river. Finally Lonzo spoke again.

"It sure looks like an early winter, don't it?"

A Little Work

It was one of those warm, wonderful days we get just before a blizzard, and I was sitting on a ramshackle bench in front of the old library on Pack Square, enjoying the weather. Then The Pundit and Lonzo heaved into view, tacking out from behind the board fence around a construction site.

Seeing me, they veered to starboard and joined me on the bench. As they sat, Lonzo wobbled a little and heaved a sigh of relief.

The Pundit looked sharply at Lonzo. "Lonzo, you feeling all right?" he asked. "Lonzo, for heaven's sake, button up your collar. Take care of yourself. We don't want anything bad to happen to you now."

I knew it was a mistake, but I couldn't help asking The Pundit why he suddenly was so solicitous of Lonzo's health.

"Lonzo," The Pundit rasped in what passes for a stage whisper with him, "is the key to fame and fortune. Lonzo is a walking Fort Knox. Lonzo, bless his leathery little heart, is a ticket to the Riviera."

I looked at Lonzo again. He seemed like the same ill-dressed, haphazardly groomed, chronic rester he always had been.

Again I knew it was a mistake, but I asked, "How, for the love of Mike, is Lonzo all of those things all of a sudden?"

The Pundit looked around carefully. Seeing no one within earshot, he whispered, "You know gasoline is going to get tight soon, don't you? I suppose you read your own newspaper enough to have discovered that?"

I nodded.

"And you know it is possible to run auto engines on alcohol, too, don't you?"

I nodded again.

"Well, son, I'm here to tell you that when it comes to producing alcohol, there is no one in these mountains, no one in the whole blue-eyed world, who knows more than Lonzo. Yes, sir, it is obvious that Lonzo is the man of the future, the coming man, one of nature's noblemen. I tell you, you give Lonzo enough copper tubing, enough sugar, and a little elbow room, and he'll have these mountains awash with alcohol.

"Ain't that right, Lonzo?"

Lonzo blinked, smiled amiably, cleared his throat with a dreadful sound, and said, "Sure enough."

He blinked again. A faraway look came over his face. He spoke again.

TWO ON THE SQUARE

"I recollect it was back in '38—or was it '39?—anyway, me and Junior had us a Silver Cloud with a double thumper running in a holler over on the far side of Black Mountain. We was putting out maybe six or seven hundred gallon, and Junior says to me . . .

"On second thought, maybe it was something I said . . . Or maybe we didn't say nothing at all to each other, maybe it was two other people . . . Well, I just can't remember now . . . It was an awful long time ago . . ."

Lonzo's voice trailed off, his head sank gracefully onto his chest, and there in the warm spring sunlight, Lonzo slept.

The Pundit looked at him thoughtfully.

"Lonzo has just got to ease up on that tonic he's been taking for his nerves," he muttered.

Then he smiled brightly.

"And as I was telling you," he said, "Standard Oil's problem is our golden opportunity, and those Arabs has done all of us here in the mountains a great service. Why, it won't be no time at all before the hills and hollers are ringing with the sound of happy, busy people, and our biggest cottage industry will be back on its feet again."

"Wait a minute," I said. "Hold it! How much do you two plan to charge for your product?"

"About three dollars a gallon would be fair, I figure," said The Pundit.

"That's crazy," I said. "No one is going to pay three dollars a gallon for alcohol just to keep an automobile running."

"Come on, Lonzo," he said. "Wake up. We have here a man who thinks that gasoline you can't get for a dollar a gallon is better than alcohol you can get for three dollars.

"Time for us to be moving on," he said.

And the two of them tacked and veered away, headed for the corner around which prosperity waits forever.

A Little Work

I saw them standing beside the reflecting pool on Pack Square. They seemed more woebegone than usual.

Lonzo looked more stunned than usual. His jaw hung slackly on his chest. Big tears flowed silently from his brown eyes down onto a not-too-clean T-shirt bearing the legend **Help Stamp Out Preppies**.

The Pundit's bottle nose was redder than ever and his rotund face was screwed up in a scowl. His big hands were nervously torturing the greasy black felt hat that usually hides his bald head.

"Bad news?" I asked.

The Pundit turned and looked at me, blinking. "We just come from the doctor's office," he said, "and we sort of got some misery."

"Which one of you is sick?" I asked.

"Well, we didn't think either one of us was sick when we went there," said The Pundit. "The odd-jobs agency sent us over to this doctor's building to mow the grass and trim the bushes. Which we did. When we finished, we went inside to get paid. But before we could explain what we wanted, the nurse there took one look at us and shoved us into one of those little rooms. She said we should hang on, that the doctor would be there in a minute. And, by Godfrey, he did come in real quick. He stepped into the room, closed the door, took a deep breath, opened the door, and yelled at the nurse about why wasn't the air conditioning turned on.

"She said it was turned on, that she had turned it up as high as it would go when we walked in. So then this young doctor sort of gulped and set about examining Lonzo. I tell you, he left no opening unplumbed. He peeked and poked and listened and thumped and said 'Cough' and 'Say ahhh!' and all like that there. He really gave Lonzo a going over. When he was finished he sort of shook his head. He told Lonzo the only thing that was holding Lonzo up was force of habit.

"He told Lonzo, 'You take Addison's Disease and you take Zoonosis. You got 'em both. What's more, you got everything in between.' That doctor told Lonzo that he was packed solid with bacteria from ear to ear.

"He said the germs in Lonzo's body probably all had their arms locked together and were pulling like crazy. If one of them ever lost his grip, the doctor said, old Lonzo would fold up like a beach chair in a hurricane."

The Pundit shuddered. "That doctor had a gift for colorful phrases,"

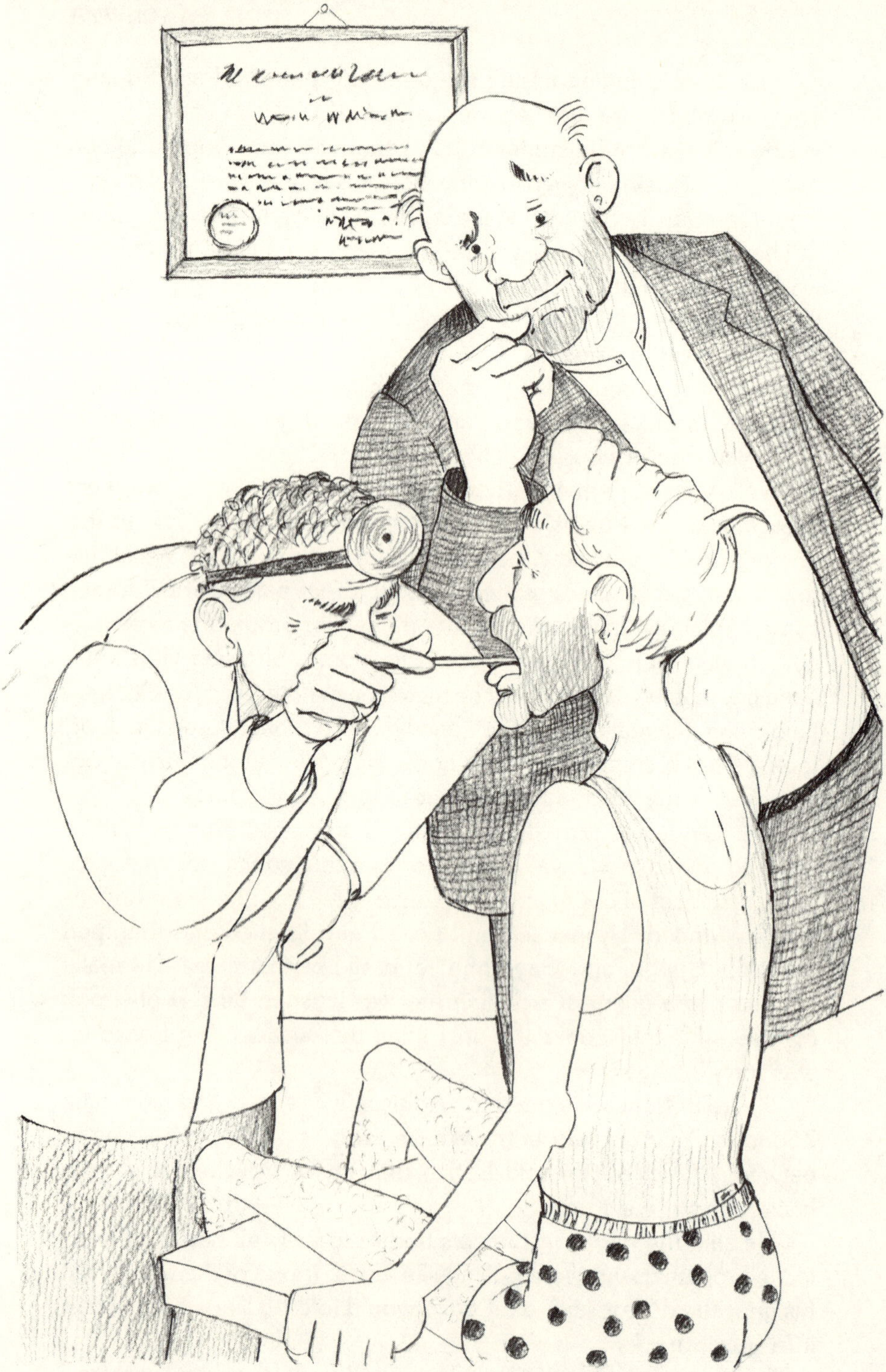

A Little Work

he said. "But I don't care for that kind of talk in a doctor's office. The doctor told Lonzo that he would have to change his ways. The doctor told him that he has to stop drinking and smoking and sleeping under bridges and in Dempsey Dumpsters.

"He said Lonzo should get a steady position, find a quiet place to stay, and get three square meals a day and lots of rest and plenty of medical attention. What Lonzo needed, the doctor said, was the quiet life, but even then he didn't think a lot of Lonzo's chances for survival.

"Lonzo asked him if he could qualify for a medical pension. The doctor looked at Lonzo kind of funny and muttered something about permanent brain damage. Then he told Lonzo that, considering Lonzo's physical condition, he wasn't qualified to join a Loafers' Club."

"What did the doctor say about you?" I asked.

"Not a thing," said The Pundit. "When he started in on me, I told him I hadn't had a physical examination since I enlisted in the Philippine Scouts back in '03, and what's more I didn't want any examination.

"I said I just didn't want to know what was wrong with me, that I didn't have time to worry about all that, that I was too busy mowing lawns. Well, the doctor looked a little insulted. He said would I please get out of the office right away, that he didn't like the idea of people dying in his examining room.

"So we left. But the real blow came as we were leaving. We were supposed to get ten bucks for the yard work. Instead, the nurse handed us a bill for thirty dollars. And we don't get any Medicare."

"And that," I said, "is why Lonzo is so broken up. It's the money, not the prognosis."

"A progwhatsis won't buy any wine," said The Pundit.

A spring breeze ruffled the surface of the water in the pool on Pack Square. Two migratory Canada geese paddled serenely around the pool, apparently enjoying the sunshine and the warmth.

Beside me on the bench two migratory North Carolina turkeys also were enjoying the sunlight and the warmth. And every time the breeze blew from them to me, it was apparent they had been enjoying something else, too.

Lonzo, as skinny as a poorhouse mouse and as angular as two tons of broken glass, was sprawled across most of his end of the bench, his sneaker-clad feet stuck out in front of him. He wore a cap extolling the virtues of a popular brand of paint, tattered jeans, and a T-shirt left over from last year's Bele Chere celebration.

The Pundit, round face beaming under a battered Panama hat, thoughtfully blew the ash off the end of a ropy cigar, cleared his throat with a sound like the ice going out on the Yukon River, and remarked that this will be a summer to test a man's sense of enterprise.

"You figuring to make a little money off the World's Fair, too?" I asked.

"Not a little," said The Pundit, "a lot. But the question is how. We thought, me and Lonzo, that we might organize the Mountain Beverage Company and act as middlemen between the manufacturers up in Madison County and the thirsty multitudes at the fair.

"Unfortunately, we were advised that that particular franchise already has been taken up, and if we tried to horn in on the deal we would be given an opportunity to make the acquaintance of a lot of medical people. So we dropped that idea."

"Amen!" said Lonzo.

"Then," said The Pundit, "we thought about offering people rides from here to the fair and back in the only steam-powered bus in the whole world. But the other day we were talking to Deputy Dan about another matter—"

"I didn't steal that steer, dang it," Lonzo blurted.

"And," said The Pundit, "he gave us some advice. He said we probably would have to get chauffeurs' licenses to do the job. That's a problem. I haven't had a driver's license since I was honorably discharged from the Philippine Constabulary back in '08, and Lonzo never has had a license that I know of."

"I had a marriage license once," Lonzo said, "but I never got around to using it."

"Anyhow," said The Pundit, "Deputy Dan also said we would have to get a certificate from the Eye See See."

"Who ever heard of getting a certificate from an eye doctor to run a bus line?" Lonzo said grumpily.

A Little Work

The Pundit grinned. "If I told Lonzo once I told him a thousand times that we ain't talking about an eye doctor, we're talking about a government agency," he said.

"But it don't make any difference. As far as we're concerned, if we see the Eye See See before the Eye See See sees us, the Eye See See ain't never going to see us. We just don't mess around with government agencies, not even the one at Langley."

"Specially the one at Langley," said Lonzo with a shiver.

"But, you see," said The Pundit, "that sort of knocks us out of the bus business to the fair, too. I swear it's getting harder all the time for an honest man to turn an honest dollar.

"However, things will brighten up. We heard from Big Time Benny Biscayne the other day. He's planning to come up from Florida for the fair, too. And whenever Benny shows up, something exciting happens."

"As I recall," I said, "the last time Big Time Benny made something exciting happen, Lonzo just missed being eaten by an alligator. That's pretty exciting, all right, but it's not the kind of excitement I'd want."

"No more alligators, dang it!" said Lonzo.

"But Benny did say something about bidding for the contract to wash all the glass in the Sunsphere—from the outside. It will be nice outdoor work, and you always did have a good head for heights, Lonzo."

"Just so there's no alligator up there," said Lonzo.

"If there is," I said, "his name will be Benny."

When I spotted them in the Pack Library, they were deep in thought, or something.

Lonzo, his chin propped up on his hands, was staring at a book titled *Home Electricity for Fun and Profit* by Sparks and Juicer. Every once in a while he would stop reading, rub his chin in a perplexed way, mumble something under his breath, and resume reading.

The Pundit was seated across the table from him, bolt upright and apparently perusing a copy of *The Wall Street Journal*. He was, in fact, sound asleep.

"What brings you two here and where have you been hiding?" I asked.

"Research," said Lonzo.

The Pundit snorted, awoke, and said, "And we have been rusticating with the Widder Lady in Whiskey Cove, that's where we've been. There's not much action downtown yet, so me and Lonzo have been staying up there, doing odd jobs for the Widder, and waiting until things loosen up."

"This last odd job we been doing is as odd as all getout," said Lonzo.

"It does seem to be sort of snakebit," The Pundit said. "We've been installing a garbage grinder under the Widder's kitchen sink, but we've had to repeat the work several times."

"Yer durn tootin'," said Lonzo. "On Mondays we install that confounded grinder and on Tuesdays we outstall it. Then we install it again and then we outstall it again. For the past couple of days we been neither installing nor outstalling—we been just plain stalling. But the Widder's getting impatient. She says it's a case of no grinder, no grub, and we're here trying to find out what we been doing wrong."

"What makes you think you've got the job wrong?" I asked.

Lonzo rolled his eyes heavenward, as if seeking Divine guidance. "Because," he snarled, "every time the Widder turns on the hot water tap, all she gets is long-hair music from some radio station over in Knoxville."

"It's a little worse than that," said The Pundit. "Whenever the Widder drinks water out of the cold water tap, her hair stands on end and blue sparks come out of her earholes. And whenever she opens the refrigerator door, all the vegetables in the vegetable drawer get shredded.

"And every time someone turns on the toaster, hot water squirts out of all the light switches in the kitchen. Read faster, Lonzo! It's getting close to supper time."

Lonzo sobbed, knuckled the side of his head, and stuck his long nose back into the book.

I stood silent for a moment, relishing the vision of the Widder Lady of Whiskey Cove with sparks coming out of her earholes.

Then I said, "Yes, indeed, it is painfully obvious that you got that grinder cross-connected somewhere, somehow."

"Oh, I ain't really worried," said The Pundit. "Me and Lonzo been in these little jams before and we always seem to come out all right, somehow."

A Little Work

So saying, he lighted one of his crooked black cigars and blew a stream of blue smoke halfway across the reading room. Whereupon a male librarian with bushy hair and a big moustache came over and threw all three of us out onto Haywood Street.

We sat on the bench in front of the library and I said, "Well, while that man was dispossessing us, I thought of a solution to your problem. All you have to do," I said, "is to connect up the grinder the way you've been doing. Then tell the Widder Lady to throw the garbage into the vegetable drawer of the refrigerator, drink the water that squirts out of the light switches, and take a music appreciation course at UNCA."

Lonzo groaned again. So did The Pundit. Then they both got up and walked away.

It was dark and cold when I came out of the newspaper office and got into my car. From off the floor in the back seat came The Pundit's hoarse voice. "Start the engine," he said.

Also from the floor came Lonzo's higher pitched tones. "Start the heater," he said.

Then both of them said in unison, "But don't turn on any lights."

For a while as the engine warmed up, I just sat there and listened to their teeth chatter like a tap dancer's toes. Finally the heater took hold, the inside of the car warmed, and the chattering in the back seat stopped.

I had last seen Lonzo and The Pundit about a month before. They then were on their way to Marathon Key to wear out the winter helping Lonzo's Uncle Cloyd wash yachts at a marina there.

Lonzo and The Pundit have gone to Florida many times, but they almost always run into disaster there.

"What happened this time?" I asked.

"We forgot to turn off the water," said Lonzo mournfully.

"Is that why you left Florida on the run . . . because you forgot to turn off the water?"

"I better explain," said The Pundit.

"Me and Lonzo were getting along fine down there at the Wackahoola River Yacht Marina on Marathon Key. We wasn't washing yachts; Lonzo's Uncle Cloyd has that job. Me and Lonzo were helping to tie up boats at the dock, refuel them, run for groceries, that sort of thing. It didn't pay much, but we were eating regular and the weather was lovely.

"Then about three days ago, a big one came in to the marina. It was about 85 feet long. Called the Bella Amici, or something like that. It was out of Miami Beach and belonged to a Mr. Barelli or something like that. Well, Mr. B. wanted fuel and more fresh water. He left orders for those items, then he and some friends got into a big, black auto and took off. So we fueled the yacht. Then we put aboard some fresh water. To do that we run a hose from a fresh water line on the dock to the filler pipe on the fresh water tank on the yacht. And that's what we did."

"Only we forgot to turn off the water," said Lonzo, on the verge of tears.

"That's right. We went home for the night and forgot to turn off the fresh water," The Pundit said.

"Well, what did that do?" I asked.

"Well, you see," said The Pundit, "when the fresh water tank was full, it simply overflowed. The overflow water ran down into the bottom of the yacht—the bilges. And during the night the Bella Amici just filled up with fresh water."

"Good Lord!" I said.

"Water, water everywhere," whimpered Lonzo.

"That's right," said The Pundit in a voice filled with regret. The Bella Amici sank right there at the dock."

"Full fathom five she went; down, down, down," said Lonzo.

"Well, surely the yacht was insured," I said. "There really wasn't any reason for you two to go on the lam."

"Mr. B. is insured all right," The Pundit said. "His insurance company is the Bet Your Life and Casualty Company of Palermo, Sicily. It's motto is 'We pay all claims—and collect all debts.' And right now I figure we owe that insurance company about a quarter of a million dollars. So just let us wait here until the Widder Lady from Whiskey Cover can come and get us. We're going to hide out in the barn for a while."

"For how long?" I asked.

"Until Mr. B. dies," said The Pundit.

9
Winters in the Sun

The Pundit's letter, as usual, came with postage due on it. It was postmarked Alligator Springs, Florida, and arrived in an envelope that had been used once, erased, and used again.

Dear Scribbles:

When we finally got to Alligator Springs after many troubles on the road, a delegation was waiting for us at the north city limits. But we came in by the south city limits, so they missed us.

There wasn't no brass band, but they did have the chief of police there. We heard later that they had planned to escort us right down into town—and right on out the other side.

Anyway, we got the jobs Big Time Benny Biscayne said would be waiting for us. Me and Lonzo is now attendants at Big Tony's Gasateria, Gourmet Restaurant, Dance Hall, and Roadside Zoo.

We pump gas, change tires (We've had a lot of experience at that), wash cars, sweep up, and generally take care of the place.

Oh yes, I almost forgot to mention that Lonzo also wrestles an alligator every Saturday night. Big Tony owns this bull alligator that must be about a million years old and is about fifteen feet long.

Lonzo is advertised as "Seminole Stan, the Scourge of the Swamp." Every Saturday night we dress him up in a tiger-striped bathingsuit with a feather in his hair and throw him into a glass tank Tony owns. Then he wrestles the alligator. Of course, Big Tony and his wife, Wanda, sit up all Friday night and Saturday morning stuffing very old fish and tranquilizers into the alligator. By Saturday night the most trouble Lonzo has is keeping the alligator awake long enough to put on a little show for the swamp angels who live around here and come in for a little entertainment.

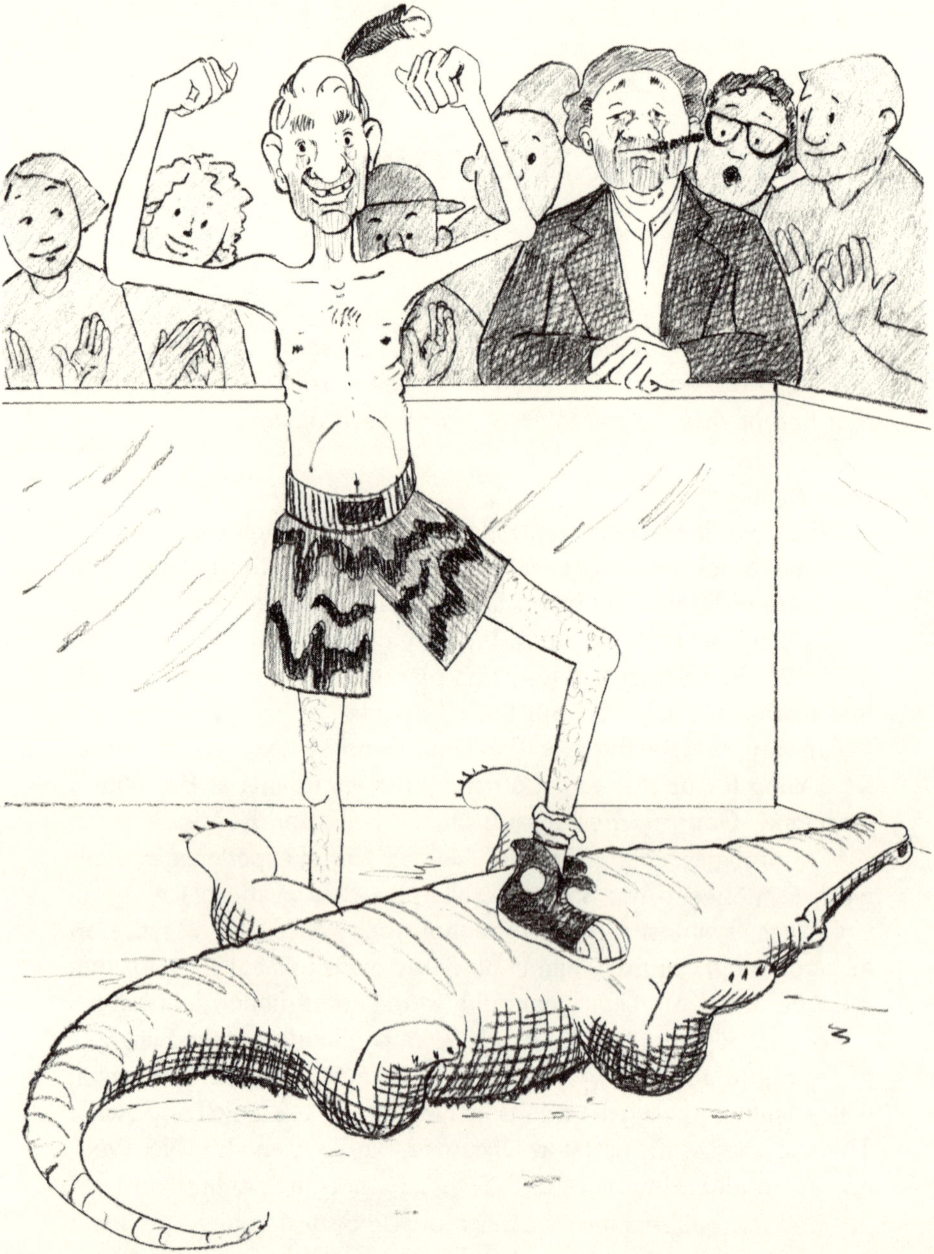

Winters in the Sun

We have trouble keeping Lonzo awake, too, because he is prone to partake of a little tranquilizer himself. Altogether, it ain't much of a show. But Big Tony says it is a nice change from the kind of wrestling that goes on in the dance hall. Besides, he says, he has been winning a little money betting on Lonzo.

Naturally, we had a little trouble persuading Lonzo to go into the tank that first time. In fact, every time someone said "alligator," Lonzo ran about forty miles down the road. Lonzo finally came around to our way of thinking after Big Tony gave him a jug of the local lightning. It is called swamp juice, and three swallows of it makes a alligator look like a pussycat. After a couple of weeks Lonzo sort of got to enjoy being the center of attraction at the Saturday night extravaganzas at Big Tony's Gasateria, Gourmet Restaurant, Dance Hall, and Roadside Zoo.

Wanda told him he was the star of the show, and Lonzo told Big Tony he wanted top billing over the alligator. I think Wanda is a little sweet on Lonzo. I swear I don't know what those women see in a skinny gink like Lonzo, but every now and then one of the older ones just goes all goopy over him.

As towns go, Alligator Springs ain't much. They is swamp on one side and swamp on another side and not much dry land on the remaining sides. It has a highway, a railroad, and the fertilizer factory, and that's about it, except, of course, for Big Tony's Gasateria, Gourmet Restaurant, Dance Hall, and Roadside Zoo.

Incidentally, it is the Christmas season and Lonzo and me are anticipating with pleasure your customary holiday remembrances. Give until it hurts, I always say.

P.S.——Don't send no gifts here to Alligator Springs! I think Lonzo and me are about to move on—fast. After I finished writing this letter I went over to the Gourmet Restaurant for a cup of coffee. Wanda was in there. She whispered in my ear that she had heard that Big Tony has started to bet on the alligator. What's more, the guy who runs the only drug store in town told her that Big Tony had canceled his standing order for tranquilizers.

I think maybe Big Tony also thinks Wanda is a little sweet on Lonzo. And we're moving on.

Yours tentatively,
The Pundit

TWO ON THE SQUARE

The letter arrived with, of course, postage due. The envelope appeared to have been stepped on several times by someone wearing golf shoes. The message was written on the back of a couple of old bills from a Florida lumber yard. It was:

Dear Scribbler:

We're still here in Florida but things aren't going well.

You remember in the last letter I wrote I told you we were about to take a hike out of Alligator Springs because Big Tony was starving the alligators Lonzo was wrestling for him and because Tony's wife, Wanda, told us Tony had stopped buying alligator tranquilizers.

Well, we did. We just packed up and pulled out in the middle of the night. We went a hundred miles down the road to a place near Port Saint Lucie.

Lonzo got another alligator wrestling job at a place called the Port Saint Lucie Gourmet Restaurant, Ceiling Fan Agency, and Outdoor Zoo. And I went to the dogs again and got a job at the Dreamsofriches Dog Track. There's a lot of dog tracks in Florida.

And things went along all right for a while.

But one night when Lonzo jumped into the pool to wrestle the alligators, those confounded lizards jumped out of the pool on the other side. They flat refused to have anything to do with him.

Then some geezer who said he was from the Florida Fish and Game Commission says he's shutting down the act entirely. It was too unsanitary for the alligators, he said.

The very next night I was walking dogs at the track when the favorite in the sixth race sank his fangs into the calf of my leg. I removed him from my leg kind of rough-like.

Over comes the track manager who says the dog is worth $10,000 and I ain't worth 10 cents and I should have been honored to have that dog bite me. He was worried about how sanitary it was for the dog, though, he says.

Well, I removed the manager kind of rough-like, too.

So both me and Lonzo was unemployed. We moved into the woods alongside a canal and toughed it out for a while. We was broke and it wasn't easy living, nohow.

Our diet was mainly green oranges and croaker fish we caught in the canal. We had no weight control problems.

Then one night the weather turned cold. Man, I mean it was really

Winters in the Sun

cold, and a little cold down here in Florida seems to hurt more than a lot of cold up there in the mountains. We started burning wood in the stove in the back of the Honkerbus. We burned all the logs we had.

The next day it was still cold. Lonzo went down the road in the Honkerbus with a borrowed chain saw, while I hung around and tried to catch some fish. He came back an hour later with the Honkerbus nearly full of neatly sawed pieces of green-painted wood. There was also a few pieces of wood painted white with black lettering on them.

The lettering said, "Property of the William J. Board Outdoor Advertising Company."

Right there I sort of got a suspicion that there might be trouble later on. But the wood burned fine and we were warm that night.

We got even warmer the next morning when they came banging on the Honkerbus back door. One of them was a deputy sheriff about nine feet wide. The other was a guy in a business suit. He was nine feet wide, too, and about ten feet tall.

The civilian says he is Bill Board, the billboard magnate, and he wants to get his hands on the skinny geek who was seen cutting up one of his billboards the day before. The geek massacred the billboard with a chain saw, he says, and it was one of his best billboards.

I say to Lonzo, "Did you cut up Bill Board's best billboard?"

"Billboards bore me," says Lonzo.

Then Bill Board has a few things to say. So does the deputy. And, finally, so does a judge in a courtroom in Port Saint Lucie.

We was sentenced to a million years, suspended, provided we restore Bill Board's best billboard and a few more, too.

So now we are in the billboard business. Bill Board says that as soon as we get the cost of that first billboard paid off, he might start paying us a salary.

In the meantime, we are almighty sick of green oranges and croaker fish.

Since we are in the advertising business now, I'll send you a message. The message is:

Send Money!

                                      Your famished friend,
                                      The Pundit

The letter had been mailed in a return envelope sent out by Sears, Roebuck, and Co. for someone to use to pay a monthly bill. But the printed address had been scratched out and my address had been written over it in a large sprawling hand I recognized immediately. It was postmarked Weekiewatchee Springs and it was from The Pundit.

Dear Inky:

I been meaning to write to you for a long time (We need money), but the holidays have been too busy. The dog track is doing a huge business. Lonzo was signed up for a Christmas Eve battle royal match against five alligators over at the truck stop, but the health department people closed the place the day before, which was no small relief to Lonzo. The health department wasn't worried about Lonzo, though. The kitchen of the place flunked an annual inspection.

And the track was closed for the New Year's holiday, so Lonzo and me drove over to Miami to visit Big Time Benny Biscayne. But Benny wasn't particularly glad to see us this time. Him and another Miami entrepreneur named Vinnie Vigorish have gone into the consumer loan business in a big way, and they have trouble collecting loan installments at that time of year.

They were awful busy catching up with some of their customers, Benny told us, but when they did the delinquents were going to be dilapidated, if we knew what he meant.

We did. Me and Lonzo have been on the wrong end of a couple of those consumer loans before and being late with a payment can cause a certain amount of agony, and the X-rays of my right leg will prove it.

So, more or less to get us off the place, Benny gave us tickets for the Orange Bowl game that night.

Lonzo said he didn't want to go to no flower show, but I explained that it was a big-time football game and that we should be grateful for the tickets.

We drove for about a hundred miles across Miami and got to the vicinity of the Orange Bowl in good time. After driving around a little, we found a nice place to park at the curb, right in front of a little white bungalow. We were trying to figure a way to lock up the Honkerbus, when a short, stocky Spanish-looking fellow came out

Winters in the Sun

of the bungalow and said howdy. He said his name was Bonifacio and he lived in the bungalow.

He said we was welcome. We thanked him. Then he said parking at that spot for the game would only cost us $7.50 and he would watch the car for us to see nothing bad happened to it while we was at the game.

Lonzo said we appreciated his hospitality and all that, but since when do people have to pay to park on a city street? Did this Bonifacio think we just got off a cattle boat or something? Was he crazy or something?

"Well, Bonifacio just looked at Lonzo hard. Then he called something in Spanish over his shoulder. Well, I picked up a little Spanish while I was in the Philippine Scouts, and it sounded like he was asking his mother to bring him a baseball.

The bungalow door opened and out came this sweet, white-haired, little old Spanish lady cradling something wrapped in a white shawl in her arms. Bonifacio took it and removed the shawl. It was a Louisville Slugger, the best baseball bat they make. It was a Ted Williams model, I believe.

Bonifacio courteously handed the shawl back to the little old lady, hefted the bat, and then tapped the business end of it on the radiator of the Honkerbus. The parking fee, he said, just went to $10 and he don't take American Express. Meanwhile his mother was muttering something about a home run.

The next closest parking place we could find was about nine miles from the stadium, and by the time we had walked all the way back we was about exhausted. We showed the tickets at one of the gates and got into the stadium, but when we went to find our seats, we run into more trouble. The tickets was for seats in section JJJ, row 56. The usher in that section looked at them and started to laugh.

There wasn't but 39 rows of seats in section JJJ, he said. He said if we really had seats in row 56 they had to be up in the Goodyear blimp. The tickets were phony, he said, and we should go find the guy who sold them to us and get our money back. I thought Lonzo was going to bust out in tears. I thought I was going to bust out in tears.

There we was, footsore and weary, in the middle of a crowd of 70,000 perfect strangers, and no place to sit.

We wandered around a while and finally, down at one end of the stadium, we saw some trucks parked. We climbed up onto the back of one and opened the jug of Mangrove Swamp Tiger Balm we had brought along for refreshment and started to console ourselves.

The consolation was going along at a great rate but we was getting cold. The nights can be pretty chilly in January, even in Miami, and we had left our coats in the Honkerbus. Someone had left a tarpaulin, on the truck bed, up near the cab, so we crawled back there, pulled the canvas over ourselves, and continued working on our consolation.

Then we both went to sleep. Well, it had been a long, hard day.

I woke up suddenly and realized that the truck was moving. There was a lot of light creeping in around the edges of the tarpaulin, and I could hear people cheering and bands playing. So I looked out. It was the half-time of the game and the truck we was on was one of the floats in the half-time parade. Up over the truck cab was a big sign that said something about "Miss Fort Pierce Orange Cooperative." And down near the end of the truck stood a pretty girl dressed in a formal dress surrounded by baskets of oranges. She was waving and smiling and people were cheering and clapping as we went by.

Well, I kicked Lonzo awake and we both stood up on the bed of the truck. Instantly the cheering and clapping changed to howls of laughter. Lonzo, that fool, was holding his hands over his head and mugging like he just won the heavyweight championship of the world.

At first the girl in the formal dress didn't know what was going on. Then she looked back and saw us. She said something I wouldn't care to repeat in a Baptist Church on Sunday and started throwing oranges at us. In no time at all about a dozen cops climbed up on the truck and pulled me and Lonzo off. It was a good thing, too. Those oranges were heavy and that girl had a better arm than most major league pitchers.

Two of them threw us into a cruiser and drove us to where we parked the Honkerbus. Lonzo wanted them to do something about the counterfeit tickets and about the parking racket Bonifacio was running, but they didn't seem to be interested. They stayed with us until we got the Honkerbus running and made sure we knew the shortest way out of town.

One of them said that Miami has enough troubles on its own and it didn't need us for relish. The next time we decided to show up on the East Coast, he said, we should visit Palm Beach. He said he'd

Winters in the Sun

give a lot to hear what the Palm Beach cops would say when they saw us.

Well, that's about the most adventure we've had for a couple of weeks. We never did find out what the score of that game was. Come to think of it, we don't even know what teams played.

Think of us often and send money when you do. We'll be back when the azaleas bloom.

The Pundit

Miami Beach

Dear Scribbles:

It is time we started home.

The Miami Beach Police Department is planning a benefit for Lonzo and me. They said it would be greatly to our benefit to get out of town.

I reckon they are tired of picking up pieces of the Honkerbus, which sheds parts like a hound sheds hair in the springtime.

I reckon they're tired of picking up Lonzo, too.

We got a job at a hotel here in Miami Beach a couple of weeks ago. We work at the hotel swimming pool and we are what they call cabana boys.

What we do is, we set up folding chairs around the pool and we rent them out by the hour to the guests. When the guests have sat around in the sun until they're done about medium rare, they get up and go back into the hotel. But first they have to pay for renting the chairs.

I think this is the first place I ever saw where you could rent a chair by the hour and not get shot for doing it.

The chairs kind of fold up. We have to unfold them in the morning and then fold them back up and put them away when the sun goes down.

Lonzo can't seem to get the hang of the thing, and I spend half my time untangling him from the chairs. The language he uses when he gets trapped in one of those chairs is shocking. I fear this trip has done a lot for Lonzo's vocabulary but not much for his soul.

The language he uses really isn't important because none of the guests here understand him, anyway. They say his accent is "quaint."

That's all right; Lonzo doesn't understand any of the guests, either. He has several times said things about the accent they have, but "quaint" ain't the word he used.

Lonzo also wants to start home. He says he wants to get back to where a man can spend an afternoon sitting on a bench without having someone else come up later and present him with a bill.

It's a funny thing about this place; everything is for rent, but nobody seems to own anything.

Speaking about benches, Lonzo and me had a experience recently. We was driving across the causeway on our way to Miami when we saw old Pearly Millican from up in Whiskey Cove. Old Pearly was just leaning against the rail, fishing, but not very hard.

We stopped to talk. Pearly told us his kids had bankrolled him and told him to get out of the snow for a while, so he come down here to spend the winter. He has a language problem, too. He can't speak Spanish.

He lives in a apartment over in Miami in a part of town where just about everybody else talks nothing but Spanish. Pearly said it had been three months since he has been able to say hello to anyone.

He said he wanted to be neighborly and he even tried to learn how to talk that lingo, but he couldn't get anyone to slow down enough so he could get a toehold on the proposition.

He kept us there talking until near midnight. Every time we started to leave, he started to cry. It was downright embarrassing.

Well, as Pearly would say, if he could, hasty la visitor and vamos con Dios and all that. We'll be seeing you soon, just as quick as we can find another crankshaft for the Honkerbus.

Cheers!
Pundit

Winters in the Sun

Weekiewatchee Springs
December 7

Dear Scrivener,

Well, we arrived here all right. The Honkerbus ran fine. We had a little problem with a deputy sheriff outside Waycross, Georgia, who wanted to know how come we didn't have any license plate on it.

Lonzo told him the Honkerbus was really a trackless railroad train and didn't need any motor vehicle license plate. By the time he got that one figured out we were in Florida.

When we got here we stashed the Honkerbus away in a mangrove swamp, set up housekeeping in a nice, dry Dempsey Dumpster, and located a reliable source of tax-free refreshments.

It looks like three days of work a week should keep us in the necessaries of life and we'll rusticate the other four days.

The day after we arrived, we took the bus over to Fishbone Beach just to look at the ocean. We was walking along a pier there when we spotted a guy sitting on a canvas camp stool with a big gunny sack between his feet.

"What you got in the gunny sack?" asked Lonzo.

"Stone crabs," said the guy.

"Yum!" said Lonzo who proceeded to talk the guy into matching quarters—his crabs against our bottle. Lonzo hardly ever loses at matching quarters, particularly when there is a bottle at stake. He won and reached for the sack.

"Hold on, there!" says the guy. "You won the crabs, but not the sack." So we rummaged around in a trash can and found a brown paper bag like the ones they give you in a supermarket. We dumped the crabs into that.

Stone crabs is about the finest seafood there is. Them boogers is the ugliest, meanest things in Christendom when they're alive, but boiled they are delicious.

Well, later we took the bus back to the Springs, and after a ways it stopped to let on some more passengers. One of them was a man my age in what, I must say, was a shocking state of inebriation.

Anyway, this man staggered down the aisle and slumped into the seat next to Lonzo, who was carrying the bag full of stone crabs on his lap. A few minutes later one of the stone crabs found a weak

TWO ON THE SQUARE

spot in the bag, stuck out a big pincher, and took a good hold on the drunk's bare arm.

The drunk felt the bite, looked down, and saw the crab pincher sticking out of the bag and munching on his arm. He went straight up in the air screaming for the driver to stop the bus and let him off because "they" finally got him.

The scream startled Lonzo who dropped the bag, which promptly split open. All those stone crabs started scootching around on the floor of the bus.

The passengers was so busy watching the drunk they didn't notice the crabs, until the crabs reached some women who were wearing sandals. Then they went straight up, screaming, with crabs grabbing onto their toes.

The bus driver slammed on the brakes, opened the bus door, and took off. We never saw him again.

A little while later a deputy sheriff drove up, looked into the bus, and yelled, "Who turned them crabs loose in there?"

"I did," said Lonzo, "and I want every dadgummed one of them back, too."

"Here's one you can have," said one of the women passengers, and she threw a crab at Lonzo. Lonzo picked up another one and threw it back. In thirty seconds the bus was full of flying crabs.

With time off for good behavior, Lonzo should be out Monday morning.

Have you had any snow yet?

Regards,
Pundit

On the Road
Sometime in January

Dear Scribbler:

Well, we finally got out of Weekiewatchee Springs.

We resurrected the Honkerbus. We discovered that Stanley, the entrepreneur of the mangrove swamp where we had stashed the thing, had appropriated some of the machinery to build a new still.

He gave us back the piping and the boiler, and he even threw in thirty-five gallons from his last batch. He said the stuff was unfit to be sold to his regular customers. Too weak, he said. After all, he has a reputation to maintain, he said.

Lonzo took a sip or two of the substandard product. After he had stopped gasping and wheezing, he said, yes, he saw what Stanley was talking about.

Why, Lonzo said, it would take at least a half-pint of the stuff to fell a healthy mule and that would never do.

Lonzo, always anxious to help, kept sipping the stuff, trying to figure out where Stanley had gone wrong with the formula. He never did come up with an answer, and he wasn't much help when it came to putting the Honkerbus back together again, either.

Anyway, we got the Honkerbus steaming, loaded aboard the thirty-five gallons of Stanley's Swampfire and rolled back into town.

I drove, of course. We never drink and drive. We don't want the governor to get after us.

I bought some half-pint bottles and had some labels printed. Lonzo recovered enough to find a bent banjo and an ocarina at the Alligator Springs Municipal Solid Waste Disposal Facility, and we took the bottles and the instruments on the road as an old-time medicine show.

I learned to play the banjo a little while General MacArthur and me was soldiering with the Filipino Scouts, and Lonzo can blow an ocarina pretty good.

Well, we tried it off the back of the Honkerbus at a couple of crossroads places and it went pretty good. We was making eating money, anyhow. Then we hit a bigger town and ran into a storm.

We wasn't halfway through the pitch when I noticed that most of the crowd consisted of men wearing sincere three-piece gray suits. I have had a lot of experience with people like that, and all of it has been bad.

This time wasn't any different.

In about thirty minutes we was in trouble with the EPA, the OSHA, the SBA, the FDA, the AMA, the FDIC, the FTC, and probably the KGB.

We was told we would have to have our product cleared by six federal laboratories, three state agencies, the state attorney general, the Department of Defense, and Dear Abby.

One wiseacre, who was standing downwind, even suggested that we ought to clear with the municipal air pollution control agency.

We decided we wasn't going to clear nothing with anybody.

We poured Stanley's mistake into the fuel tank of the Honkerbus, lit up a clear blue flame under the boiler, and steamed out of that place at flank speed.

Now we are working our way north, sort of following the crops.

I think we have enough fuel to get us back to Asheville, if Lonzo don't drink it first.

Yours cheerfully,
The Pundit

December 28
Dogbiscuit Downs

Dear Ed:

Well, despite all the crepe-hanging and the dire predictions we heard from our friends before we started, the Honkerbus got us here.

The driveshaft fell off (again) as we drove through the main gate here at Dogbiscuit Downs, and you can't hardly see the back of the thing for oil smoke, but we made it.

Fortunately it was all downhill.

Things are going along here pretty well. Lonzo and I are in-and-out men at the kennels. We carry in the dog food, then we carry out the other stuff. It's amazing how little dog food it takes to make a whole lot of the other stuff.

We work in the kennels all day and then at night we go over to the grandstand and watch the dogs chase the mechanical rabbit. Did you know that people actually bet money on these dogs? It's amazing. The only way I'd make a bet at a dog track is if they let me bet on the rabbit.

The weather has been mostly pleasant here, but the other night it got real cold. We have been sleeping in the Honkerbus, which we pushed around to the back of the track and parked. But it got so cold that night that Lonzo went over to the kennels to sleep with the dogs.

Unfortunately, as soon as Lonzo walked in, the dogs started making a terrific racket and they wouldn't stop. Pretty soon the track security officer came over and threw Lonzo out of the kennels.

He said the dogs are all thoroughbred greyhounds and they have their standards. It was all right for Lonzo to bring food to the dogs, but they certainly didn't propose to sleep with him.

Lonzo said he has been thrown out of much classier kennels before, anyway.

The other day we got a day off and hitched a ride over to the Springs, where we took a cruise on a glass-bottomed boat. We saw the wonders of the underwater world, the fish and the plants and the weeds and the old rubber tires and the junked cars and the old bedsprings.

Lonzo asked the boat driver if that was fresh water, and the driver said it certainly was, just like the water that comes out of the spigot in the kitchen. Lonzo said he didn't believe he'd ever take another drink of water.

The boat driver took a look at Lonzo and said he doubted if Lonzo ever had taken a drink of water in his whole life. Lonzo said something about the boat driver's parents, and the boat driver stopped the boat and helped Lonzo to get off. We was fifty feet from the shore at the time.

On the way back to Dogbiscuit Downs, Lonzo said he was getting feelings of rejection.

I am beginning to get feelings of malnutrition. I just can't make it on a steady diet of Purina and stolen oranges.

Sometimes we feed meat to the dogs. They call it beef, but I sort of suspect that it's what's left of the losers at the horse track over on the beach.

Neither Lonzo nor me can stomach it.

However, next weekend we are going to hitch down to Miami and visit Big Time Benny Biscayne. He will entertain us at the arches restaurant.

In the meantime I must remark that we have not yet received your customary generous remembrance for the holidays. I'm sure it's simply a matter of uncertainty about where we are. Get up the money. Please.

                                                    Doing poorly,
                                                    The Pundit

The box had been shipped from Sarasota and it looked a little beaten up. It arrived, of course, with $4.20 worth of shipping charges due.

The grapefruit it contained, however, tasted great.

There was a note inside the box, a crumpled piece of paper covered with The Pundit's scrawly handwriting.

Lonzo saw this box sort of fall off the back of a truck, and we immediately thought of you two.

As you no doubt saw from the front of the box, we are no longer at the dog track at Dogbiscuit Downs. We was terminated as the result of a slight case of mismanagement.

The other morning Lonzo had thirty-five dogs with him in the exercise yard when a real rabbit walked by the gate.

About that time Lonzo realized he had mismanaged the latch on the gate. So did the dogs. The rabbit, closely followed by thirty-five pedigreed greyhounds, took off in the general direction of the Everglades.

When last seen they were going down the main street of Weekiewatchee Springs clocking about 60 miles an hour, and the rabbit was beginning to look worried.

Lonzo and me saw right away that the owners of the dogs probably would complain to the management, so we drew our time, fired up the Honkerbus, and headed out across the peninsula.

Unfortunately the Honkerbus wouldn't go as fast as those dogs went, and we was closely followed by a caravan of dog owners throwing rocks at us. Chased us nearly all the way to Tampa. It's a good thing there wasn't any glass in the windows.

For a while it looked like we had a job in Tampa pulling up old metal for the "Plane-a-Day-in-Tampa-Bay" Salvage Company.

Then we discovered we was supposed to hitch up to some tanks of air and dive under the water.

Well, Lonzo just flat balked at that.

"I thought you said you two was good divers," the foreman said to us.

"Nobody said anything about diving," Lonzo said. "We thought you was asking us if we were good diners!"

While we were swimming to shore, Lonzo said he was beginning to get feelings of rejection again.

So we went down the coast to St. Petersburg.

There we got jobs with the city parks department running the shuffleboard courts. They give us each hard hats like construction workers wear, some keys to the equipment room, and turned us loose. In no time at all we had people playing shuffleboard all over the park.

Things were quiet for a while, then an old party holding a shuffleboard stick came over and asked Lonzo to judicate a little disagreement he was having with some friends he was playing against. We walked over to where the game was, and the old parties each stated their case and demanded a ruling.

I know nothing about shuffleboard and Lonzo knows less. I was about to suggest that they take the matter up in municipal court or something, when Lonzo takes another squint and says, "It looks like a jump ball to me."

That's when we found out why the city issued us the hard hats. Those old parties take the game seriously, let me tell you. And it never has been smart to crack wise at people who are standing there with sticks in their hands.

After Lonzo recovered from the concussion, we drew time again and went on down the road.

Now we are in Sarasota and we are, as they say in show biz, at liberty. If we get much more liberty, we are going to starve like free men.

We went over to the winter quarters of the circus the other day and asked for work. They said the only thing they had open was a job feeding the big cats in the animal act.

Lonzo was all for taking the job, but this time I flat balked. I just don't have the heart to risk another case of mismanagement with the latch on a cage door.

Living with Lonzo is trying enough—I have no ambition to die with him.

We'll be seeing you soon, it looks like.

The Pundit

January Something

Dear Scribbles:

Well, our sojourn here at warm, friendly Citrus City probably has come to an end. By the time you read this we probably will have fired up the Honkerbus and taken to the open road again.

We don't want to go, dang it. But we got no choice. And it's all because of a apple-cheeked, sweet-faced, blonde biddy named Griselda Hockenlocker who is the welfare lady in these parts.

Me and Lonzo have had lots of dealings with welfare ladies in the course of our long careers. Seems like half the beginning welfare ladies south of the Mason-Dixon Line at one time or another tried to get us to straighten up and lead a sanitary life.

They come out of college with a brand-new diploma, take one look at us, roll up their sleeves, and go to work. Eventually most of them give us up as a bad job and leave us alone.

But not Griselda. She won't go away and she won't play fair, and we are going to have to hit the road to get her out of our hair.

It all started one morning about a week ago when she woke us up by kicking on the side of our dumpster. (I forgot to mention that this Hockenlocker lady is constructed along the general lines of a steamroller and wears steel-toed shoes.)

Well, she made such an infernal racket that Lonzo and I climbed out of our boudoir even though it was not one of our days to work. Then she started in on us with the chin music.

And this lady can talk faster than she can kick, which is saying a lot.

What she wanted was just for us to stop living in the dumpster, find regular jobs, stop fermenting our orange juice, and start taking baths. Otherwise, she said, there was no place for us in Citrus City.

Lonzo said we'd be purely delighted to do all that—next week. But in the meantime would she please go away and be quiet because she was making his head ache worse than usual?

Nothing doing, she said. She'd read all about people like us in college, she said, and she knew we'd promise anything just to get rid of her.

Then I made like I went to sleep standing up, and Lonzo threw one of his fake fits.

Miz Hockenlocker went away, saying she could see that we wasn't

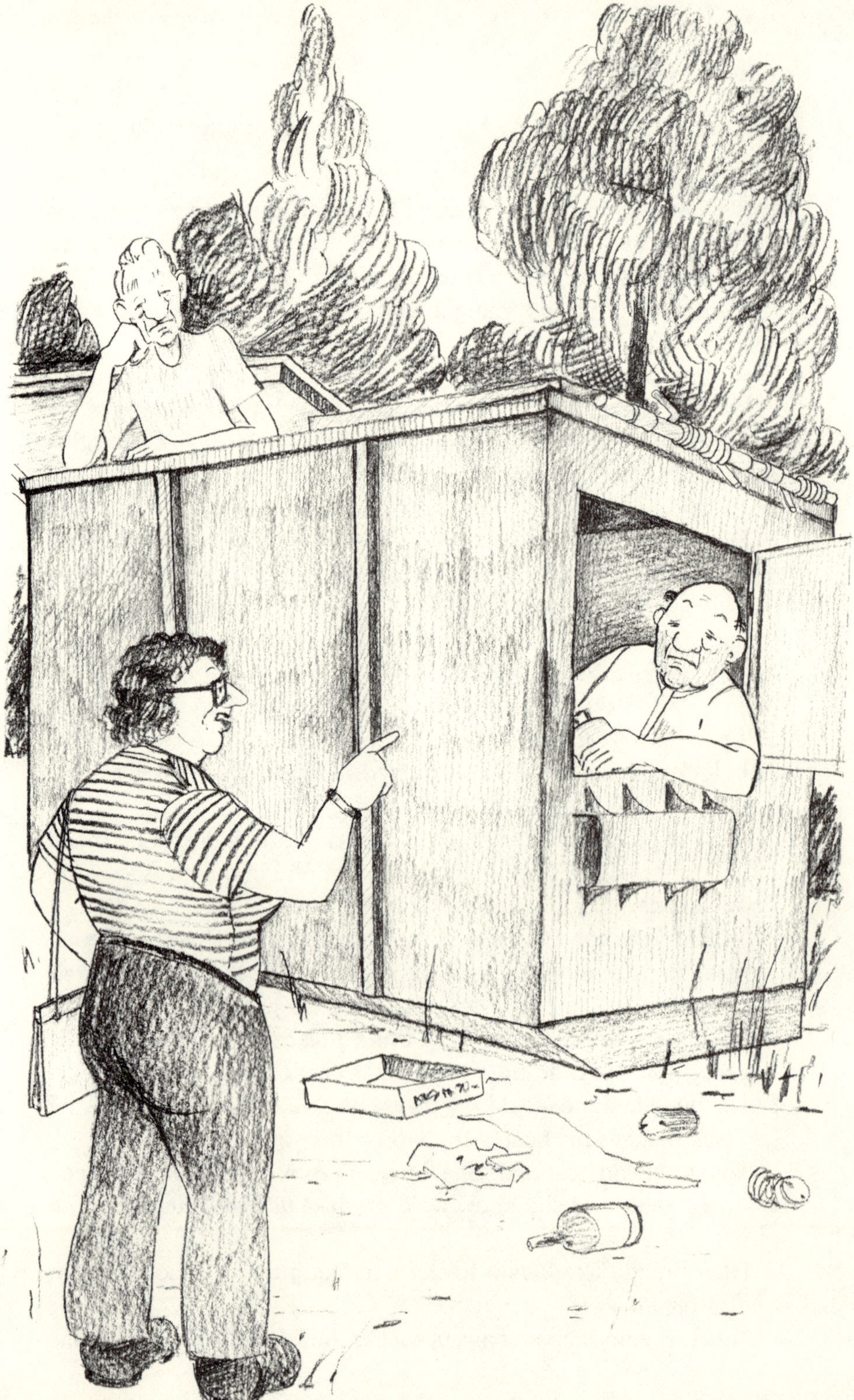

ready to talk reason yet, but that, by gum, we would be, or her name ain't Griselda Hockenlocker.

The next day Citrus City changed its trash pickup schedule. They had been emptying the dumpsters every day about 4 p.m. in our neighborhood. That next day they emptied ours at 6 a.m.

I don't know if you ever had the experience of having your sleeping chamber picked up by a huge truck, lifted thirty feet in the air, shaken like a terrier shakes a rat, banged three times on the steel side of the truck, and then turned upside down.

If you haven't, you ain't lived yet.

That sort of thing gets your attention. Lonzo says it gave him a bad case of what he calls insomonia. That was a week ago and we ain't had a decent night's sleep since. Griselda, like that man Shakespeare said, hath murdered sleep.

If we don't get up before 6 a.m., we get hoisted into the wild blue yonder. And there ain't any alarm clocks in Dempsey Dumpsters. Whenever we hit the ground Griselda is there, rattling away about leading the sanitary life.

Lonzo is so nervous he keeps falling off his picking ladder in the orchard. The rest of the pickers are calling him "Orange Crush."

So I guess it's time to go—either that or get steady jobs and start taking baths.

Regards,
Pundit

All characters within this book are purely fictional, with the exception of the author and certain political and governmental personalities whose existence is a matter of public record. Any association of a living person with any other character within this book is purely the result of the reader's imagination, as no intent exists on the part of the publisher, author, or artist to portray any identifiable real life person within the text or illustrations.